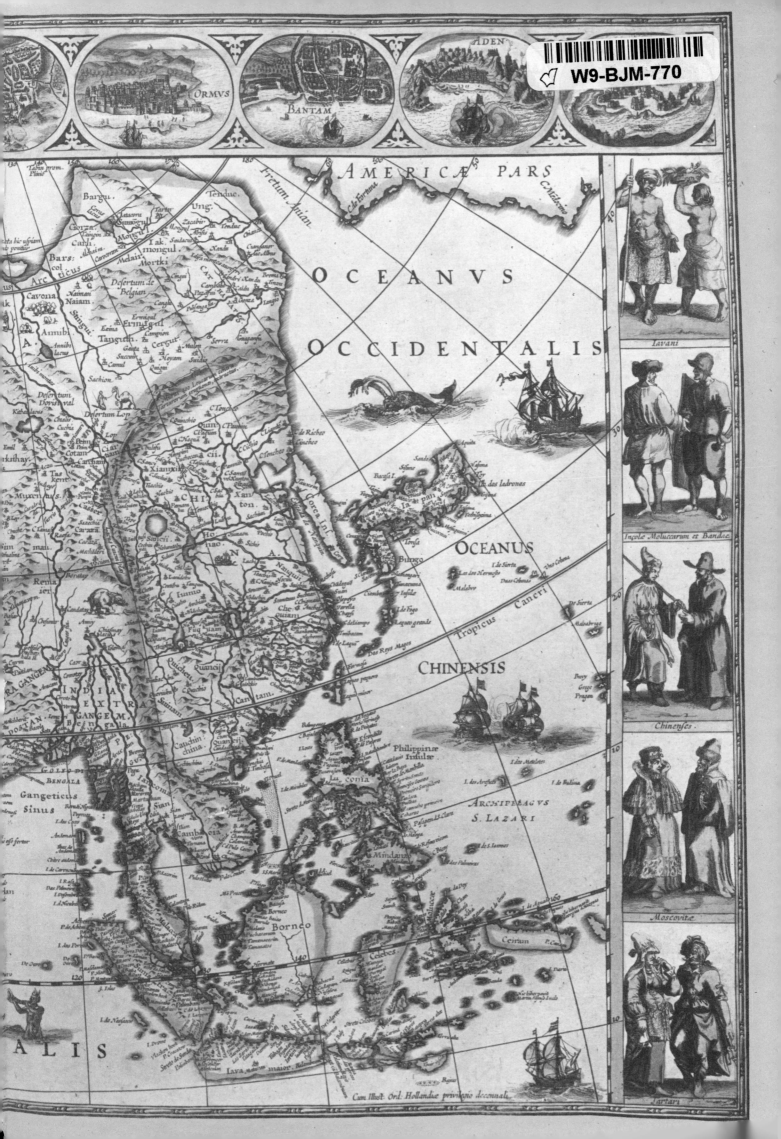

ORMVS

BANTAM

ADEN

AMERICÆ PARS

C. Mendocio

Fretum Anian

OCEANVS

OCCIDENTALIS

OCEANUS

Tropicus Cancri

CHINENSIS

Philippinæ Insulæ

ARCHIPELAGVS
S. LAZARI

Mindanao

Borneo

Celebes

Ceiran

Iavani

Incole Moluccarum et Bandae.

Chinenses.

Moscovitæ

Tartari

Gangeticus Sinus

GOLFO DI
BENGALA

INDIA
EXTRA
GANGEM.
Bengala.

ALIS

Iava maior.

Cum Illust. Ord. Hollandiæ privilegio decennali.

ATLAS OF DISCOVERY

ATLAS OF DISCOVERY

Introduction by Sir Francis Chichester

Text by Gail Roberts

Maps by Geographical Projects

Crown Publishers, Inc., New York

About this Atlas

The *Atlas of Discovery* tells the story of exploration from the very earliest times to the present day. The first three chapters are organized chronologically, from the first wanderings of primitive men, and civilization's earliest recorded journeys, up to the first circumnavigation of the world in A.D. 1519-22. Then, through chapters 4 to 11, the story unfolds geographically, region by region. The final chapters, 12 and 13, deal with exploration of different kinds—man's investigation of the oceans, and his first ventures into space. At the beginning of each of the first 11 chapters—those dealing with geographical exploration—an illuminated globe highlights in blue the areas where the journeys described in that chapter took place, and on the relief maps in these chapters the areas of interest are highlighted in green. To make cross reference between maps and text easier, the name of each explorer whose journey is mapped is printed in bold type.

Frontispiece: During the Great Age of Discovery in the 1400's and early 1500's, in ships similar to this, the sea route to India was discovered, the Americas reached, and the first circumnavigation of the world was made.
Right: From the discovery of the world's continents and islands, Europeans turned to the exploration of the newly discovered lands. Here, explorers stand at the foot of a waterfall deep in the South American interior.

Editor   **Gail Roberts**
Cartographic Editor   **Shirley Carpenter**
Design   **Roger Hyde**
                          Douglas Sneddon
Maps by Geographical Projects

ISBN 0-517-50563-0

Library of Congress number 72-96669

© 1973 Aldus Books Limited, London
Maps © 1973 Geographical Projects Limited, London
First published in the U.S.A. 1973
by Crown Publishers, Inc.,
419 Park Avenue South, New York, N.Y. 10016.
Printed and bound in Spain by Roner S.A. Madrid.

CONTENTS

The Spirit of Adventure

Sir Francis Chichester's thoughts on the challenge of life

"I think a cruise is delightful, and I have enjoyed a number, both as air-pilot and in sail. But it is not to be compared with racing, record-breaking, or doing something that has not been done before, for excitement, interest, sport, and the satisfaction of achievement. Those of you who have both raced and cruised know exactly what I mean; you have only to recall the excitement and sport and fatigue that you have had out of four hours racing compared with four hours of a leisurely sail."

This is how, in 1969, Sir Francis Chichester summed up the moving spirit of his life, the search for challenge and achievement that he shared with so many of the adventurers of the past. He was to have written the foreword to this book about those great adventurers, the pioneers of world discovery, but unfortunately he never saw it completed. During the spring and summer of 1972, while making his public preparations for his latest adventure, a third and final entry in the Singlehanded Transatlantic Race, Sir Francis was privately battling with the fatal illness that forced him to retire from the race and caused his death two months after his return to England. After his death, his son Giles compiled these words from his writings.

"I look back and find that romance, romantic adventure, has been the keynote of my life." Even in Sir Francis' childhood, this was true. His first solo expedition with an adventure in it happened when he was 11 years old. "I used to wander all day through the woods in North Devon by myself . . . I caught a snake. This viper bit me and for 20 hours, so I was told, it was touch and go whether I would survive. This seemed strange when very few people died from snake bites in England, and it was caused by the fact that I had traveled seven miles, as fast as I could, running and on a bicycle, hampered, perhaps, for the first part of the journey by the snake that I was still carrying."

Aviation was still in its infancy when, in 1929, Sir Francis took up flying. He was quick to sense the excitement of solo flight. "I can still feel the thrill of many of the 'firsts' of that time. Such as the first solo landing and then the first time I went up alone at night. The tremendous thrill of landing in the dark, no luxuries like lights to help one take off or land . . . Of course, doing things by oneself, I find that one

C. Horn
20 March 1967

ARCTIC CIRCLE

TROPIC OF CANCER

PACIFIC

EQUATOR

OCEAN

TROPIC OF CAPRICORN

NEW
ZEALAND

FALKLAND
IS.

ANTARCTIC CIRCLE

ATLAN

Miles Equatorial Scale

▲ *Sir Francis Chichester on board* Gipsy Moth IV, *the boat in which he made his voyage around the world. Sir Francis had been a keen aviator before taking up sailing, and all his boats were named after the Gipsy Moth airplane in which he flew from England to Australia in 1929-30 and made the first east-west solo flight across the Tasman Sea.* Gipsy Moth II, *bought secondhand after World War II, was his first boat, but it was in the new* Gipsy Moth III *that Sir Francis won the first Singlehanded Transatlantic Race in 1960. After the second singlehanded race across the Atlantic in 1964, when he finished second, Sir Francis conceived his plan for a round-the-world voyage, and* Gipsy Moth IV *was born. After the circumnavigation,* Gipsy Moth IV *was put into dry dock at Greenwich, beside the wool clipper* Cutty Sark.

is much more efficient. I seem to come to life when I am thrown onto my own resources." "Although to my regret, I never achieved a big first in solo flying, I did pull off one or two minor firsts which I found thrilling and satisfying. I was the first person to fly solo from New Zealand to Australia across the Tasman Sea. Then I had all the sport and thrills I could wish for when I made the first long-distance solo flight in a seaplane. This was from New Zealand to Japan in 1931. But the first which gave me the greatest satisfaction was that of devising a system of astronomical navigation to find a $3\frac{1}{2}$-thousand-acre island in the Tasman Sea while flying alone and solely depending on sextant observations of the sun."

From flying, Sir Francis Chichester turned to sailing, and it was as a sailor that he achieved the feat for which he will be longest remembered, his circumnavigation of the world in 1966-7. "The thrill of *Gipsy Moth's* voyage around the world is a priceless treasure for me. I believe this is

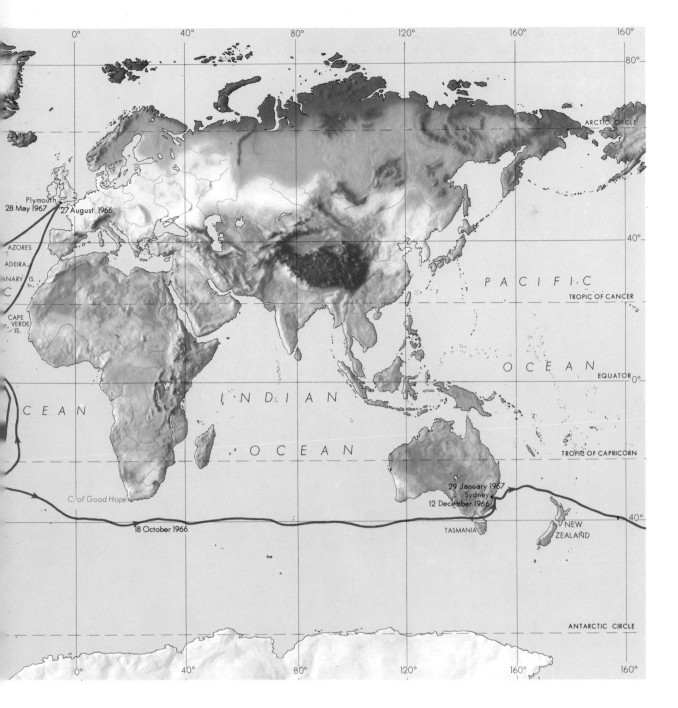

Plymouth
28 May 1967   27 August 1966

AZORES
ADEIRA
ANARY IS.

CAPE
VERDE
IS.

C. of Good Hope

18 October 1966

29 January 1967
Sydney
12 December 1966

TASMANIA

NEW
ZEALAND

ARCTIC CIRCLE

TROPIC OF CANCER

PACIFIC

OCEAN

EQUATOR 0°

INDIAN

OCEAN

TROPIC OF CAPRICORN

ANTARCTIC CIRCLE

because there were some unique features about the voyage. Other yachts have sailed around the world by Cape Horn, but this was the first time it had been done by a small boat in two passages. And then the speed meant a lot to me, circumnavigating at twice the speed of the next fastest small vessel. The thrill of these things can never be repeated. How many people could name the second person to climb Mount Everest, or the second person to fly alone across the Atlantic, or for that matter the second person to fly alone from England to Australia [this was Sir Francis himself]. The hard fact is that once something has been done, much of the first-time magic has gone."

For Sir Francis, there were common factors in all he had set out to do, and he summed up the most important of these in his last book, published in 1971. "At the head of the list came the attraction of doing something that had never been done before, because of the appeal of the untried, the unknown, and the excitement."

▲ *The route Sir Francis Chichester followed on his voyage around the world. When Sir Francis sailed from Plymouth on 27 August 1966, his aim was to make a circumnavigation using the route of the wool clippers which used to ply between England and Australia. He hoped to equal their passage time of 100 days from Plymouth to Sydney and, perhaps, to make the fastest ever circumnavigation of the world by a small boat. Despite setbacks, he arrived in Sydney only seven days behind schedule, and on 29 January 1967 he set sail from Sydney bound for Cape Horn. He rounded the Horn on 20 March in a howling gale, then set his course north. On 24 April, he crossed the equator, and on 28 May he was back in Plymouth. On 7 July, in recognition of his magnificent achievement, he was dubbed knight by the Queen.*

9

1 The Beginning

Long, long ago, in the dawn of his existence on earth, man first set out into the unknown. In those far-off days, tens of thousands of years before the birth of Christ, almost every journey was a journey of discovery. Men knew only their immediate neighborhood—the river where they fished, the forest where they hunted, the spring where they drank. Although their homes were only primitive shelters, still they represented security in a world full of danger. When a man left his familiar surroundings, he was at the mercy of the unknown.

Yet, despite their fears, men did venture beyond the safety of the area they knew. They forged paths across the trackless wilderness, and sailed down turbulent rivers. Their expeditions were motivated not by love of adventure, but by need, as they sought food and shelter, or fled from danger. They journeyed to no special country, in search of no definite goal. Their travels ended where they found a safe place to make their homes. By 10,000 B.C., man had discovered the secrets of cultivating crops and of domesticating animals, and permanent farming settlements had replaced the nomadic hunting communities of earlier years. Still, however, periodic upheavals took place; these carried men far into the unknown world.

The men who made these, the world's first journeys of exploration, could not write, and left no record of the paths they had followed, or of the lands through which they had passed. Present-day knowledge of their wanderings is derived from archeological findings, but no such information was available to the primitive travelers themselves. A man's journeys died with him, and although one traveler might follow in the footsteps of another, he had no warning of the difficulties he would meet on his way. Every journey was a new and terrifying undertaking. Thousands of years were to pass before men recorded their travels, and a picture of the world could be built up.

Even with the beginning of recorded journeys, and the consolidation of knowledge, exploration was a slow process. Equipment was primitive, and direction finding difficult, so that at sea mariners dared not venture out of sight of land, and on land travelers were in constant danger of getting lost. Ships were frail, and shipwreck frequent, while on land travelers often faced hazardous terrain. Always there was the danger of death if food and water should run out.

In spite of such great difficulties, the early explorers pushed back the frontiers of the unknown. They learned about the lands they lived in, then about other lands beyond. From the isolated communities of earlier times, they forged a known, civilized world, whose boundaries spread wider with each succeeding year. The story of how man's knowledge of his world increased is the story of discovery. Its first chapter begins with the appearance of civilization on earth.

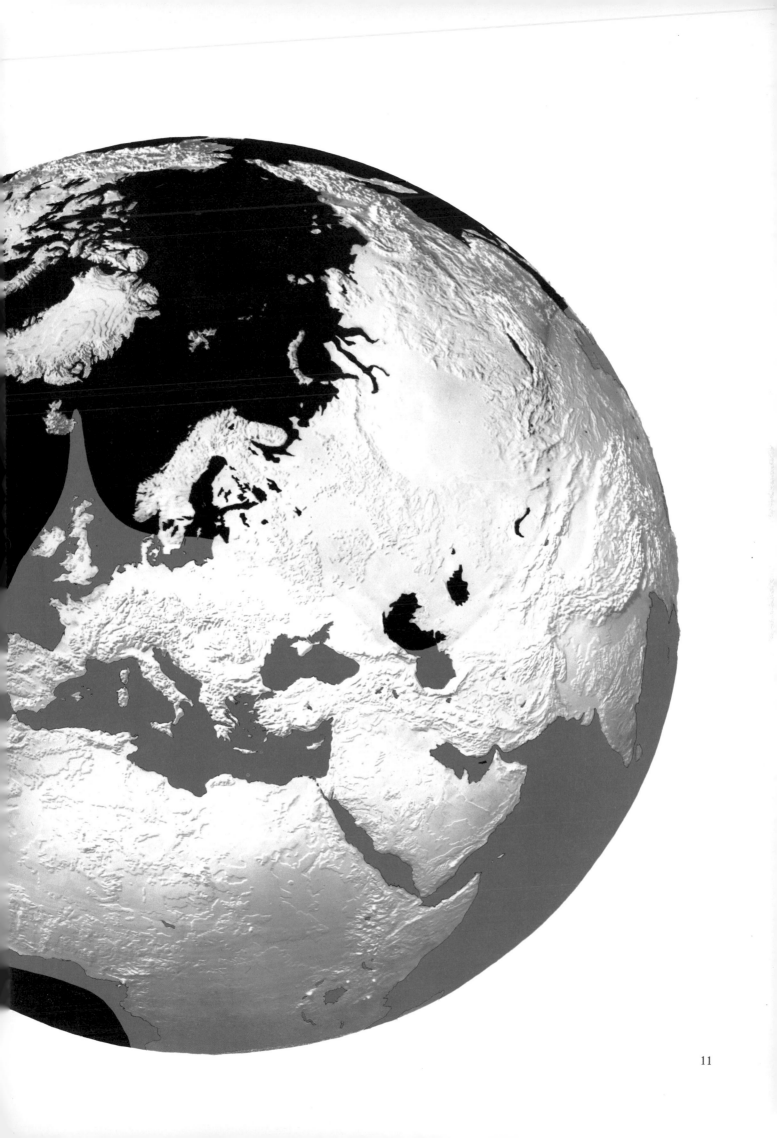

First Steps

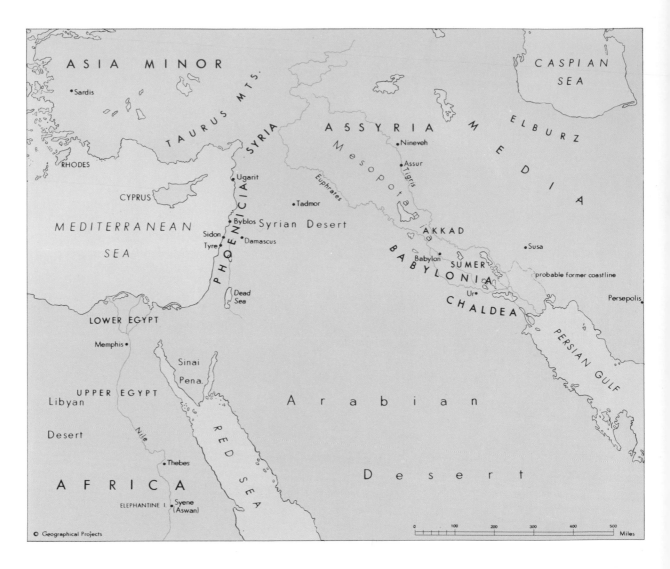

▲ Early Middle Eastern civilizations.

Civilization first grew up between 5000 and 6000 years ago in the so-called Fertile Crescent of the Middle East, an arc of rich land curving from the Nile Valley, through the coastlands of the eastern Mediterranean and the valleys of the Euphrates and Tigris rivers, to the Persian Gulf. There, for the first time, cultured, organized societies emerged in which the nomadic hunting and agricultural existence of earlier times was replaced by a planned economy, and a sophisticated way of life. Village settlements became towns, a system of government evolved, and religion, learning, and the arts flourished. Writing was invented, with the result that journeys of exploration could at last be recorded. With this, the story of discovery becomes clearer.

In ancient times, the Persian Gulf probably extended farther northwest than it does now, and the Tigris and Euphrates rivers entered it at two separate places instead of, as today, through a single mouth. The region between the two—known as Meso-

potamia, meaning "between the rivers"—included the lands of Akkad and Sumer. In Sumer, one of the world's earliest civilizations emerged. Its life centered around its great rivers, and on these rivers the first journeys of the Sumerians took place. But as their civilization developed, they needed raw materials unobtainable at home, and they began to venture farther afield in search of them. In time, they were sailing the Persian Gulf to trade with India.

As trade led to exploration, so too did conquest, for the expansion of civilization resulted in an increase in knowledge of the world. Around 2700 B.C., nomadic invaders from Akkad conquered the Sumerians, but within 600 years they, too, had been overthrown. The Elamites, their conquerors, in turn fell to new invaders, the Amorites, who made Babylon their capital, and ruled until about 1750 B.C. Babylonia was to come into power again in the 600's B.C., when the Chaldeans made Babylon their capital, initiating the great period of new Babylonian rule.

Before 2900 B.C., in the region of Assur on the upper Tigris, the foundations of the great empire of Assyria were laid. Through trade with Sumer, the Assyrians adopted Sumerian civilization, and in time they began the spread of Assyrian rule. In the 700's B.C., they established an empire extending from the Persian Gulf to the Nile, but in the 600's, they fell to attacks from the Babylonians and Medes.

Civilization first emerged in Egypt, in the valley of the Lower Nile, at approximately the same time as in Sumer, and Egypt was to become one of the most highly developed, as well as one of the longest-lived, nations of ancient times. The life of the country revolved around the Nile River, and on that river the Egyptians made their first voyages. Later, however, like the Sumerians, the need to trade drove them beyond the Egyptian shores. It was they who made the first seagoing voyage ever recorded. In 2600 B.C., an Egyptian fleet voyaged to **Byblos** in Phoenicia for cedarwood from the mountains of Lebanon, and brought 40 shiploads of timber back to Egypt. The Egyptians made other expeditions, too, most of them, like the voyage to Byblos, in search of raw materials unobtainable at home.

Around 2270 B.C., several such trading expeditions were made by **Herkhuf** (dates unknown), governor of Egypt's southern province. Herkhuf traveled south up the Nile, returning with ivory, ebony, and frankincense. He even brought back a pygmy from one expedition.

From Punt, to the southeast of Egypt, the Egyptians obtained the incense that they used in religious ceremonies. The first recorded expedition to Punt took place as early as 2500 B.C., in the reign of **Sahure** (dates unknown). Nearly 500 years later, an Egyptian named **Hennu** (dates unknown) sent a ship to Punt for myrrh. The most famous expedition to Punt was, however, the one commissioned by **Queen Hatshepsut** (dates unknown) in 1493 B.C., and commanded by **Nehsi** (dates unknown), who brought back myrrh trees for Hatshepsut's temple.

Despite their trading voyages, however, the Egyptians were unwilling sailors, and played little part in opening up the Mediterranean Sea. In time, they even left their trading voyages to others, first to the Minoans of Crete, and later to the Phoenicians.

The Minoans were the pioneers of Mediterranean exploration, for Crete's prosperity depended on trade and, for this island civilization, trade depended on seagoing voyages. Their supremacy only lasted until about 1400 B.C., however. Then, the Minoan civilization was destroyed, by an earthquake, or perhaps by an invasion from mainland Greece.

After the fall of Crete, the Phoenicians, the most skillful sailors of ancient times, dominated the Mediterranean. Phoenicia was a narrow country, bounded by the Mediterranean on the west and by the mountains of Lebanon on the east and, when the population outgrew the resources of the land, the Phoenicians looked to the sea for their living. Often employed as carriers by other countries, they also traded in cedarwood from the mountains of Lebanon, and in red-purple cloth, colored with a special local dye. Phoenician seamen explored the Mediterranean from end to end, and even ventured through the Strait of Gibraltar into the unknown Atlantic Ocean. Experts who have discovered similarities in building styles in the Middle East and the Americas

▲ *Egyptian ship of about 2000 B.C.*

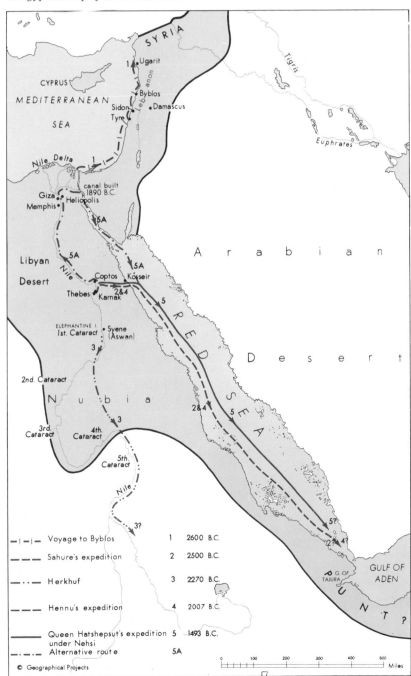

—l—l—	Voyage to Byblos	1	2600 B.C.
————	Sahure's expedition	2	2500 B.C.
—·—·—	Herkhuf	3	2270 B.C.
— — —	Hennu's expedition	4	2007 B.C.
————	Queen Hatshepsut's expedition under Nehsi	5	1493 B.C.
—··—··—	Alternative route	5A	

© Geographical Projects

13

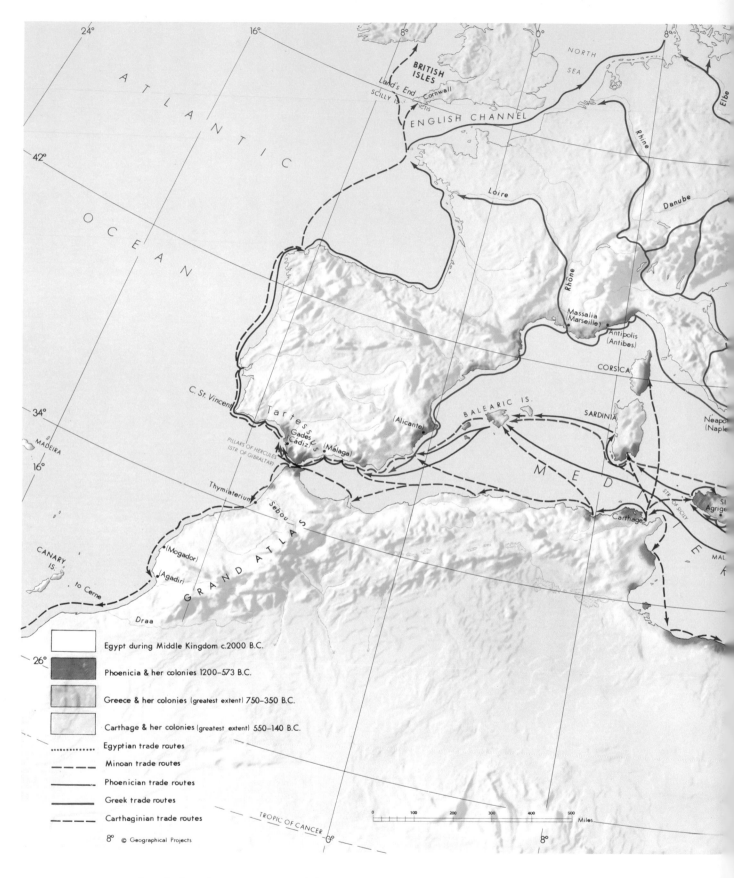

ATLANTIC

OCEAN

NORTH
SEA

BRITISH
ISLES

Land's End
SCILLY IS. Cornwall
Ictis

ENGLISH CHANNEL

Loire

Rhine

Elbe

Danube

Rhône

Massalia
(Marseille)

Antipolis
(Antibes)

CORSICA

SARDINIA

Neapol
(Naple

BALEARIC IS.

M E D

C. St. Vincent

Tartessus

(Alicante)

MADEIRA

Gades
(Cádiz) (Málaga)

PILLARS OF HERCULES
(STR. OF GIBRALTAR)

Carthage

STR. OF SICILY

SI
Agrige

Thymiaterium

Sebou S.

MAL

CANARY
IS.

(Mogador)

(Agadir)

GRAND ATLAS

E
K

to Cerne

Draa

Egypt during Middle Kingdom c.2000 B.C.

Phoenicia & her colonies 1200–573 B.C.

Greece & her colonies (greatest extent) 750–350 B.C.

Carthage & her colonies (greatest extent) 550–140 B.C.

.... Egyptian trade routes

– – – Minoan trade routes

———·— Phoenician trade routes

——— Greek trade routes

– – – Carthaginian trade routes

TROPIC OF CANCER

0   100   200   300   400   500
                                          Miles

8°   © Geographical Projects

even wonder whether they, or other seamen of their time, may have sailed right across the Atlantic. Such voyages are as yet mere conjecture, but we do know that the Phoenicians traveled down the Gulf of Aqaba and into the Red Sea and, although no proof of such an expedition has yet been found, the Greek historian Herodotus records that a Phoenician fleet sailed

right around Africa 600 years before the birth of Christ.

In the 500's B.C., Phoenicia fell to the Babylonians. Thereafter, the Phoenician colony of Carthage took up the challenge of the unknown. Situated in present-day Tunisia, in North Africa, Carthage founded a powerful empire that stretched across North Africa, and reached up into

Spain. The Carthaginians controlled trade in the Mediterranean, but the great sea beyond the Strait of Gibraltar interested them more. Carthaginian sailors discovered Madeira, the Canary Islands, and the Azores, and in about 450 B.C., a Carthaginian named Himilco may have sailed north to Britain. Certainly, at about that time, an explorer

called Hanno voyaged out through the Strait of Gibraltar, and far down the African coast.

Trade or conquest inspired most of the early journeys of exploration, but in Hanno's voyage, another cause is seen. For although Hanno had set out with the intention of founding colonies, he sailed on south even after his mission was completed. For the first time, a simple love of discovery had prompted a journey into the unknown.

This new spirit was embodied in the travels of the Greeks, whose passion for adventure was to lead them far beyond the Mediterranean world. The Greek civilization originated in the Balkan Peninsula in southern Europe, but as time passed, the Greeks founded colonies in Asia Minor, and later spread throughout the Mediterranean Sea. They also explored the Black Sea, and traveled north through Europe to the Baltic, the North Sea, and the English Channel. Their civilization was characterized by a spirit of inquiry and a natural curiosity, and this was evident whenever the Greeks explored.

15

The World of the Greeks

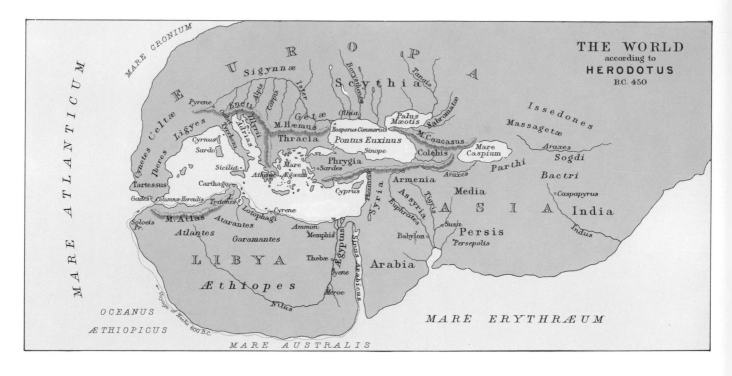

THE WORLD
according to
HERODOTUS
B.C. 450

The Greek historian Herodotus (484?-424? B.C.) wrote his *Histories* in the mid-400's B.C. His book was intended first and foremost as the story of the Greeks' long struggle with the Persian Empire, but Herodotus also included everything he had been able to find out about the geography, history, and peoples of the world. His work, with the map that can be reconstructed from his descriptions, provides our most detailed picture of the world of the Greeks.

Herodotus was not only a great writer, but he was also an adventurous traveler. His researches for his book took him from his home in Halicarnassus in Asia Minor—the peninsula of western Asia between the Black Sea (Herodotus' Pontus Euxinus) and the Mediterranean—through much of the known world. His geographical descriptions are based on the observations he made on this journey, combined with what he learned from people he met. From this information, he built up a picture of the world that is very near the truth. The area he knew was small, but his knowledge of it was amazingly complete.

Herodotus scoffed at the popular belief that Europe, Asia, and Africa (which he called Libya) were all the same size, and made up a circular world. His view of the earth was closer to our own, although, because his knowledge was limited, he described Europe as being as long as

Asia and Africa together. Of the north and east he knew little, mentioning neither Britain nor Scandinavia, and confessing ignorance of eastern Asia. In the geography of India, Herodotus made a surprising mistake. Although he knew that a Greek mariner called **Scylax** (dates unknown) had sailed down the Indus River and around Arabia into the Red Sea, Herodotus maintained that the Indus flowed southeast.

In two respects, Herodotus' knowledge was considerably in advance of his time. He realized that the Caspian was an inland sea and not, as many geographers thought, a gulf connected to the ocean that was supposed to encircle the earth. Also, he stated that Africa was surrounded by sea, and cited the Phoenician voyage commissioned by Necho in 600 B.C. as definite proof of this. Some 500 years after Herodotus wrote, the geographer Ptolemy, whose knowledge was more detailed than Herodotus', mistakenly joined southern Africa to Asia, making the Indian Ocean into an inland sea. Herodotus' knowledge of the course of the Nile was, however, as hazy as that of the Indus. According to him, it rose south of the Atlas, and flowed across Africa before turning north to flow through Egypt toward the Mediterranean Sea.

Nearly 50 years after Herodotus' travels, another Greek made a journey that did much to increase knowledge of the east. A soldier

▲ *World map, reconstructed from descriptions in Herodotus'* Histories.

named **Xenophon** (434?-355? B.C.) led a force of 10,000 Greek troops from the heart of the Persian Empire overland to the Black Sea. The Greeks had joined the Persian prince **Cyrus** (424?-401 B.C.) in a war against his brother King Artaxerxes II but on Cyrus' death in battle at Cunaxa, they were stranded far from home. They then elected Xenophon to lead them back to Greece. The way overland through Asia Minor was long, and Xenophon therefore decided to try to reach the Black Sea, from which the Greeks could easily find their way home. Although the route was unknown, and the conditions harsh, Xenophon managed to complete the grueling journey. He even made notes about the lands through which he and his 10,000 men had passed, and which had formerly been unknown to the Greeks.

Late in the 300's, another Greek made a journey that helped to fill in the gaps in Herodotus' description of the north. His name was **Pytheas** (dates unknown), and he set out from Massalia (Marseille) in about 325 B.C. Opinions differ as to the route he followed, but it is thought he sailed up the western coast of Europe, and along the coast of Britain before continuing into the northern seas. He had heard of an island called Thule, supposed to be the "outermost of all countries", and

ATLANTIC

OCEAN

24° 66° ARCTIC CIRCLE

16°

8°

0°

8°

16°

24°

32°

ARCTIC CIRCLE 66°

THULE (ICELAND)

FAEROE IS.

SHETLAND IS. 2

THULE?

THULE? 2

S c a n d i n a v i a

58°

SCOTLAND

Duncansby Hd.

N O R T H

S E A

BALTIC SEA

IRELAND

ENGLAND

1

HELGOLAND 2

Land's End Cornwall

N. Foreland

1 2

2?

Rhine

50°

ENGLISH CHANNEL

USHANT 1

2

1

Corbilo
(St. Nazaire) Loire

2?

2? 2?

BAY OF
BISCAY

2?

Rhône 2?

2? 2?

2? Massalia

C. St. Vincent

MEDITERRANEAN

SEA

PILLARS OF HERCULES
(STR. OF GIBRALTAR)

2

1

42°

34°

0 100 200 300 400 800
Miles

0°

8°

16°

50°

—————— 1 Pytheas' route 325 B.C.

—————— 2 Alternative routes which some authorities
believe Pytheas followed

he thought that if he reached that land, he might discover the farthest limits of the world.

Thule was probably Iceland, although some think it was Norway, and evidence has been produced to support both claims. It is not certain, however, whether Pytheas did get there, for further details of his voyage are obscure. When he returned to Massalia, far from being honored for his feat, he found his stories were received with disbelief.

While Pytheas was making his voyage of discovery north, another Greek was exploring in the eastern extreme of the world known to the peoples of the Mediterranean. No two expeditions could have been more different. Pytheas' small ship compares strangely with the massed troops of the Macedonian-Greek army. Pytheas' contemporary reputation is in contrast to the renown of **Alexander the Great** (356-323 B.C.).

Alexander was born in 356 B.C., son of King Philip II of Macedonia.

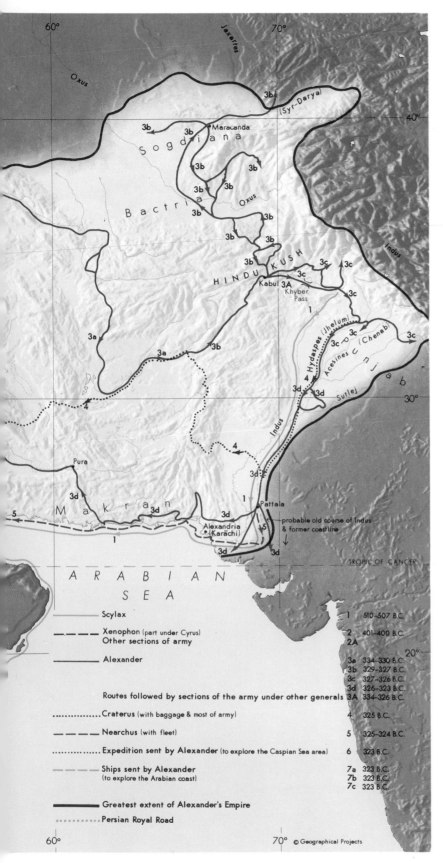

When Alexander heard of Darius' death, he proclaimed himself king of Persia. His pursuit of the Persian monarch had led him deep into the Persian Empire, but although his conquest was complete, he did not turn back. Instead, he spent several years exploring east into Sogdiana and Bactria, then in 327 B.C., crossed into northern India. There, wearied by the long years of war, his men rebelled. They would follow him no further.

Ordering troops to march along the banks of the Indus as a safeguard against attack by hostile tribes, Alexander and the rest of his men sailed down the river in a fleet of especially constructed ships. From the Indus delta, he sent the sick and wounded with **Craterus** (?-321 B.C.) by the overland route to Persia, while he himself led his best troops along the unexplored Makran coast. **Nearchus** (dates unknown) was to sail to the Persian Gulf. In 324 B.C., the army was reunited in Susa.

Alexander was as much an explorer as a conqueror, and his journeys almost doubled the area known to the Greeks. He routed his marches through as much unknown country as possible, and arranged that a

▼ *Alexander the Great.*

On his father's death, he inherited not only the kingdom but also a plan to unite the Macedonians and Greeks against the Persians, who had overrun the Greek colonies in Asia Minor, and whose armies threatened Greece. When Alexander crossed the Hellespont (Dardanelles) in 334 B.C., the conquest of Persia was his goal.

Alexander's army swept through the Persian Empire, liberating the Greek colonies in Asia Minor and pressing south into Syria and Egypt, where he established Greek rule. Returning north, he defeated the Persian army at Gaugamela, but King Darius escaped and fled east. Soon afterward, he was murdered.

record be kept of all the new things he saw. After his return from India, he sent expeditions to the Caspian Sea, and down the Arabian coast, but when he died in Babylon in 323 B.C., his curiosity about the unknown was still unsated. No one knows what discoveries he might have made had he lived.

SCOTLAND

NORTH SEA

BALTIC SEA

BRITAIN

WALES
ENGLAND

Thames

ATLANTIC

ENGLISH CHANNEL

lost in A.D. 9

OCEAN

G A U L

Rhine

Danube

A L P S

Col de la
Traversette

Rhône

ILLYRIA

PYRENEES

Massalia

LIGURIAN
SEA

L. Trasimeno

Danube

Saguntum

CORSICA

Rome

Cannae

BALEARIC IS.

SARDINIA

Gades
(Cadiz)

STR. OF GIBRALTAR

Alicante

M E D I T E R R A N E A N

New Carthage
(Cartagena)

Caesarea

SICILY

M A U R E T A N I A

Carthage

NUMIDIA

Zama

GRAND ATLAS

SAHARAN ATLAS

Ge

CRETE

Roman Republic in 218 B.C.

Roman Empire at its greatest extent A.D. 117

Carthage and her colonies 218 B.C.

Hannibal   1 218–202 B.C.

Aelius Gallus   2 25–24 B.C.

Suetonius Paulinus 3 A.D. 42

Julius Caesar's campaigns in Gaul, Spain, Britain & Armenia 61–47 B.C.

Julius Caesar's campaigns in the civil war against Pompey 49–45 B.C.

© Geographical Projects

0   100   200   300   400   500
Miles

The Roman Empire

The ancient Mediterranean world was to see the rise of one more great power—Rome. From about 500 B.C., the city of Rome had gradually increased the territory it ruled, but when it looked beyond the frontiers of Italy, it saw the might of Carthage in its way. Three wars—the Punic Wars—arose from the Romans' struggle to overcome Carthage.

The Punic Wars, though fought over known territory, gave rise to one of the greatest feats of military exploration ever. In 218 B.C., on the outbreak of the second war, the Carthaginian general **Hannibal** (247-183 B.C.) led his troops from Spain, across the Pyrenees and through Gaul (France), and over the Alps, the great mountain range guarding Italy's northern frontier. He planned a surprise attack on the Romans, and knew they would never expect him to use such a hazardous route. Despite the dangers his army faced, it made the 135-mile crossing in only 15 days.

Even Hannibal's inspired leadership could not hold back the power of Rome, however. In 201 B.C., Carthage lost the war and, little more than 50 years later, the city itself was destroyed. Now Rome reigned supreme in the Mediterranean. As the Romans were more interested in conquest than in exploration, most of their journeys were military expeditions—with discovery an occasional bonus.

One such expedition was that of **Aelius Gallus** (dates unknown) to southern Arabia in 25-4 B.C. Gallus failed in his object of capturing Marib, center of the valuable Arabian trade, so although he traveled over much new country, his expedition was judged a failure. The crossing of the Atlas by **Suetonius Paulinus** (dates unknown) in A.D. 42 was far more acclaimed, even though his only aim was to explore.

One Roman general did see his conquests as more than military achievements. This was **Julius Caesar** (100-44 B.C.). It was Caesar who conquered the country the Romans called Gaul, and who in 55 B.C. first led his troops into Britain. The accounts he wrote of the lands he visited are some of the earliest descriptions of them in existence.

Caesar's battles against the northern barbarians were followed by a more bitter struggle—civil war. Fearing that he had grown too powerful, the Roman rulers appointed **Pompey** (106-48 B.C.) to throw him down. For four years the opposing forces battled throughout the empire. When the war ended, Pompey was dead, and Caesar was in control of Rome.

The Far East

Around 1700 B.C., in the fertile valley of the Hwang Ho, the earliest Chinese civilization of which there is archeological evidence emerged. Cut off by the deserts and mountain ranges of central Asia, China grew up independently of the contemporary Mediterranean world. It was not until the 100's B.C. that it emerged from its isolation and made its first contacts with the civilizations of the West.

By that time, China's rulers had pushed out its frontiers far beyond their original limits in the valley of the Hwang Ho. In the north, part of the Great Wall of China had been built to protect the empire against barbarian attacks, yet in the 100's B.C., China's ruling Han dynasty was still engaged in a constant struggle against the Huns, a warlike people from northern Asia. It was the Han emperor Wu Ti's search for an ally in this struggle that led the Chinese to make their first journeys westward.

The people with whom Wu Ti hoped to unite against the Huns were the Yue-Chi, a nomadic race from central Asia. In 138 B.C., he sent **Chang Ch'ien** (dates unknown) on a mission to the Yue-Chi, but at the start of his journey, Chang spent 10 years as prisoner of the Huns. Although he did eventually reach the Yue-Chi, his embassy met with little success. But he did learn much about the hitherto unknown lands and peoples that he saw, and his knowledge was instrumental in the setting up in 105 B.C. of the Silk

▼ *Hsuan-tsang.*

Route across central Asia, linking China to the West.

Along this great trade route were carried the precious supplies of silk that Roman Europe craved and that China alone could produce. But other luxuries besides silk could be obtained in the East. At first, they were brought to Europe by Arab traders, but as demand increased, Europeans themselves began to travel to the lands where the Eastern treasures were found.

By the time of Christ, mariners bound for Asia had discovered the advantage of the seasonal monsoon winds. The South West Monsoon, which blows in summer, would carry them across the Indian Ocean to their destination, and they could use the North East Monsoon in winter to return. In time, they sailed around the tip of India and discovered that the monsoons could be used to travel from India to Southeast Asia across the Bay of Bengal. The Malay Peninsula was rounded, and the seamen from the West pushed northward. By A.D. 120, China had been reached.

In A.D. 476, Rome fell to the barbarians. Darkness descended in Europe, and European voyages of exploration virtually ceased. Asia, too, was in turmoil, but one Chinese traveler did explore—in defiance of the emperor's orders forbidding him to leave China and journey in the troubled lands.

Hsuan-tsang (A.D. 600?-664), a Buddhist monk whose aim was to learn more about his religion, set out from China in A.D. 629. He was making for India, the birthplace of Buddhism. Hsuan's 16-year journey took him west to Bactria, then over the Hindu Kush and east into Kashmir. He studied for two years there, and visited cities and monasteries in the valley of the Ganges River. He traveled down the east coast of India, bordering the Bay of Bengal, and returned north up the west coast to recross the Hindu Kush and head for home. In 645, Hsuan arrived back in China. So important was his expedition considered that, far from being reprimanded for ignoring the ban on his journey, he was received with great honor.

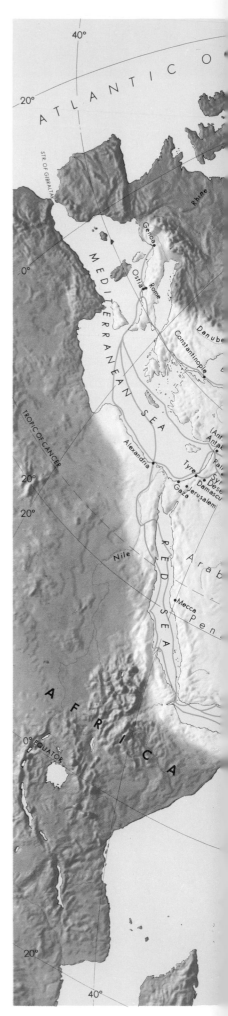

ARCTIC CIRCLE

80°   0°   20°   40°   60°   80°   100°   120°   140°   160°   180°   60°

80°

ARCTIC CIRCLE

S O R K N E Y IS
SHETLAND IS.

a n d i n a v i a

ALTIC SEA

U R A L M O U N T A I N S

40°

160°

Volga

CASPIAN SEA

Dnepr

A R T H I A

Volga

M o n g o l i a   Gobi Desert   M a n c h u r i a

Kyzyl Kum

Tashkent

Samarkand

Turfan   2   built c.300 B.C.   built c.290 B.C.

40°

esiphon

Merv

Oxus

Balkh

Bactria

HINDU

Peshawar

Kashmir

Multan

Indus

la

A R A B I A N
S E A

Malabar Coast

Madras

C. Comorin

CEYLON

N D I A N   O C E A N

T I E N - S H A N

Kashgar   Taklamakan
Desert

Khotan

PAMIRS

KUSH

Indus

2

Benares   Ganges

2

B A Y   O F

B E N G A L

STR. OF MALACCA

Malay Pena.

Shang (An-yang)

Hwang Ho

Changan

Yangtze R.

built 112 B.C.

built 7/3

EAST
CHINA
SEA

TROPIC OF CANCER

20°

Canton

P A C I F I C

O C E A N

S O U T H   C H I N A   S E A

G. OF
SIAM

EQUATOR 0°

60°   80°   100°

120°

Chang Ch'ien 1 138–126 B.C.

Hsuan–tsang 2 A.D. 629–645

Trade routes

Great Wall of China

Boundary of early (Western) Han dynasty c.100 B.C.

Boundary of later (Eastern) Han dynasty c. A.D. 100

0   250   500   750   1000   1250   1500
Miles

© Geographical Projects 120°

2 The World Sleeps

In A.D. 476, Rome was taken by the barbarians. Her mighty empire, which had once united Europe and the Mediterranean area, crumbled and fell. Europe sank into turmoil. The turbulence and unrest of those years echoed throughout the known world and, as the dust settled, a new picture emerged. In Europe, many small kingdoms had grown up, each supplying its own needs, and caring little for other lands. In the Middle East, however, the concept of empire was reborn. There, in the 600's, in Arabia, the prophet Mohammed preached the religion of Islam. His Arab followers, in their desire to spread his teachings, conquered vast territories. By the 900's, the Islamic Empire stretched from western India, through southwest Asia, and across northern Africa to the Atlantic Ocean. Its rule even extended up into Spain, across the Strait of Gibraltar.

For Europeans in the years following the fall of Rome, the world was a narrow one, turned inward on itself. Bounded on the west by the wild waters of the Atlantic Ocean, and on the east by the barbarian-infested plains of Asia, its life centered on the Mediterranean Sea. In this world, there was little place for exploration. Journeys were dangerous and their outcome uncertain. What travel did take place was, like the conquests of the Arabs, inspired mainly by religion. The growing Christian communities sent out missionaries to convert the heathen, and pilgrims ventured abroad to visit the holy places of their faith.

Although Christianity did inspire some travel, it had the adverse effect of halting the increase of geographical knowledge. This was because Church leaders were afraid that discoveries might disprove accepted belief, as set out in the Bible. They based their view of the earth on Biblical descriptions and, as the travels of ancient times were forgotten, strange superstitions became rife. Europeans thought that the earth was flat, and that if they sailed too far in any direction they would fall off the edge. They feared strange monsters and other imaginary dangers, and their fear, added to the terror of other, actual perils, made the prospect of travel terrible. Most Europeans dared not venture beyond the bounds of the world they knew.

Yet, even in those troubled times, the spirit of discovery never completely died in Europe. A few courageous travelers did brave the unknown, journeying far beyond the limited horizons of their time. Some sailed out into the Atlantic, to Iceland, Greenland, and probably to America. Others traveled east, across central Asia to China, well known in times past, but long cut off from Europe. Their journeys had few lasting results, for the paths they had pioneered were soon forgotten. But they did succeed in overcoming the barriers of fear and superstition that had isolated Europe. By their travels, they proved that the frontiers of Europe were not the limits of the world.

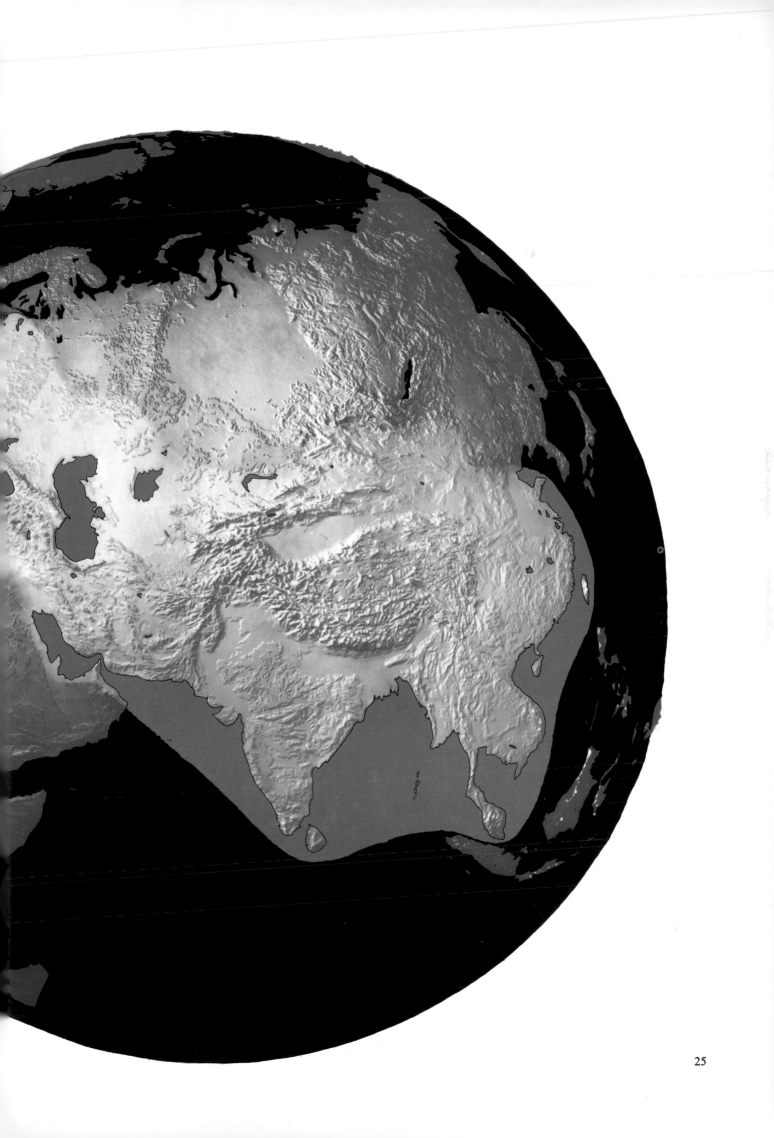

The Western Travelers

In the 500's, in search of converts to Christianity, the Irish set sail. Theirs were, however, no ordinary missionary voyages. When they launched their frail boats onto the Atlantic Ocean, the Irish were braving an unknown world.

The most astounding Viking journeys were made in the Atlantic, but their expeditions were not all ocean voyages. Vikings also traveled through Europe, as far as the Mediterranean Sea. ▼

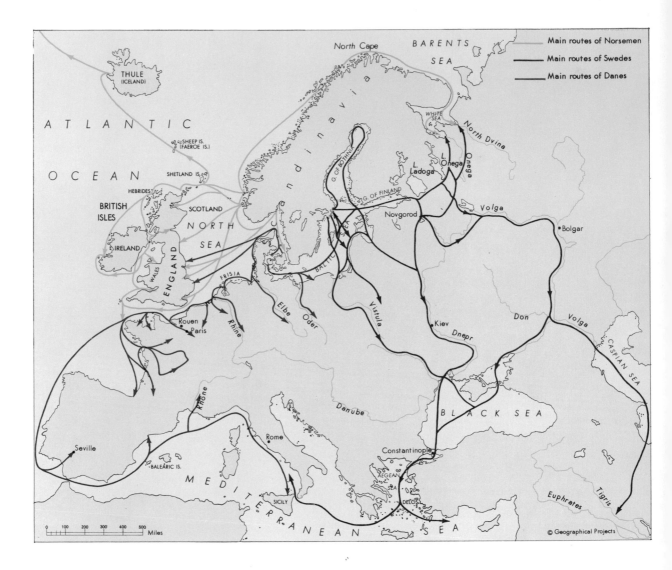

From the monasteries of Ireland, Irish monks had first spread the word of God among their neighbors in Cornwall, in southwest England, Wales, and northern France. As time passed, however, they began to travel farther afield in search of new lands in which to preach. Some of their journeys are recorded in monastery archives, but others survive only as legends.

One of the most famous Irish legends recounts the voyage of **Saint Brendan** (484–577). From monastic records, Brendan is known to have visited Scotland, Wales, and Brittany. The legend, however, tells of journeys to more distant lands, to the Sheep Islands (probably the Faeroe Islands), the Paradise of Birds (perhaps the Shetland Islands or the Outer Hebrides), and other mysterious lands far out in the Atlantic Ocean. So widely is Brendan supposed to have traveled, it seems likely that he has been credited with the voyages of other, unknown Irish seafarers besides his own.

Definite proof does, however, exist of other Irish voyages to northern islands. In 563, Saint Columba founded a monastery on Iona, and from there the Irish set out to convert the Scottish people of the mainland. In time, the Irish-Scots began to travel north. By about 700, they are known to have reached the Faeroe Islands. Some 70 years later, they arrived in Iceland. They called it Thule.

At about this time, the seafarers who were to continue the Irish explorations first appeared on the waters of the Atlantic. They were the Vikings, from Scandinavia in the north. The Viking homelands were poor and overcrowded, and the Vikings found it more profitable to raid their more prosperous neighbors than to try to scratch out a living at home. From the late 700's, they terrorized Europe, sweeping south to Spain, Italy, and North Africa. The Swedish Vikings, unlike the Danes and Norsemen (Norwegians), were interested in trade, and traveled overland to the Caspian and Black seas and beyond. It is probably from one of the Swedish tribes, the Rus, that the name of Russia comes.

While at first the Vikings were concerned solely with plunder, later they voyaged in search of new lands to settle. They pushed west, and word of their coming must have reached Iceland for, by 870, Iceland had

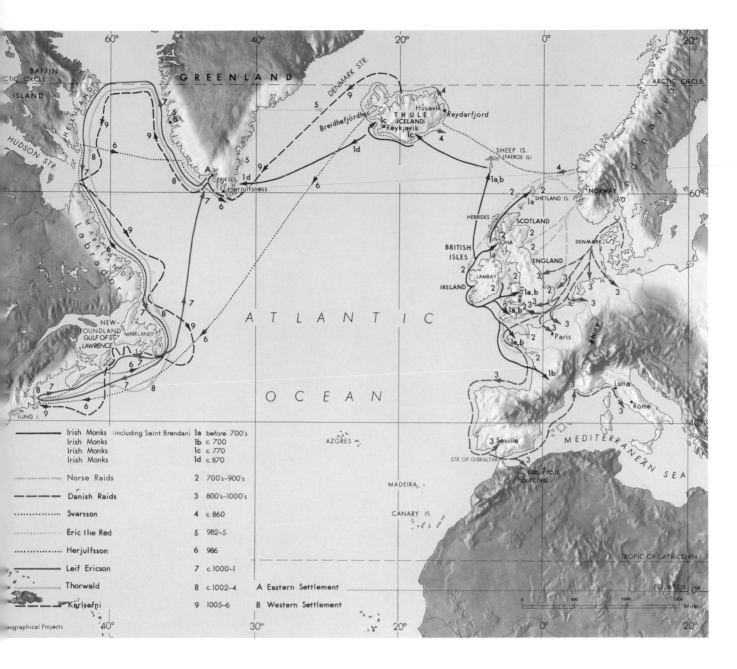

been abandoned by the Irish, who fled farther west. According to the sagas, which tell the story of Viking voyaging, the Vikings themselves discovered Iceland by accident. In about 860, **Gardar Svarsson** (dates unknown) was blown off course, and landed on the island's southeast coast. Others followed him and, within 70 years, Iceland was a thriving Viking colony.

By the end of the 900's, the Vikings were again seeking new lands. When **Eric the Red** (dates unknown) was exiled from Iceland in 982, he set out west. He landed in the country discovered by the Irish in their flight from Iceland more than 100 years before. Eric called it Greenland, and in 985 he returned to colonize the island. On the west coast of Greenland, the colonists founded two communities, which they called the Eastern Settlement and the Western Settlement.

From Greenland, it was only a short step to the shores of America and, so the sagas say, the first Vikings made the crossing the year after Eric had founded his Greenland colony. But **Bjarni Herjulfsson** (dates unknown), who made the first landfall, never went ashore. It was left to **Leif Ericson** (dates unknown), son of Eric the Red, to take that adventurous step.

In about 1000, Leif Ericson set sail for Herjulfsson's new land. He made three landfalls on the American coast—Helluland, which was probably part of Baffin Island; Markland, which was probably in Labrador or Newfoundland; and Vinland, farther south. The climate was mild in Vinland, and Leif's men spent the winter there before setting out for home.

Leif's glowing reports of Vinland inspired his brother **Thorwald** (dates unknown) to try his luck in this new land. He found it so beautiful that he wanted to make his home there. But tragedy overtook the Vikings when, in a clash with the Indians, Thorwald was killed.

The American Indians were to destroy Viking hopes of settling in Vinland. In 1005-6, the attempt of **Thorfinn Karlsefni** (dates unknown) to found a colony had to be abandoned when fighting broke out between Indians and colonists. Although other Vikings did make their way to Vinland, their push west was nearly over. Within a few years, America had been forgotten.

27

The World beyond Europe

The East remained a mystery to the peoples of Europe long after the Irish and Viking voyages into the Atlantic in the west. The atmosphere in Europe from about A.D. 500 onward—the period often called the "Dark Ages"—did not favor exploration, for religious teaching fixed its own limits on the world. It would take impending disaster to force Europeans to travel east.

In those years, the study of geography suffered from a notably unscientific approach. Maps were made by scholars, and scholars were invariably monks, who accepted without question the Church's view of the world. Even though great journeys of exploration were undertaken by the Moslem Arabs throughout this period, the knowledge of the Moslems was ignored in Europe.

European map makers based their work on Christian principles, and interpreted Biblical statements and descriptions literally to build up a picture of the world. Typical of cartographers' work during this time are the so-called "Beatus" maps. These maps—drawn between the 900's and 1200's—were copied from one used by Beatus of Valcavado

(dates unknown) to illustrate his *Commentary on the Apocalypse* of 776. Beatus was a Spanish Benedictine monk who, with his followers, had a profound effect on religious cartography. Beatus maps are symbolic, oriented to the sacred East where Palestine, the birthplace of Christianity, is situated. Ironically, although Christian maps of those years were thus oriented to the East, Palestine and the sacred shrines of Christendom were almost always under Islamic rule.

Because east is placed at the top in Beatus maps, they are easier to read if they are given a quarter turn to the right. Thus, the position of the continents corresponds to a modern map of the world. To the north lies Europe, cut by a narrow, riverlike Adriatic between Italy and Acaia (Greece), and divided from Asia by an enlarged Hellespont (Dardanelles), and a small Black Sea. Asia, in turn, is divided into two parts, Asia Minor and Asia Major. Somewhere between the two, the Garden of Eden, with Adam, Eve, and the serpent, is shown.

West of Asia Major lies the continent Beatus called Libia, of

which, according to his map, Africa was only a part. South of this continent lies an ocean, beyond which another land, called the "fourth part of the world", is shown. According to the inscription on this region, nothing is known of the fourth part of the world because of the heat of the sun. The inscription records, however, that there live the Antipodeans, "of whom so many tales are told".

Around the simplified and truncated world of the Beatus maps lies an ocean, which here teems with islands, fish, and boats. Off the coast of Europe, this ocean is named the Oceanus Britannicus, and it is thought that one of the islands in it represents the British Isles. Off the coast of Libia lie the Insulae Fortunatarum—the Fortunate Islands, a name by which the Canaries were once known. In general, however, the picture of the world in Beatus maps was so defective that, with only such maps to help them, it is understandable why Europeans were reluctant to venture out into the world.

World map, after that of Beatus, made in France between 1028 and 1072. ▼

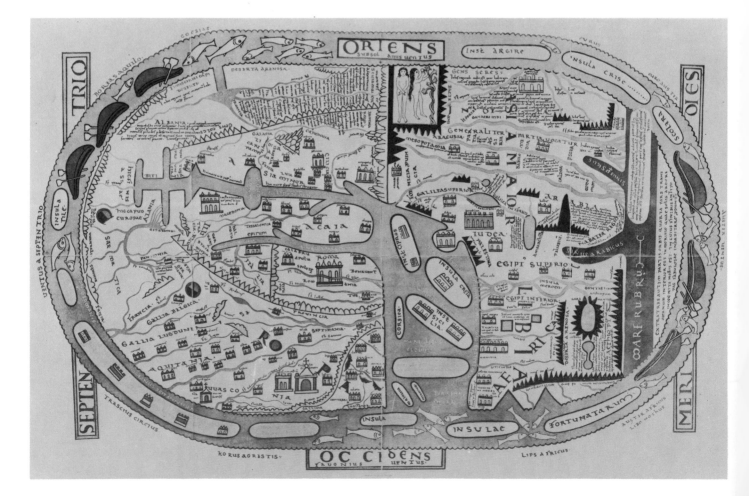

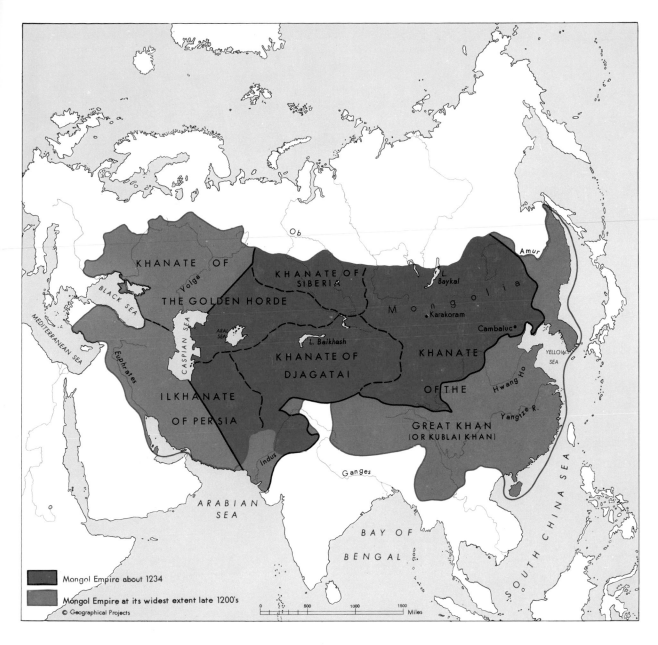

KHANATE OF
THE GOLDEN HORDE

KHANATE OF
SIBERIA

Mongolia

Karakoram

Cambaluc

KHANATE OF
DJAGATAI

KHANATE

OF THE

ILKHANATE

OF PERSIA

GREAT KHAN
(OR KUBLAI KHAN)

BLACK SEA

MEDITERRANEAN SEA

CASPIAN SEA

ARAL SEA

L. Baikal

L. Balkhash

Volga

Euphrates

Indus

Ganges

Hwang Ho

Yangtze R.

YELLOW SEA

Amur

Ob

ARABIAN
SEA

BAY OF
BENGAL

SOUTH CHINA SEA

Mongol Empire about 1234

Mongol Empire at its widest extent late 1200's

© Geographical Projects

0   500   1000   1500   Miles

元太祖

鐵木真

In the 1200's, from their bleak homeland on the Mongolian steppes, the Mongol warriors swept through Asia. They conquered all in their path. Cities, countries, empires —all fell before their advance.

The man behind the Mongol rise to power was Genghis Khan. Born in 1162, he became khan (ruler) of the Mongols in 1206. He reorganized Mongol society along feudal lines, and welded the nomad Mongol warriors into one of the most efficient fighting units the world has known. By 1234, seven years after his death, the Mongol Empire reached from the Yellow Sea to the Caspian.

Under Genghis Khan's successors, the Mongol lands stretched farther still. Too large to be governed by one central administration, the empire was divided into five smaller khanates under Kublai Khan, Genghis' grandson. Each owed allegiance to the Great Khan, supreme ruler of the

◀ *Genghis Khan.*

Mongols, whose personal domain was the easternmost of the five.

In the north, the khans of Siberia ruled a region that lay southwest of present-day Siberia. In central Asia, Genghis Khan's son Djagatai and his heirs held sway. Southern Russia was ruled by Genghis Khan's grandson Batu. He set up the Golden Horde, so called because he made his original headquarters (called *ordu* by the Mongols) in a great golden tent. The Ilkhans of Persia ruled what is now Iran. Ilkhans means "obedient khans", for, like the other Mongol rulers, the Ilkhans were vassals of the Great Khan.

At first, Europe knew nothing of this great Eastern empire. But as the Mongols drove west, and devastated the frontier lands of eastern Europe, they forced the Europeans to recognize their might. So, with their very existence threatened, the Europeans for the first time looked out fearfully into the vast, unknown Eastern world.

Into the East

In 1241, the Mongol advance west halted. The Great Khan Ogotai was dead, and the Mongol leaders hurried back to their homeland for the election of a new Great Khan. In the lull that followed, the first Europeans ventured east.

The city-state of Venice, home of the Polo family, was well situated as a center for trade between East and West. By the mid-1200's, it ruled the world's greatest commercial empire. ▼

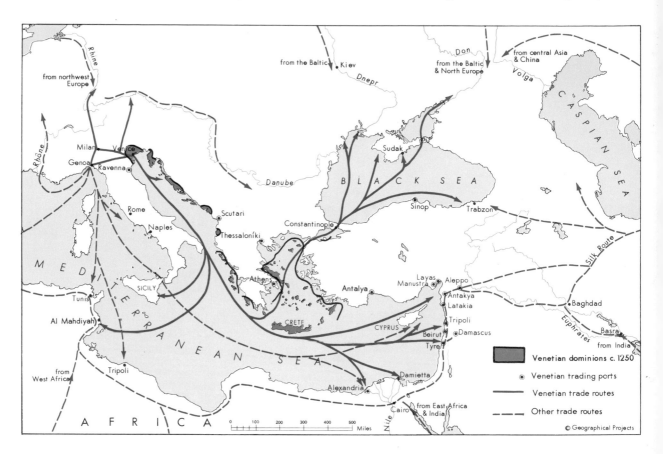

The European leaders knew nothing of events in Mongolia, and had no idea what had made the Mongols call off their advance. As far as they knew, the rampaging hordes might at any moment resume their progress west. It was in an attempt to prevent such an occurrence that Pope Innocent IV sent a mission to the Mongol rulers in 1245. He charged his envoy, **Giovanni de Piano Carpini** (1182-1252), to persuade the Mongols to give up war, and to convert them to the Christian faith. Carpini reached the Mongol summer court at Syra Orda in time to see the coronation of Kuyuk, the new Great Khan. But his long and dangerous journey was all for nothing, and he had to return to Europe with his mission unfulfilled.

William of Rubruck (1215-1270) led a missionary expedition to the Mongols in 1252, but met with no more success. The Mongols refused to become Christians, and the letter Rubruck carried back to his patron, King Louis of France, held a threat of war. Rubruck was, however, the first European to visit the Mongol capital, Karakoram, and to write an account of his experiences in the East.

In 1259, Kublai was elected Great Khan of the Mongols, and under his rule, peace came to the Mongol domains. His new capital, Cambaluc (*Khanbalik,* the "City of the Great Khan"), was a magnificent and wealthy place, to which Kublai welcomed foreign travelers, traders, and priests.

The first Europeans to visit Cambaluc—and, indeed, the first to reach China (which they called Cathay)—were two Venetian merchants, **Nicolò** and **Maffeo Polo** (dates unknown). In 1255, the Polos left Venice for a trading trip to Constantinople. Their expedition was to last 14 years, and would take them far beyond their original goal. They traveled into lands never seen by Europeans, and met the Great Khan, Kublai. When they set out for home, they promised to return to his court.

In 1271, Nicolò and Maffeo Polo, accompanied this time by Nicolò's son **Marco** (1254?-1324?) set out once more for the East. Their journey was to change the course of history. It gave Europe a picture of the East that was fabulous beyond the wildest imaginings, and destroyed for ever the narrow insularity of the Mediterranean world.

The Polos stayed at Kublai Khan's court for 16 years, during which time Marco acted as the khan's adviser, and traveled on diplomatic missions throughout the Far East. In the account of the Polos' travels which was recorded by the writer Rusticello, Marco tells of their adventures, mentioning the strange people and places they saw, and giving geographical descriptions and information on trading possibilities. Many thought it exaggerated, but when asked if he wanted to alter anything, Marco replied: "I did not write half of what I saw."

Other Europeans, too, were welcomed at Kublai's court, among them the missionary **John of Montecorvino** (1247-1328?). John, a Franciscan friar, made his journey to China by sea. There, he founded a church, and succeeded in making many converts to the Christian faith.

Under Kublai Khan, the long disused trade routes across Asia were re-opened, and caravans journeyed between East and West. With one such, the Polo brothers traveled east. ▶

	Carpini	1	1245-7
	Rubruck	2	1252-5
	Polo brothers, N. & M.	3	1255-69
	Polo, Marco (with Polo brothers)	4	1271-95
	Polo, Marco	4A	
	Montecorvino	5	1291-4

© Geographical Projects

3 The Great Age

In the 1400's and early 1500's, in one glorious surge of voyaging and discovery, the invisible frontiers that had so long surrounded Europe finally fell. The first steps forward were tentative enough, but once the barriers of fear and superstition had been breached, progress was swift. In 50 short years, European sailors rounded the Cape of Good Hope and sailed to India, crossed the Atlantic to the Americas, and at last, in the heroic culmination of this great age, sailed all the way around the world.

No single factor was responsible for this sudden burst of exploration—rather, it was the product of a combination of circumstances and events. To begin with, the Europe of those years was no longer the narrow, inward-looking world of earlier times. The new lands the Vikings had discovered in the west had been forgotten, but the travels of Marco Polo and his contemporaries had reminded Europeans that in the east lay countries whose wealth and splendor surpassed those of Europe herself. Trade with those countries, which had lapsed since the days of the Roman Empire, was re-established. By the 1400's, many of the necessities, and most of the luxuries, of European life were imported from the East.

The importance of the Eastern trade was to prove a major factor in the revival of European interest in the world. All Eastern goods reached Europe through the ports and markets of the Middle East and, in the 1400's, these vital commercial centers were in Moslem Arab hands, as they had been for some 700 years. It was only on terms dictated by the Moslems that Europe could obtain Eastern goods at all and, as the Moslems would trade solely with the Italian city-states of Venice and Genoa, other European countries had to buy through them. Prices rose each time the goods changed hands, and by the 1400's, Europeans were reasoning that if they could find a new route to the East, bypassing these avaricious middlemen, they would be able to buy more cheaply directly from the producers of the goods.

Not only did Europe have a vital reason to take an interest in discovery, but at the same time, seemingly unrelated events combined to enable exploration to take place. The reappearance in Europe of Greek and Roman works on geography, mathematics, and astronomy, lost since the fall of the classical world, provided important new sources of knowledge, vital to the study of geography and to the science of navigation. Developments in shipbuilding also helped. During this period, for example, was built the first caravel, a light, seaworthy ship that sailed well both before and into the wind, and was also suitable for long voyages across dangerous seas. It was in Portugal and Spain that the first caravels were developed, and from these countries, with their long seafaring tradition, the voyages that marked the beginning of what we now call the Great Age of Discovery took place.

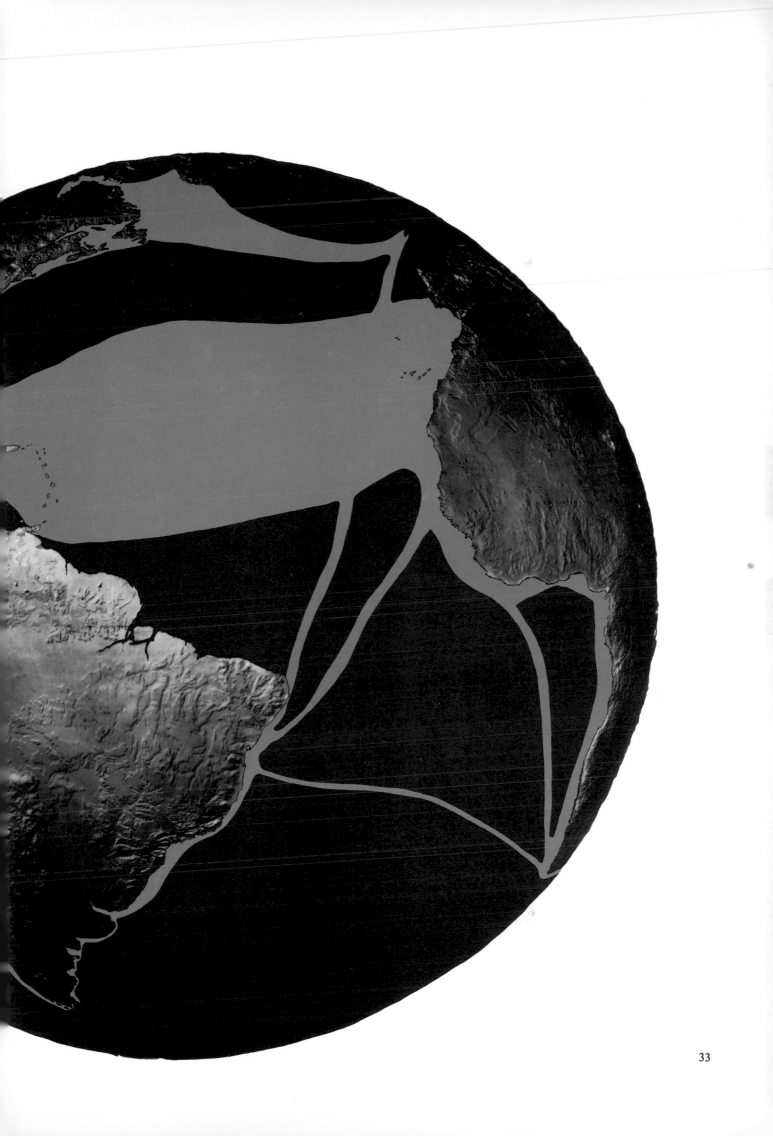

A Sea Route to India

Prince Henry of Portugal never went on a voyage himself, nor did he direct the journeys that finally opened a sea route to the East. But it was his pioneering work that paved the way for those journeys, and it was due to him that the Great Age of Discovery began.

Henry was born in 1394, the third son of Portugal's King John I. As a young man, he took part in an expedition that captured the Moslem stronghold of Ceuta in North Africa. From this he learned much about Africa, and about the Moslem Empire, which was richer and stretched farther south than he had ever dreamed. When he returned home, he pondered how he could use his new knowledge to benefit his country, and to further his crusading aims. For, like many Europeans, he hated the Moslem "unbelievers", and longed to destroy their power.

By sending his ships south down the African coast, Henry reasoned, he might discover the Moslem Empire's farthest limits, and there find a weak spot at which he could direct an attack. There, too, he might find allies, for, like most Europeans in the 1400's, he believed that somewhere in Africa lay a Christian kingdom ruled by a priest-king called Prester John. Henry was sure that if an embassy could reach that legendary monarch, he might be persuaded to join the Portuguese crusade against the Moslems.

A Holy War against Islam was not Henry's only reason for his interest in the south, however. Like most pioneers of discovery, he was fascinated by the unknown, and he thought exploration might lead to new and profitable trade. In the southern lands, there would be fresh sources of commerce—and competitors would probably be few. Henry may even have envisaged the possibility of opening a new route to the rich countries of the East.

Soon after 1418, Henry settled at Sagres, to the west of Lagos. There he built an observatory and naval arsenal, and founded his "school of navigation". Little is known about the school, for the Portuguese were secretive about everything concerning exploration. But there Henry brought together experts on maps and navigation, and trained the pilots who would undertake his voyages.

Portugal was a nation of seafarers and, for his voyages, Henry knew that he could count on reliable ships, and on experienced crews. But those very men put the first difficulty in his way. They refused to sail beyond Cape Bojador, a headland on the African mainland south of the Canary Islands and, at that time, the southern limit of the known world. The Portuguese knew of no sailor who had passed Cape Bojador and lived. Some thought the seas beyond boiled and steamed, others that any white man who traveled farther south would turn black. Portuguese mariners called the southern ocean the "Sea of Darkness", and would not sail there.

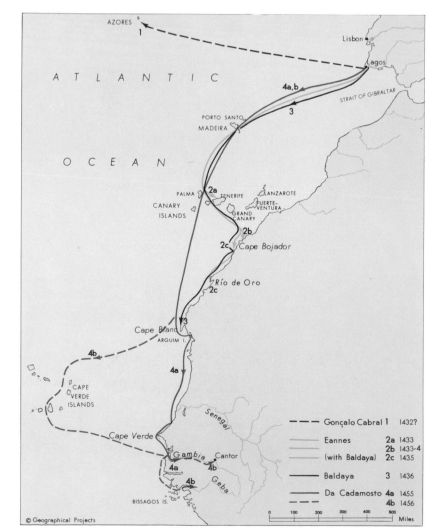

▲ *Prince Henry the Navigator.*

Prince Henry's first task was to dispel these fears. He sent out ship after ship to round Cape Bojador, but none of his captains would do it. Some went crusading against the Moslems, others sailed to Madeira or the Canary Islands and, by 1432, **Gonçalo Cabral** (dates unknown) had reached the Azores. But not one man dared to venture beyond the dreaded cape.

In 1433, however, the breakthrough in Henry's campaign was made. In that year, **Gil Eannes** (dates unknown), a squire of Prince Henry's household, who on his first voyage

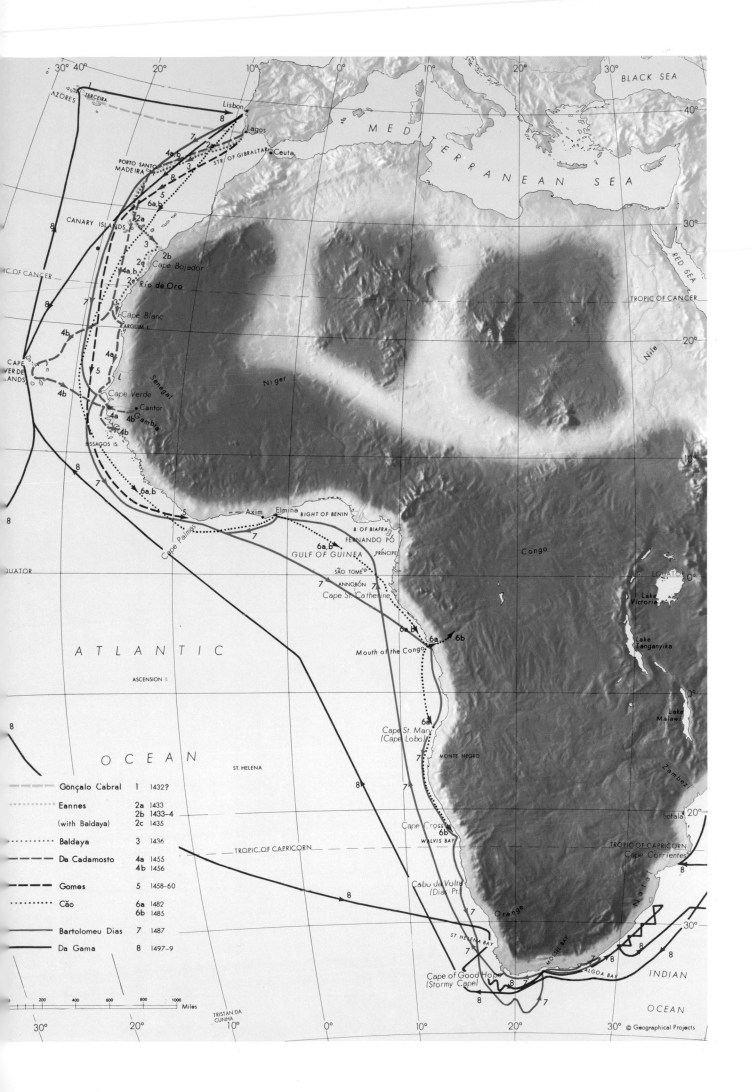

BLACK SEA

MEDITERRANEAN SEA

RED SEA

TROPIC OF CANCER

Nile

Niger

Senegal

Gambia

Cantor

BISSAGOS IS.

Cape Verde

Cape Blanc
ARGUIM I.

Río de Oro

Cape Bojador

Río de Oro

CANARY ISLANDS

PORTO SANTO
MADEIRA

Lisbon
Lagos
STR. OF GIBRALTAR
Ceuta

AZORES
TERCEIRA

TROPIC OF CANCER

CAPE
VERDE
ISLANDS

ATLANTIC

OCEAN

ASCENSION I.

ST. HELENA

Cape Palmas
Axim   Elmina   BIGHT OF BENIN
B. OF BIAFRA
FERNANDO PÓ
GULF OF GUINEA   PRÍNCIPE
SÃO TOMÉ
ANNOBÓN
Cape St. Catherine

EQUATOR

Congo

Lake
Victoria

Lake
Tanganyika

Lake
Malawi

Mouth of the Congo

Cape St. Mary
(Cape Lobo)
MONTE NEGRO

Cape Cross
WALVIS BAY

Cabo da Volta
(Dias Pt.)

Orange

Zambezi

Sofala

Natal

TROPIC OF CAPRICORN
Cape Corrientes

TROPIC OF CAPRICORN

INDIAN

OCEAN

© Geographical Projects

ST. HELENA BAY

Cape of Good Hope
(Stormy Cape)

MOSSEL BAY
ALGOA BAY

Gonçalo Cabral   1   1432?
Eannes   2a   1433
    2b   1433-4
(with Baldaya)   2c   1435
Baldaya   3   1436
Da Cadamosto   4a   1455
    4b   1456
Gomes   5   1458-60
Cão   6a   1482
    6b   1485
Bartolomeu Dias   7   1487
Da Gama   8   1497-9

200   400   600   800   1000
Miles

TRISTAN DA
CUNHA

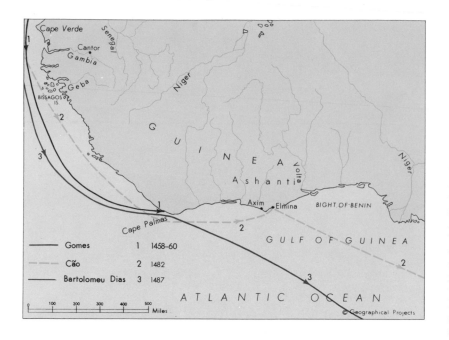

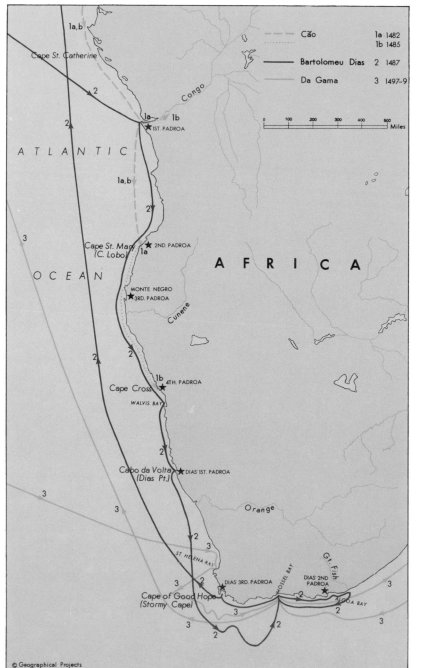

had failed to pass Cape Bojador, was so ashamed at Henry's disappointment in him that he set out immediately on a second voyage south. In 1434, he was able to bear the glad news back to Portugal—Cape Bojador had been rounded at last.

Eannes' achievement was small in terms of discovery, but immeasurable in its effect. Once he had shown that Cape Bojador could be rounded, the way was open for others to journey south. In 1435, Eannes made another voyage, landing on the African coast south of Cape Bojador. There, he and **Alfonso Gonçalves Baldaya** (dates unknown) saw tracks of men and of camels. In 1436, Baldaya tried unsuccessfully to meet the people of the region, but he did sail farther south to Cape Blanc—beyond the southern limits of the Moslem world—and he returned home with thousands of sealskins, the first commercial cargo to be brought to Europe from that part of Africa.

In the 12 years after Baldaya's expedition, the Portuguese pushed south beyond Cape Verde but, after 1448, troubles at home prevented Prince Henry from commissioning further voyages. For the next seven years, although some trading expeditions did take place, few discoveries were made. The Portuguese had realized that there was wealth in slaves, and with no shortage of potential victims in the known regions, most seamen found no need to sail farther south.

By 1455, however, Prince Henry was able to turn his attention once more to the unknown. In that year, a Venetian mariner named **Alvise da Cadamosto** (1432?-1511?) entered his service. Da Cadamosto made two voyages for the Portuguese, reaching the Gambia River on the first in 1455. The following year, he sailed up the river to trade with an African tribe. On this second voyage, Da Cadamosto also continued to the Geba River, but he turned back to Portugal on finding he was unable to trade. In the account he wrote of his travels, Da Cadamosto claims that he discovered the Cape Verde Islands, but he was probably not the first seaman to reach this island group.

Two years after Da Cadamosto's second voyage, a small fleet led by **Diogo Gomes** (1440-1482) sailed as far as Cape Palmas. This was the southernmost point that Prince Henry's sailors would reach. In 1460, the year of Gomes' return, the Portuguese pioneer died. He had paved the way for the great voyages that would open up the world, and it is a tribute to his achievement that, although he never sailed on the voyages he had planned, he is known to history as Prince Henry the Navigator.

After 1469, the Portuguese crown for a time abdicated direct responsibility for exploration. In that year, King Alfonso made a five-year agreement with Fernão Gomes whereby, in return for exclusive trading rights on the African coast and sole control of the profits, Gomes was to explore 400 miles of new coast each year. But although the arrangement worked well, the contract was not renewed when it expired. Instead, King Alfonso put exploration in the hands of his son John, who shared Prince Henry's enthusiasm for discovery and crusading and who hoped, too, that he might be able to capture a share of the Eastern trade for Portugal.

At first, John had little time for his new task. His country was at war; then, in 1481, his father died and he succeeded to the throne. The following year, King John II commissioned his first expedition. Its leader, **Diogo Cão** (?-1486), was to discover more than twice as much new coast in a single voyage as Fernão Gomes' seamen had been required to in a whole year.

Cão sailed south past Cape St. Catherine, the southernmost point that the Portuguese had reached, and continued to the mouth of the Congo River. There, he set up a *padroa* (stone pillar) bearing the Portuguese arms. On Cape St. Mary, still farther south, he set up a second padroa before returning home. In 1485, Cão made another voyage, erecting two more padroas, one on Monte Negro, north of the Cunene River, and the other on Cape Cross.

Cão's voyages convinced King John that Africa's southernmost point could not be far off, and with this in mind, he briefed his next expedition. **Bartolomeu Dias** (1450?-1500) was to round the continent and sail north. Once the Indian Ocean was reached, John thought, the way to the East would be clear.

Dias set his course close to the African coast, but off Cabo da Volta, his ships were caught in a storm. Helpless before its fury, they were blown south for nearly two weeks. When the wind died down, no land could be seen. Dias had been blown past the tip of Africa, the point the Portuguese had striven so long to reach.

When Dias sighted land again, he was halfway along Africa's southern coast, and he sailed east beyond Algoa Bay before turning for home. As the fleet made its way west, a great cape came into view. Dias named it Stormy Cape, because of the storm that had hidden it on the voyage out. But King John changed its name to Cape of Good Hope, for with its discovery, the possibility of finding a sea route to the East was greatly increased.

In 1495, King Manuel I succeeded to the Portuguese throne. He was known as "the Fortunate", and in the realm of exploration, the nickname was well deserved. For it was during Manuel's reign that the long years of patient creeping down the African coast brought their reward, and the longed-for sea route to the East was found at last.

The man who commanded the momentous voyage across the Indian Ocean was **Vasco da Gama** (1469?-1524). He was born in the seaport of Sines, but little is known of his career before King Manuel chose him as leader of the first expedition to India. He must, however, have had some experience at sea to be picked for a mission that was of such great importance to the Portuguese.

Da Gama sailed from Lisbon on 8 July 1497, in command of four small ships. As far as the Cape Verde Islands, they steered southwest. But soon afterward, Da Gama made a wide sweep out into the Atlantic away from the African coast, perhaps to try to avoid the calms and adverse currents Dias had encountered in the Gulf of Guinea. Not until 7 November did the fleet reach St. Helena Bay on the southwest coast of Africa, north of the Cape of Good Hope.

The Portuguese fleet rounded the Cape of Good Hope on 22 November, and sailed up the east African coast. They gave the name *Natal* to the area of the coast they passed on Christmas Day. In March, they arrived at the seaport of Kilimane. There, they could learn nothing of the way to India, so they continued to Mozambique, a predominantly Moslem port visited regularly by Arab ships trading between India and the African coast. The Portuguese had reached the regions where the Moslems dominated trade.

Although Da Gama and his men were welcomed warmly at first, their chances of receiving help vanished when they were found to be Christians. In Mombasa, too, the hostility of the Moslems was strong; but in nearby Malindi, the Portuguese managed to obtain a pilot who would guide them across the Indian Ocean to their destination.

On 21 May 1498 the Portuguese ships anchored off Calicut on India's southwest coast. Dangers and difficulties faced them still—both in India where the Moslems, rather than the Hindu rulers, controlled all trade, and on the terrible voyage home. But nothing could obscure the greatness of their feat in opening the long desired direct sea route to the rich countries of the East.

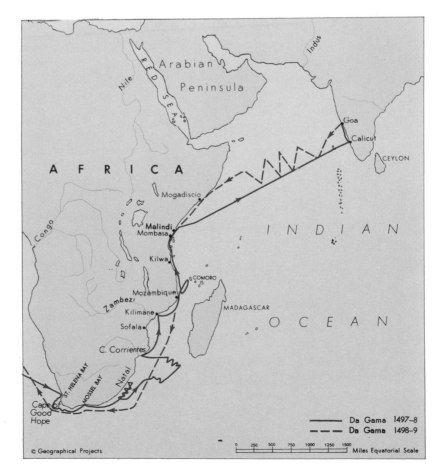

© Geographical Projects

———— Da Gama 1497–8
– – – – Da Gama 1498–9

0 250 500 750 1000 1250 1500 Miles Equatorial Scale

The New World

Christopher Columbus (1451-1506) landed on the island of San Salvador in the Bahamas on the morning of 12 October 1492. He thought he was in the Orient, for he had set out to find a westward route to the rich lands of the East. Little did he dream that he stood on an island that lay, not in the East Indies, but on the edge of a vast new world.

The first European landfalls in the New World were made on the Caribbean islands. Columbus landed on the island in the Bahamas that the inhabitants called Guanahani (now San Salvador), and named two islands for the king and queen of Spain. ▼

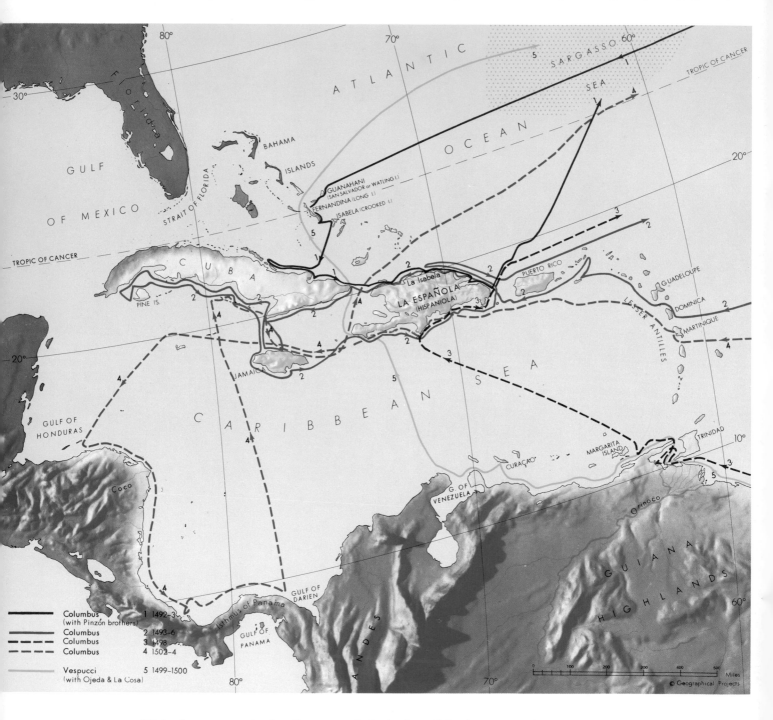

	Columbus (with Pinzón brothers)	1	1492-3
	Columbus	2	1493-6
	Columbus	3	1498
	Columbus	4	1502-4
	Vespucci (with Ojeda & La Cosa)	5	1499-1500

Columbus was not the first European to reach the Americas, but in the 1400's, Europeans knew nothing of the Vikings' earlier voyages, and the very existence of the new land those bold seafarers had tried to settle had been forgotten. When Columbus set sail in 1492, he was sure nothing lay between Europe and the treasure-rich East.

It had taken Columbus years of struggle to gain the financial backing he needed to make his great voyage. He had long dreamed of finding a westerly route to the Orient, and all he read and saw only strengthened his belief that such a route existed. But the monarchs of Portugal and England, to whom he first took his plan, were skeptical of its feasibility.

It was not until 1492 that King Ferdinand and Queen Isabella of Spain were persuaded to sponsor his grandiose scheme.

In Spain, Columbus was supplied with three caravels, the *Santa María, Niña,* and *Pinta.* Two Spanish seamen, **Vicente** and **Martin Pinzón** (1460?-1524? and 1440?-1493), were to captain the *Niña* and *Pinta,*

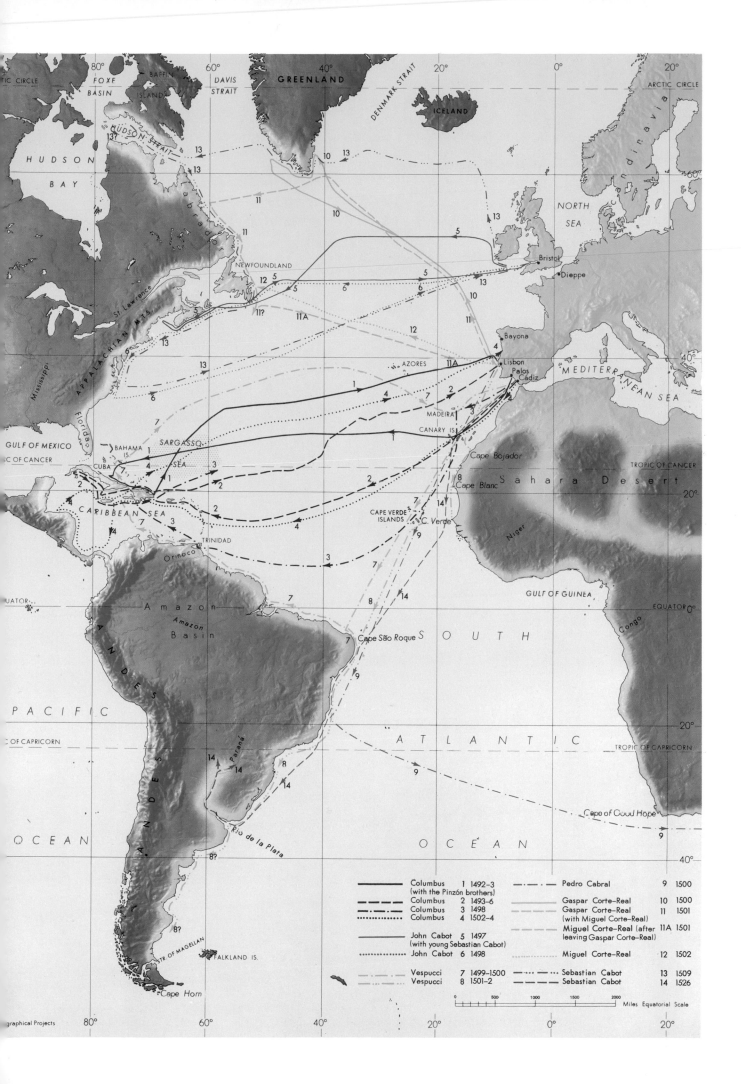

Columbus   1   1492-3
(with the Pinzón brothers)
Columbus   2   1493-6
Columbus   3   1498
Columbus   4   1502-4

John Cabot   5   1497
(with young Sebastian Cabot)
John Cabot   6   1498

Vespucci   7   1499-1500
Vespucci   8   1501-2

Pedro Cabral   9   1500

Gaspar Corte-Real   10   1500
Gaspar Corte-Real   11   1501
(with Miguel Corte-Real)
Miguel Corte-Real (after   11A 1501
leaving Gaspar Corte-Real)

Miguel Corte-Real   12   1502

Sebastian Cabot   13   1509
Sebastian Cabot   14   1526

0   500   1000   1500   2000
Miles Equatorial Scale

graphical Projects

while the *Santa María* was commanded by Columbus himself. On 3 August 1492, the little fleet set sail.

The first landfall of the three ships was the Canary Islands, where they were delayed for a month while repairs were made to the *Pinta*. The work completed, on 6 September they set out across the unknown sea. At that time, long voyages out of sight of land were rare and, as the days passed without even a glimpse of a distant island, Columbus' men became uneasy. They did not share their commander's confidence in his dream, and they began to wonder whether they would see Spain again.

At last, however, on 12 October, the ships reached land. They were lying off San Salvador in the Bahamas, and Columbus went ashore to take possession of the island for Spain. From San Salvador, he sailed on to Cuba, and then east to another large island which he named La Española (Hispaniola) in honor of the country that had sponsored his voyage. On Hispaniola, misfortune struck. The *Santa María* was shipwrecked, and when Columbus set sail for Spain on 16 January 1493, he was forced to leave 40 men behind. On his return to the island during his next voyage, he found they had all been killed.

Storms and high winds battered the *Niña* and *Pinta* as they struggled back across the Atlantic, and it seemed a miracle to their crews when they reached the Azores. From the Azores, Columbus continued to Portugal, visiting the Portuguese court. There, he was honored by King John who, a short time before, had turned down his amazing plan.

It was not until March that Columbus arrived in Spain, and not until April that he reached the court to give an account of his voyage. He believed that he had landed in the Orient, that Cuba was mainland China, and Hispaniola the island of Japan. Although he had found none of the precious goods for which the East was famed, he was sure that other voyages would open up trade and give Spain her share of the Eastern wealth. The Spanish monarchs had no reason to doubt Columbus. They were delighted by the success of his voyage, and the trading possibilities it opened up. They rewarded him lavishly, honoring him with the title "Admiral of the Ocean Sea".

Christopher Columbus was to make three more voyages to the "Indies" far in the west. On the first of these, he discovered Dominica, Guadeloupe, Puerto Rico, and Jamaica. He also established the settlement of La Isabela on Hispaniola's northern coast, some distance away from the place where his men had been killed. But he was to prove himself less successful as a colonial administrator than as a seaman. His attempts to put down a revolt in Hispaniola in 1498 during his third voyage ended in his being arrested and transported back to Spain in chains. Although he redeemed himself enough for the Spanish monarchs to permit another voyage—on which he reached mainland America—he never regained their lost favor.

It is generally thought that, when Columbus died in 1506, he was still unaware that the lands he had reached were part of a huge continent lying between Europe and Asia. The Spaniards continued to refer to the new lands as the "Indies", identifying them with the East Indies, where the spices Europe needed were grown. Even when they were recognized as the outposts of a new land mass, their importance was at first ignored. Only later did the full significance of Columbus' discovery become clear.

Meanwhile, the search for a westward passage to the East went on. In 1497, the race was entered by England in the person of the Venetian navigator **John Cabot** (1450-1498). Cabot and his son **Sebastian** (1476?-1557) sailed from Bristol across the North Atlantic to Nova Scotia and Newfoundland. On his return, Cabot claimed to have found the land of the Great Khan, and the following year King Henry VII authorized a second voyage to the area. But the journey produced neither precious goods nor ambassadors from the khan, and Henry lost interest in exploration.

Sebastian Cabot, however, did not. In 1509, he sailed, as his father had done, from Bristol, but he set his course farther north. Touching on southern Greenland, he continued west, and is thought to have sailed into Hudson Strait before turning south down the Labrador coast. Although he returned safely, he must have been convinced of the impracticability of the northern route. On his next attempt to reach the Indies, he sailed south, exploring the Rio de la Plata in South America.

Exploration in the northwest was kept alive by the Portuguese. In 1500, **Gaspar Corte-Real** (1450?-1501?), who had probably heard John Cabot's claim of having found the Great Khan's realm, sailed north to Greenland, continuing up the coast until he was forced by icebergs to turn back. The following year, he

An allegorical engraving, hailing Christopher Columbus as the discoverer of the New World. ▼

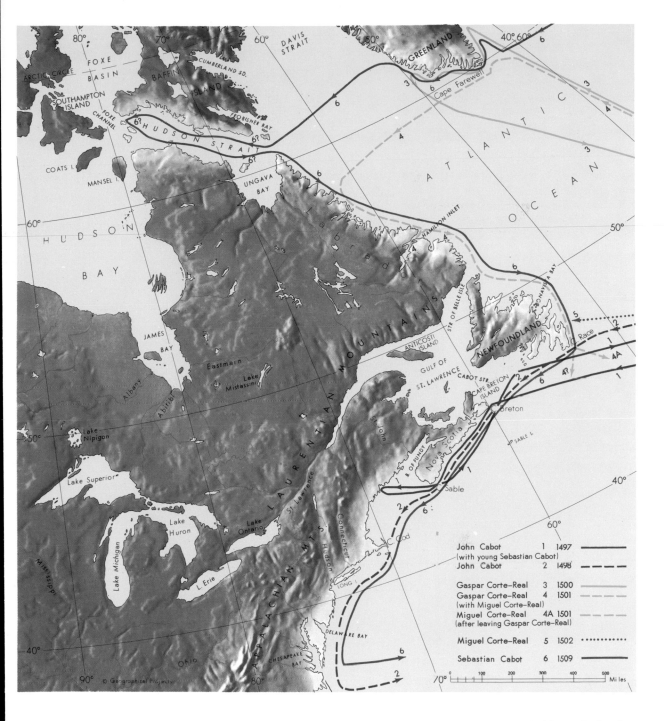

made another voyage to the north, this time with his brother **Miguel** (?-1502?). Sailing to Greenland as before, the brothers then crossed to Labrador, and cruised down the coast to Newfoundland. There, they took prisoner a number of Indians and, while Miguel returned to Portugal with their captives, Gaspar sailed on south. When he had failed to return by May 1502, Miguel set out in search of him. Nothing was heard of either brother again.

With each new voyage across the Atlantic Ocean, it became clearer that Columbus had been mistaken in believing he had reached the East. In 1500, on his way to India, **Pedro Álvares Cabral** (1467?-1519?) tried to follow Da Gama's route, making a wide sweep west into the Atlantic, but he sailed much farther west than

Da Gama and landed on the coast of Brazil. According to the Treaty of Tordesillas of 1494—which attempted to resolve disputes over ownership of newly discovered lands by granting Spain the right to those west of an imaginary line some 350 leagues west of the Cape Verde Islands, and Portugal the right to lands east of that given line—Brazil fell within the Portuguese sphere of influence. Therefore, acknowledging Brazil as a completely new land, and moreover one that by rights "belonged" to Portugal, Portugal sent out an expedition to ascertain its size.

On this Portuguese expedition of 1501 sailed the man who was to give his name to both the great continents of the New World. **Amerigo Vespucci** (1451-1512) was a Florentine merchant who had studied geography and

navigation as a hobby and who, late in life, had turned explorer. He had already made a voyage to the New World in 1499-1500 with **Alonso de Ojeda** (1465?-1515) and **Juan de la Cosa** (?-1509), Columbus' pilot on his second expedition. On this, Vespucci's second expedition, he claims to have sailed as far south as 50°S. This claim is generally unaccepted, as indeed are Vespucci's reports of two other voyages he made to the Americas.

Whatever the truth about Vespucci's voyages, his account of them was widely believed in his own time. It even led the geographer Waldseemüller to regard him, rather than Columbus, as the discoverer of the great land mass in the west, and to suggest that it should be called America in honor of his explorations.

41

Juan de la Cosa's Map

Christopher Columbus must have made maps of his discoveries, but only one of his sketches exists today. A contemporary record of the lands he reached does, however, still survive. It is a world map, drawn in 1500 by Juan de la Cosa, and this makes it particularly interesting, for La Cosa was no stay-at-home cartographer, but had actually seen the lands he depicted. He had acted as Columbus' pilot on his second expedition, and had later sailed with Ojeda and Vespucci to the "New World" far in the west.

La Cosa's map depicts not only Columbus' discoveries, but also shows Da Gama's voyage to the East, and it is the oldest map in existence to record both these events. By the time it was drawn, enough was known of Africa for La Cosa to depict the west coast accurately. Even his portrayal of the east coast, navigated for the first time by Da Gama only two years earlier, is

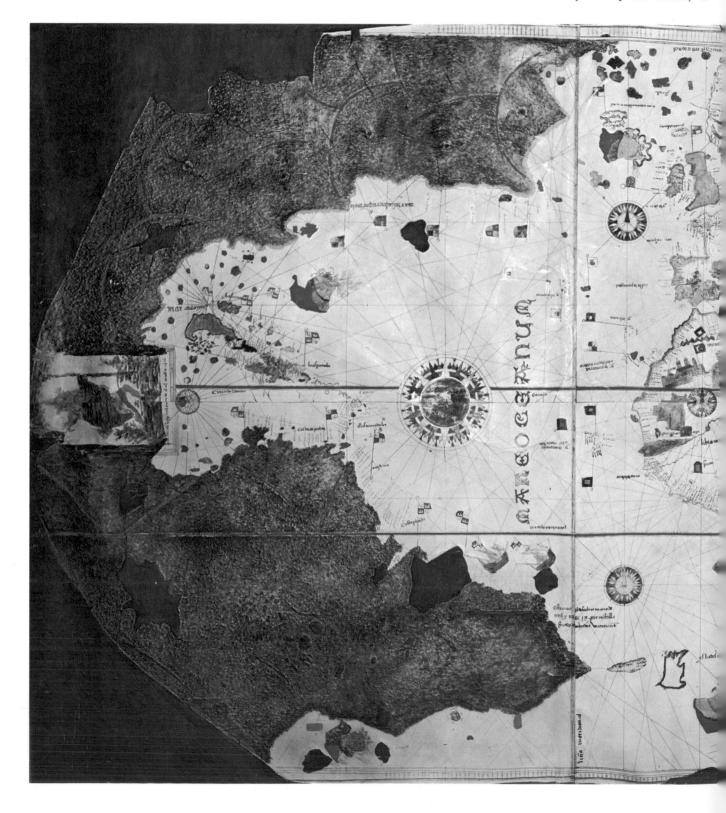

essentially correct. His principal interest lay, however, in the newly discovered Americas, and he drew them on a larger scale—perhaps as a way of showing that they were what his map was really about.

In the west of the map, the land fades into the edge of the parchment. This avoids the question of whether Columbus had discovered a new continent or whether, as he himself believed, he had reached Asia. Spanish discoveries up to 1499 in South America—and his own voyages to the New World—enabled La Cosa to map the South American coastline, and John Cabot's landfalls of 1497 are marked in the north. However, La Cosa was probably ignorant of the geography of the Yucatan region of Central America, for a picture of Saint Christopher hides the coast.

Cuba is shown as an island, although it was not proved to be separate from the mainland until 1508, the year before La Cosa's death. One explanation that has been put forward for La Cosa's knowledge is that Portuguese mariners reached North America before Columbus, and that La Cosa based his depiction of certain regions on information they provided.

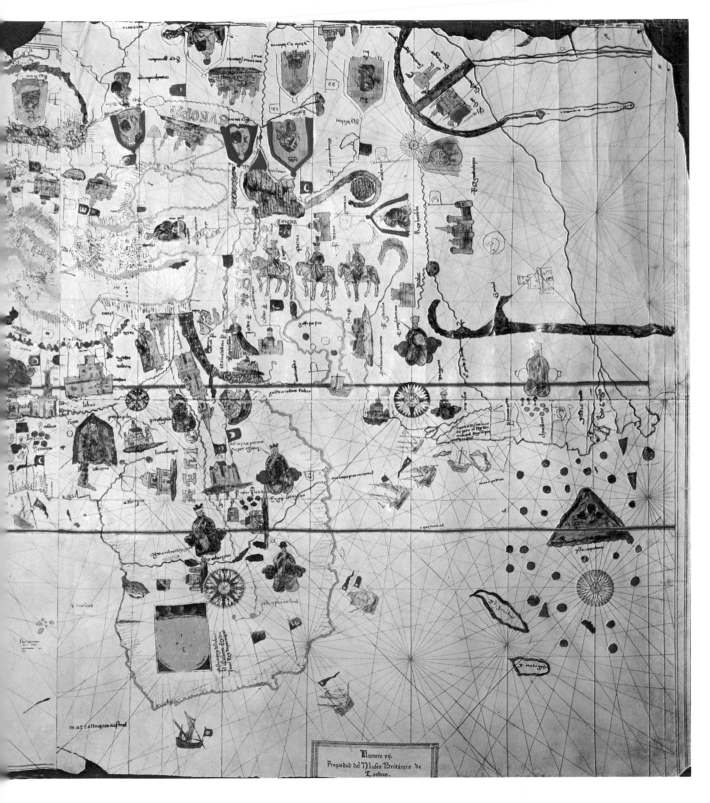

Around the World

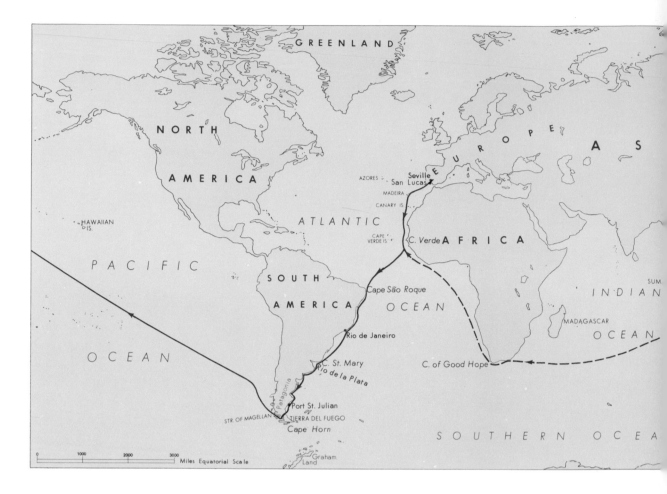

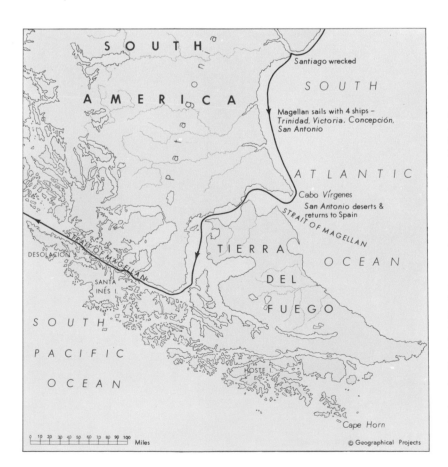

Even after the discovery of America, the attention of Europe was still concentrated on the East. The Portuguese controlled the Cape route, and the English the North Atlantic, but it was still possible that a passage to the southwest might exist. In 1519, **Ferdinand Magellan** (1480?-1521) set out to find one—his voyage was the first circumnavigation of the world.

Magellan had taken part in many Portuguese expeditions to the East, but he had been refused the rewards usual for such services. Enraged, he had made his way to Spain, seeking backing for a voyage to find a westward passage to the East.

The Spanish king warmly approved Magellan's scheme and, by 1519, the expedition was under way. After a three-month voyage, Magellan's ships reached the bay of Rio de Janeiro. Sailing south, they spent 23 days exploring the estuary called Rio de la Plata, believing it was the strait they sought. But now the days were growing shorter and, on 31 March 1520, the fleet put into Port St. Julian for the winter. Provisions were running low, and Magellan incurred

◄ *The Strait of Magellan.*

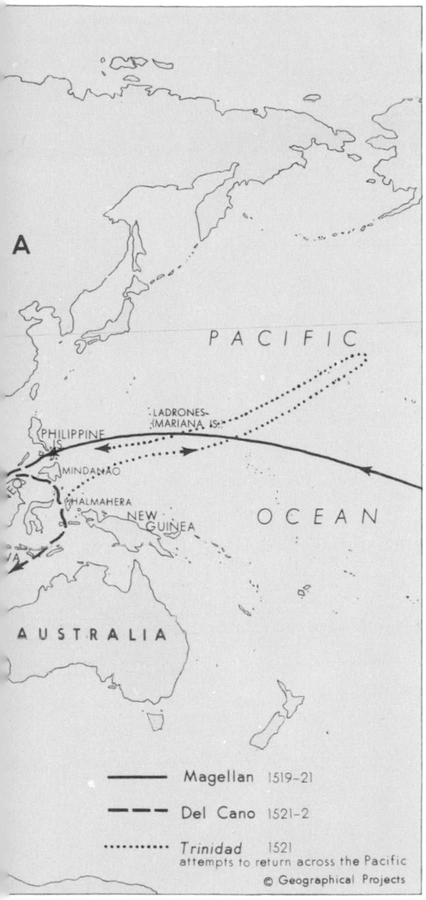
A
PACIFIC
LADRONES-
(MARIANA IS.
PHILIPPINE
IS.
MINDANAO
HALMAHERA
NEW
GUINEA
OCEAN
AUSTRALIA
Magellan 1519–21
Del Cano 1521–2
Trinidad 1521
attempts to return across the Pacific
© Geographical Projects

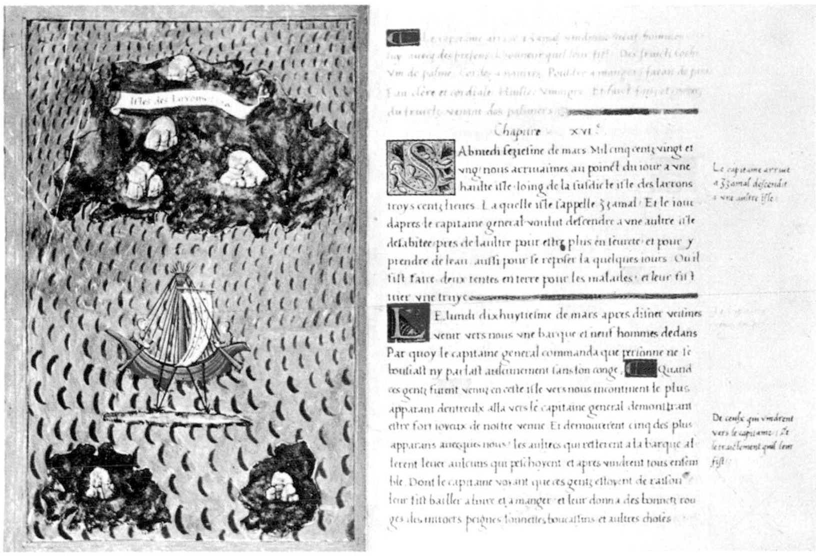
Isles des Larrons

Chapitre xvi.

Sabmedi sezietme de mars Mil cinq centz vingt et vng/ nous arriuaimes au poinct du iour a vne haulte isle loing de la susdicte isle des larrons troys centz lieues. La quelle isle sappelle Zzamal/ Et le iour dapres le capitaine general voulut descendre a vne aultre isle desabitee pres de laultre pour estre plus en seurete/ et pour y prendre de leau/ aussi pour se reposer la quelques iours. Ou il fist faire deux tentes en terre pour les malades/ et leur fit tuer vne truye

Le lundi dixhuytiesme de mars apres disner veismes venir vers nous vne barque et neuf hommes dedans Par quoy le capitaine general commanda que personne ne se bougeast ny parlast aulcunement sans son conge. Quand ces gentz furent venuz en ceste isle vers nous incontinent le plus apparant dentreulx alla vers le capitaine general demonstrant estre fort ioyeux de nostre venue. Et demourerent cinq des plus apparans avecques nous/ les aultres qui resterent a la barque allerent leuer aulcuns qui peschoyent et apres vindrent tous ensemble. Dont le capitaine voyant que ces gentz estoyent de raison leur fist bailler a boire et a manger et leur donna des bonnetz rouges des miroers peignes sonnettes boucassins et aultres choses

◀ *Ferdinand Magellan died before his voyage was complete, but its inspiration was his, and it is to him that honor is due. The strait he discovered was too dangerous for regular use, but he proved that a strait existed and, although he was not the first man to see the Pacific, he named it, and was the first to sail across it. When he succeeded in reaching the East by sailing west, he provided conclusive proof that the earth is a sphere.*

▲ *In 1524, two years after the* Victoria *returned to Spain, Antonio Pigafetta, a member of the crew, wrote an account of the magnificent voyage for King Charles V. This page from his book, which was published by King Charles, shows the islands that Magellan named the Islas de los Ladrones—the islands of thieves. There, as later on many of the other Pacific islands, the people stole all they could from the European seamen.*

his men's hatred by reducing their rations. Soon mutiny broke out, and only Magellan's prompt action avoided the voyage ending there and then.

When the fleet continued south in mid-October, it was only three days before a waterway was sighted, opening to the west. It was a hazardous, winding passage, but it proved to be the longed-for strait. On 28 November 1520, Magellan's ships emerged into the Pacific Ocean.

For week after week, the Spanish ships sailed northwest. The food was exhausted, the men dying of hunger and disease. But they saw no land where they could take on supplies. It was early March before they reached the Ladrones (the Mariana Islands).

From the Ladrones, Magellan continued to the Philippine Islands. There, for him, the long voyage ended. In a battle between local rulers, Magellan was killed. His men sailed on to the Moluccas, where they loaded up with spices. Then the *Trinidad* set out across the Pacific, while the *Victoria,* under **Sebastián del Cano** (?-1526), continued west. On 6 September 1522, the *Victoria* reached harbor in Spain.

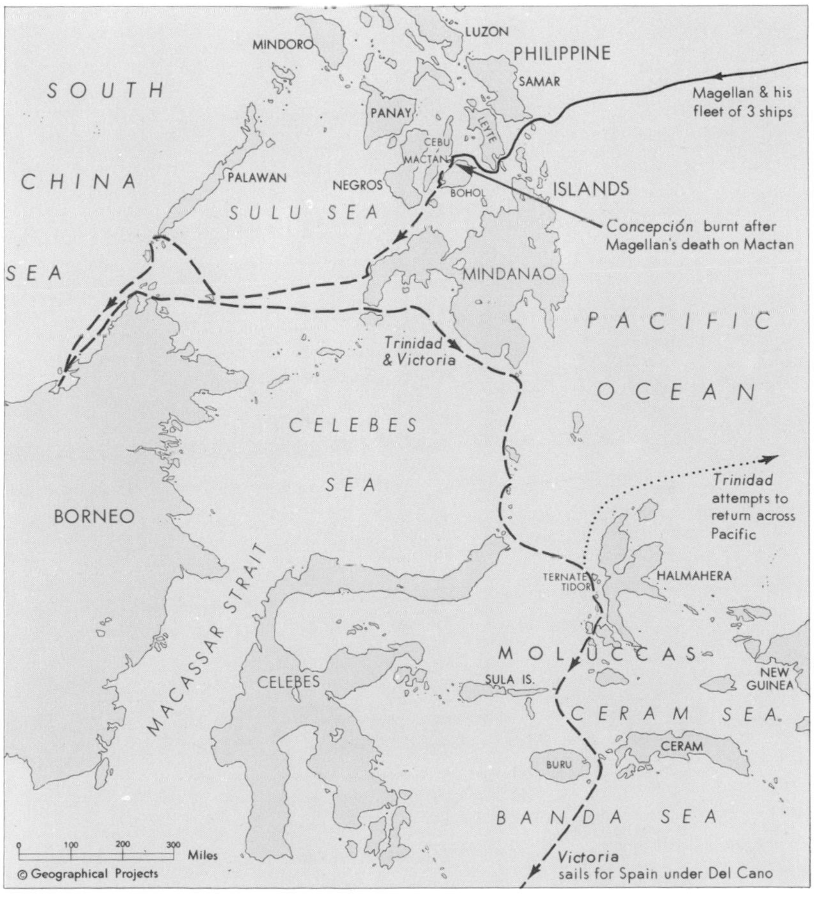
MINDORO
LUZON
PHILIPPINE
SAMAR
SOUTH
PANAY
LEYTE
Magellan & his
fleet of 3 ships
CEBU
MACTAN
CHINA
PALAWAN
NEGROS
BOHOL
ISLANDS
SULU SEA
Concepción burnt after
Magellan's death on Mactan
SEA
MINDANAO
PACIFIC
Trinidad
& Victoria
OCEAN
CELEBES
SEA
Trinidad
attempts to
return across
Pacific
BORNEO
TERNATE
TIDOR
HALMAHERA
MACASSAR STRAIT
MOLUCCAS
NEW
GUINEA
CELEBES
SULA IS.
CERAM SEA
CERAM
BURU
BANDA SEA
100 200 300 Miles
© Geographical Projects
Victoria
sails for Spain under Del Cano

The Philippines and Moluccas. ▶

4 The Riches of the Orient

Vasco da Gama's voyage to India was the culmination of years of effort and of hope. For Portugal, it was the crowning triumph of the campaign of discovery Prince Henry the Navigator had initiated, and the end to which all her later voyages had been bent. Yet, while marking the close of one chapter in the story of Europe and the East, it also heralded a new one. The sea route to India had been discovered; now the expansion to the Orient could begin.

Strange though the Asian seas were to Europeans of the 1400's, they were far from being totally unknown. The journeys European sailors had made to India and China in the days of the Roman Empire had long been forgotten, but since then, the monsoon routes had been followed by the Arabs sailing eastward, and by Chinese sailors voyaging west. According to the Arab historian al-Masudi, who wrote in the 900's, Chinese ships were visiting the Euphrates River in the A.D. 400's, and Chinese records of the 600's and 700's describe the course these ships would have followed from Canton. Early in the 1400's, when Prince Henry the Navigator was just beginning his push to the southward, the Chinese admiral Cheng Ho made voyages to India, and as far west as the Persian Gulf and Africa's eastern coast.

In Europe, however, nothing was known of these journeys—the European explorers had to rediscover the eastward routes for themselves. They had to contend with the hardships and dangers that inevitably accompanied ocean voyages and, moreover, they faced the implacable hostility of the Moslems. For trade as far east as the Indies was under the control of the Moslems, who bitterly resented Europeans intruding on their preserve. The Europeans, however, looked on Asia as the treasure house of the world, and their desire for a share in her riches led them to disregard the dangers that they faced. These travelers were the children of a materialistic age, when interest in discovery was subordinate to the desire for wealth. Because of this, the East was opened up by commercial voyages that had trade as their first aim. These trading expeditions took Europeans to the East Indies, and to China and Japan, extending the frontiers of knowledge in the struggle for mercantile growth.

The European powers did not set out to establish their rule in the Orient, since they were interested first and foremost in the setting up of trade. But as nation after nation joined the race eastward, Europeans came to realize that profitable trade was an impossibility without direct political rule. For only through the control that this would give them could a commercial monopoly be achieved. Thus, in the wake of trade, European government reached the East. It paved the way to a dominion lasting 300 years.

47

Reconnaissance

Asia, home of mystery, of adventure, of riches beyond compare, in the 1500's what great visions were conjured up by the mere mention of its name. The fire of its fascination burned in the imagination of the West, kindled by the men who had first traveled its unfamiliar, and often dangerous paths with their tales of the strange and splendid things they had found there. Those same bold pioneers, in their journeys, had spearheaded the European advance east.

The first European after Marco Polo to write a realistic description of the East was **Odoric of Pordenone** (1274?-1331), a Franciscan friar who made a 12-year missionary journey to India, the East Indies, and China, returning to Europe overland. Then, early in the 1400's, **Niccolò de Conti** (dates unknown), an Italian nobleman, spent

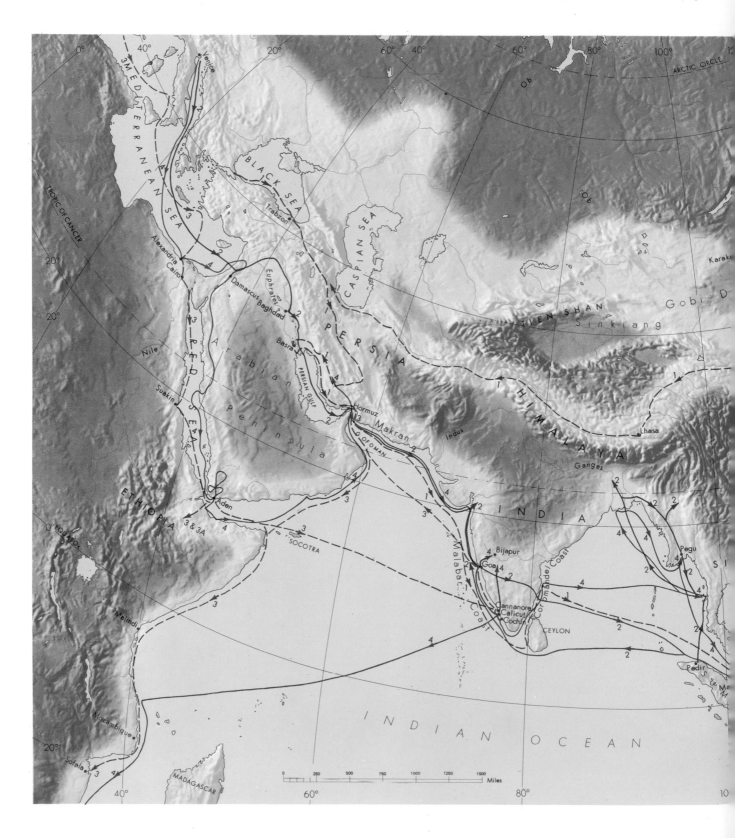

25 years wandering through India and Southeast Asia, and wrote an account of his travels as important to map makers as Marco Polo's had been. But the first detailed knowledge of the Indian trade and the Indian Ocean came from the Portuguese.

Pedro de Covilham (1450?-1545?) and **Affonso de Paiva** (dates unknown) were sent by King John II to find Prester John's kingdom, and to discover whether a sea route around Africa did exist. De Covilham visited India and Persia, then sailed to Sofala, while De Paiva searched for Prester John. Returning through Cairo, De Covilham learned that De Paiva had died, so he sent his report to Portugal, then set out to find Prester John. In Ethiopia, a Christian country in which the Prester John legend had originated, he entered the emperor's service, remaining there until his death.

The report De Covilham sent to Portugal, with that of Bartolomeu Dias, helped in planning the voyage to India in which Da Gama opened direct trade with the East. The true source of the spice trade, though,

▲ *Nutmeg, cinnamon, and other spices highly valued in Europe.*

was not India, but a series of island groups in the East Indies. Named the Moluccas, they were known as the Spice Islands because of their main resource.

The first European to visit the Spice Islands may have been **Ludovico di Varthema** (dates unknown). In 1502, Di Varthema left Italy to see the world, and he visited Arabia, Persia, India, and Pegu besides the Spice Islands, sailing back to Europe around the Cape of Good Hope. His book, *Itinerario,* was full of valuable information, and very successful.

By the mid-1500's, Europeans had reached even farther than Di Varthema—two Portuguese had visited Japan. The first was **Fernão Mendes Pinto** (1509-1583), unjustly dubbed "Prince of Liars" because his book about his travels was so widely disbelieved by his contemporaries. The second was a missionary, **Saint Francis Xavier** (1506-1552), who made many converts in Japan, and preached in the Spice Islands too. When he died, he was preparing a mission to the Chinese.

49

Gastaldi draws Asia

During the 1500's, in Italy, and in particular in Venice, the art of map making flourished. Not only had the city long been a crossroads on the trade routes between East and West, thus receiving all the latest geographical information, but also the techniques of map printing by wood and copper engraving reached new heights there. One of the greatest of the cartographers working in Venice during this period was Giacomo Gastaldi (1500?-1565?), a native of Piedmont, in northwestern Italy. During his career, which began in 1544 with a map of Spain, Gastaldi drew nearly 100 maps, depicting the world, Europe, Africa—and the distant Asian lands.

Gastaldi's map of Asia was published between 1559 and 1561, on six separate sheets. This one—showing Southeast Asia—appeared in 1561. Gastaldi was familiar with G. B. Ramusio's recent Italian edition of Marco Polo's book, and on his map he tried to show all the places Polo had described, taking their names from Ramusio's text. He was able to draw on other, more up-to-date sources as well, among them Niccolò de Conti's account of his journey to the East.

Although Gastaldi's map is not strictly accurate, it represents a considerable advance on earlier drawings of the Orient. Asia as we know it today was at last taking shape. India and Ceylon, and the general outline of the Malay Peninsula, and of part of China, can easily be recognized, and the huge group of islands that stretches away from the mainland of Southeast Asia clearly corresponds to the East Indies. On looking at those islands more closely, however, we can see how Gastaldi's map differs from the truth. He places many of the islands wrongly, and shows more large islands than there really are. Such errors were inevitable in the days when accurate position finding was difficult, and map makers relied partly on hearsay. Two separate islands were often believed to be joined together before the strait dividing them was discovered, while one, sighted twice, but with its position calculated differently on each occasion, might be shown as two.

In places, Gastaldi uses short descriptions to amplify his drawing, and in these, fact and hearsay blend strangely. For while he writes—correctly—that in the Moluccas lie numerous kingdoms in which spices are found, he also reports Marco Polo's warning of the strange spirits that he believed to lurk in the deserts of central Asia.

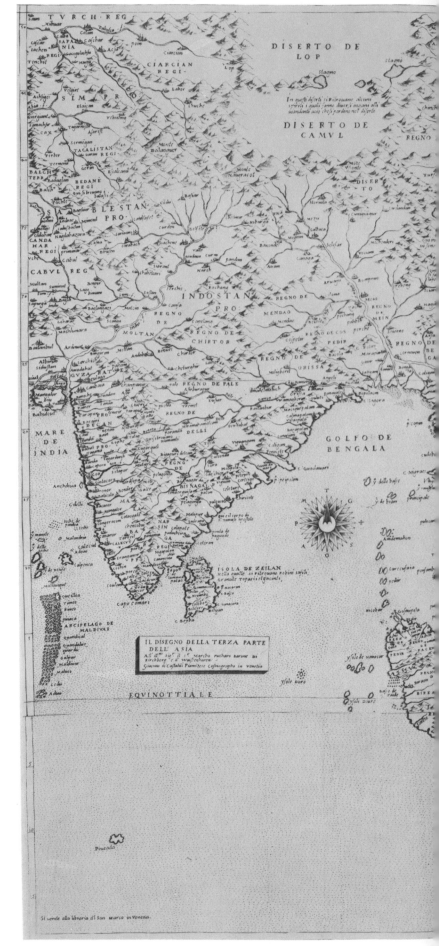

Through Trade to the Indies

Vasco da Gama sailed back to Europe with his ships heavily laden with the treasures of the East. The search for a sea route to India was finally over, and now the dawn of a new era broke. This new era was in spirit one of commerce, not one of exploration, yet discovery did follow in the wake of trade. Also, as each European nation attempted through territorial expansion to protect its mercantile interests in Asia, the foundations of great colonial empires were laid.

Long before Da Gama's voyage, mariners had used the seasonal monsoon winds when sailing in the Indian Ocean, and it was in the path of these winds that trade routes grew up. Ships bound for India used the South West Monsoon, which blows from May to October, to make their outward voyage, and returned in winter with the North East Monsoon. ▼

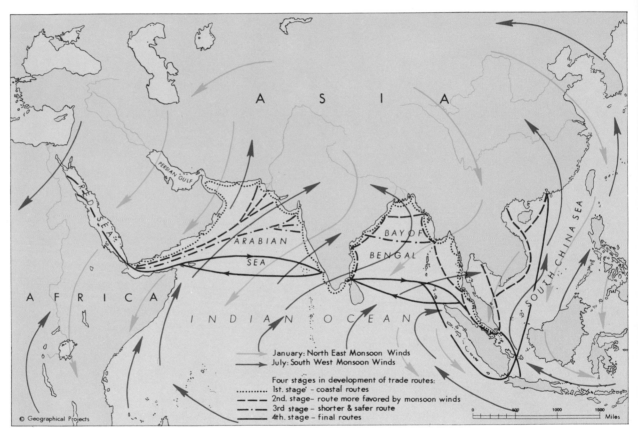

January: North East Monsoon Winds
July: South West Monsoon Winds

Four stages in development of trade routes:
.... 1st. stage - coastal routes
– – – 2nd. stage - route more favored by monsoon winds
–·–·– 3rd. stage - shorter & safer route
———— 4th. stage - final routes

© Geographical Projects

0   500   1000   1500
Miles

When the Portuguese reached India by a direct sea route, they won a substantial lead over the other countries of Europe in the race for the Indies trade. To exploit this advantage, they followed up Da Gama's voyage with a second expedition, led by **Pedro Álvares Cabral,** in 1500. His was the fleet that made the first European landing in Brazil. In Calicut, the goal of his expedition, Cabral's attempts to set up trade were unsuccessful, but in Cochin, he was luckier. He sailed back to Portugal with his ships laden with precious goods.

Despite the success of these early voyages, however, Portugal still had no guarantee of a share in the Eastern trade. The Indian Ocean sea routes—and with them the import trade into Europe—remained in Moslem hands, as did commerce in

Hormuz and Aden, the trade's western centers, and in the ports of India. More important, the Moslems ruled many of the lands where the Eastern goods originated, as well as the port of Malacca, the foremost trade center of the East. To insure success for its traders, Portugal would have to wrest control of the Indian Ocean from the Moslems, and then extend its authority to the countries of the East.

It was to this end that in 1505, King Manuel appointed Francisco de Almeida first permanent Portuguese representative in the East. Almeida first tried to break the Moslem grip on the Indian Ocean, and this he achieved in 1509 by the defeat of a combined Egyptian and Indian fleet off Diu. During his term

Afonso d'Albuquerque. ▶

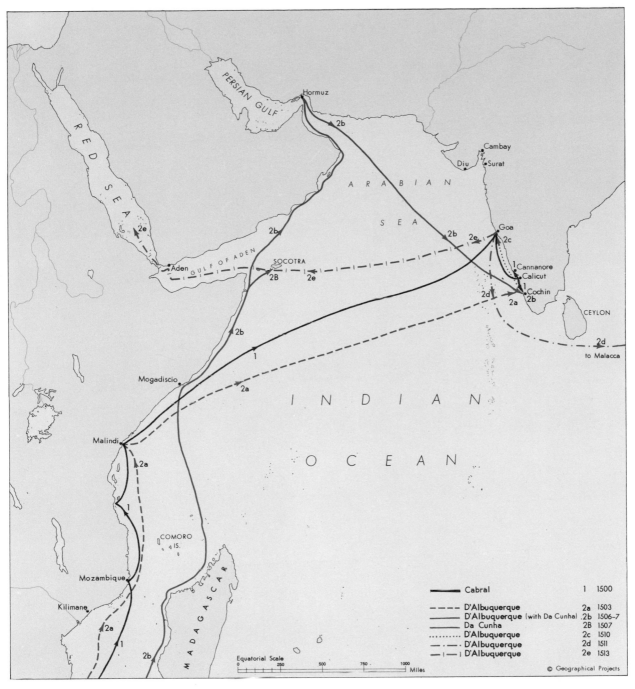

▬▬▬ Cabral	1	1500
▬ ▬ ▬ D'Albuquerque	2a	1503
▬▬▬ D'Albuquerque (with Da Cunha)	2b	1506-7
▬▬▬ Da Cunha	2B	1507
·········· D'Albuquerque	2c	1510
▬·▬·▬ D'Albuquerque	2d	1511
▬ ı ▬ ı ▬ D'Albuquerque	2e	1513

© Geographical Projects

of office, too, the first Portuguese fleet reached Malacca, but it had little success in opening trade. In fact, the Moslems were so hostile to **Diego Lopez de Sequeira** (dates unknown), the fleet's commander, that they tried to destroy his ships and many Portuguese were killed.

Almeida had broken the Moslem stranglehold on the Indian Ocean trade routes. His successor, **Afonso d'Albuquerque** (1453-1515), established the Portuguese in the ports that dominated the trade. In 1507—before taking up his post—D'Albuquerque had captured Hormuz from the Moslems, and in that same year **Tristão da Cunha** (1460?-1540?) had taken the island of Socotra at the mouth of the Gulf of Aden. D'Albuquerque was later to try to capture Aden, but without success. In 1510, however, he captured Goa. Then, with

his control of the Indian Ocean established, he led an expedition to Malacca itself. In 1511, that vital link in the trade routes fell to the Portuguese.

Under D'Albuquerque, for the first time a European power gained supremacy in the East and, from this day on, the area of European influence and rule gradually grew. In 1509, the Portuguese had established a factory (trading post) at Pedir, an important pepper-trading center in Sumatra, and after 1511, numerous other commercial settlements were made throughout the islands of Southeast Asia.

In 1513, the first Portuguese ships reached China, but their attempts to trade were hindered by Chinese hostility to foreigners. Not until 1557 were the Portuguese allowed to open a factory. Even then, it was not

situated on the mainland, but on the island of Macao. In Japan, Europeans were welcomed more warmly, as Mendes Pinto's account of his travels shows, but the Portuguese could not persuade the Japanese to give them preference in trade. However, in Ceylon, the "Pearl of the Orient", the Portuguese quickly established their rule. They took over most of the western half of the island in an attempt to establish a monopoly over the valuable trade in cinnamon.

Portugal's was a sea empire, based on trade routes linking commercial ports, and as such, vast supplies of men and arms were necessary to secure its far-flung bounds. For a small country, the expense was too great to bear for long, particularly as the Portuguese monarchs simply seized the riches for themselves rather than plowing the profits back

53

into the empire. Consequently, as time passed, the profits themselves began to decrease. Lacking money to buy arms, or to employ men to defend its possessions, Portugal was at the mercy of any nation that made a bid for the Indies trade. The challenge this afforded was taken up by the Dutch.

Dutch pilots had long been employed on Portuguese ships, and the Dutch were therefore well informed about Portugal's Eastern trade. They had another source of information in *Itinerario*, a book by Jan Huyghen van Linschoten, a Dutchman who had worked for some years for the Portuguese in Goa. His descriptions of the Indies, and the maps illustrating his text, provided the necessary spur for the

Dutch to send an expedition east.

In 1595, a group of Amsterdam merchants commissioned the first Dutch voyage to the East Indies. Led by **Cornelius Houtman** (1540?-1599), the expedition was almost a complete disaster—the ships returned with only small cargoes of spices, and more than half the men died. But it did prove to the Dutch that the Portuguese were not all-powerful in the Eastern seas.

During the next few years, the Dutch sent numerous expeditions to the East, backed by a number of separate companies, each trading from a different port. The competition between the companies themselves was as strong as that between the Dutch and the Portuguese. Some fleets, like the one of **Jacob**

van Neck (dates unknown) and **Wybrand van Warwijck** (dates unknown), traveled by the Cape route, while others sailed west through Magellan's strait. Van Neck and Van Warwijck's expedition was a great success, establishing friendly relations in the Indies, and yielding a profit of 400 per cent. Of the westward expeditions, however, only two reached the East. One was that of **Oliver van Noort** (dates unknown), who went on to become the first Dutchman to circumnavigate the world.

The Dutch fleets that sailed to the Indies were at first concerned solely with trade, but when their sponsors realized how many islands grew spices, they saw that a commercial monopoly would be neces-

54

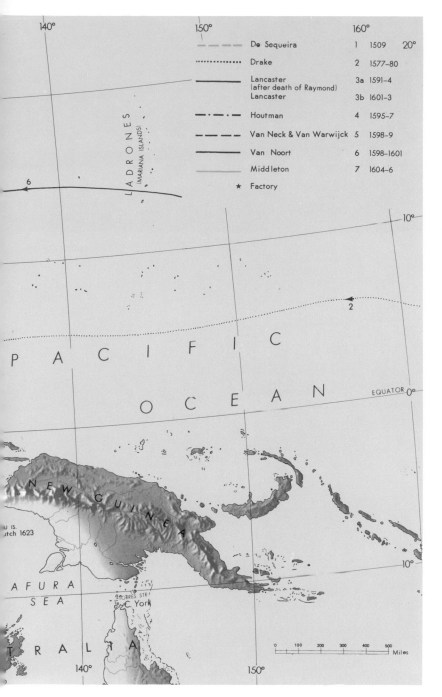

– – – – De Sequeira	1	1509
·············· Drake	2	1577–80
———— Lancaster (after death of Raymond)	3a	1591–4
Lancaster	3b	1601–3
–·–·–· Houtman	4	1595–7
– – – Van Neck & Van Warwijck	5	1598–9
———— Van Noort	6	1598–1601
———— Middleton	7	1604–6
★ Factory		

sary if they were to make the profits they had hoped for. Thus, like the Portuguese before them, the Dutch began to build trading posts. Gradually, their hold on the area tightened, and eventually most of the East Indies was to come under Dutch rule.

By the end of the 1500's, the English had also developed an interest in the East. They obtained their first information from **Francis Drake** (1540?-1596), who had called at the Moluccas on the last stage of his voyage around the world, and as early as 1591 an English fleet had sailed east to trade. But **George Raymond** (dates unknown) was drowned, and although **James Lancaster** (1550?-1618) reached the East, he had little success. Nevertheless, the English tried again. The publication in English of Van Linschoten's *Itinerario*, added to reports of Dutch successes in the Indies, inspired the formation of a company to organize the Indies trade. In 1600, the "Governor and Company of Merchants of London trading into the East Indies" —as the English East India Company was formally known—were granted a royal charter by Queen Elizabeth I.

Unlike the Dutch, who wanted to capture from Portugal the carrying trade between Asia and Europe, the English were interested in expanding their own exports, and in particular, in finding new markets for their woolen cloth. This did not prevent them from taking an active interest in the spice trade of the Indies, and the East India Company's first fleet, commanded by James Lancaster, returned home with its holds full of pepper. Surprisingly, although it was trespassing on ground the Dutch considered to be theirs, it had met with no resistance from the Dutch.

It was the English challenge, however, that forced the Dutch to realize that their hold on the Indies trade would be greater if the resources of their various companies were pooled. In 1602, therefore, they founded their own East India Company to take over the work of the numerous smaller concerns. By 1604, when **Henry Middleton** (?-1613) made the English East India Company's second expedition, the Dutch presented a united front, and Middleton had considerable difficulty in trading. As English traders gradually moved into Dutch territory, the situation became increasingly strained. By the mid-1600's, however, the Dutch had emerged triumphant, and the English East India Company had directed its attention to another part of the East.

◄ *Ships of the English East India Company at sea.*

55

MOGUL EMPIRE

HIMALAYA

Indus

Lahore
Br.

•Ajmer
Br. 1614

1c?

←Fatephur Sikri
1b

Agra
Br. 1602

•Lucknow
Br. 1856

1C

Jumna

Cooch
Behar

Brahma

24°
TROPIC OF CANCER

GUJARAT

Ahmadabad
Br. 1612

Patna
Br. 1620

Ganges

1C

1C

Cambay
Port. 1539
Br. 1612

2

Baroda
Br. 1612

Chandernagore
Fr. 1688
Serampore
Dan. 1616

Dacca
Br. 166

Gogeh
Dutch 1631
Diu
Dutch 1535
Port. 1535

2

GULF OF CAMBAY

2

Hooghly-Chinsura Port.
Calcutta
Br. 1690

•Broach

Mouths of the Ganges

66°
1a

Surat
Port. 1540
Br. 1618–83

2

Damão
Port. 1527–58
Dutch 1558

1b

Bassein Port. 1527
Bombay Port. 1530–1664 Br. 1669

Chaul
Port. 1509
Dutch 1509–1737

16°
2

GHATS

Vishākhapatnam
Br. 1668

1C

ARABIAN

Western

Bijapur

Rajapore
Br. 1637

Golconda

Krishna

EASTERN

Yanoan
Fr. 1706

1b

1a

Goa
Port. 1510

Masulipatam
Port. 1570–1605
Br. 1611
Dutch 1605–1781

BAY OF

1C

•Vijayanagar

LACCADIVE

SEA

ISLANDS

Malabar

I?

Armagon
Br. 1620

Mangalore
Port. 1527–65

Madras
(St. George)
Br. 1639

Pulicat Dutch 1609

Coromandel

BENGAL

Cannanore Port. 1505
Mahé
Fr. 1725
Calicut
Port. 1498–1616
Br. 1824

Dutch 1663

Pondichéry
Fr. 1672, 1674
Br. 1761

8°

Cochin
Port. 1500–3
Dutch 1663
Br. 1824

Tranquebar
Dan. 1616

Coast

Quilon
Br. 1503
Port. 1512
Dutch 1661

1C

Jaffna Port. 1560
Dutch 1658

Tuticorin
Br. 1658
Dutch 1781–1817

Trincomalee•
Dutch 1639

C. Comorin

CEYLON
Port. 1518
Dutch 1644–1795
Br. 1796

————— Newberry   1a   1583
(with Fitch, Leeds & Storey)
Newberry   1b   1585
(with Fitch & Leeds)
Newberry   1c   1585
(sets out to return home)
Fitch   1C   1585–91
(after leaving Newberry)

Negombo
Dutch 1635

Senkadagala

Colombo
Port. 1517
Dutch 1656
Br. 1796

Galle
Port. 1518–1640
Dutch 1640
Br. 1796

1C

·············· Jourdain   2   1608–12

© Geographical Projects

74°

82°

0   100   200   300   400   500
Miles

90°

The English and India

When the English turned from the Indies in search of new openings for trade, it was to the Indian subcontinent that they looked. India had as yet been little affected by the spread of European power in the East, for although the Portuguese had kept a tight grip on India's western ports, their main interest was always the East Indies. The riches of India were still virtually untouched, and to the English, the commercial possibilities seemed great.

England had learned much about the prospects for Indian trade from **Ralph Fitch** (?-1606). Fitch left England in 1583 with a party headed by **John Newberry** (dates unknown), who had already made a journey in the Middle East, and including **James Storey** (dates unknown) and **William Leeds** (dates unknown). Their goal was India, but their journey also provided information about the ancient but, to western Europeans, hardly known, overland route from the eastern

through. So long was he away that on his return he found that he had been presumed dead, and all his belongings sold.

It was not until 1608 that the English attempted to set up a trading post on the Indian coast. This unsuccessful venture, led by William Hawkins, is recounted in Hawkins' papers, and in those of another traveler, **John Jourdain** (dates unknown), who in about 1610 visited the Mogul court, and wrote glowingly of its wealth. Two years later, the English won the first of two naval victories against the Portuguese, and so impressed the Mogul emperor Jahangir, that he granted them facilities to trade. Factories were founded at Cambay, Baroda, Surat, Ahmadabad, and Ajmer.

In 1615, King James I sent England's first official ambassador to the Mogul court to negotiate a general trading agreement. Although no treaty was signed, the Moguls did promise support and protection

▼ *Akbar, Mogul emperor.*

▼ *Jahangir, Mogul emperor.*

Mediterranean, which it was hoped might prove an alternative to the sea route around the Cape. In Hormuz, the men were arrested, and they arrived in India as prisoners; but an Englishman working in Goa managed to obtain their release. Storey left the party in Goa, but the others traveled to Fatephur Sikri, seat of the court of the Mogul emperor Akbar, whom they presented with a letter from Queen Elizabeth of England. Then, they separated. Leeds remained with the court, and Newberry set out for home, disappearing on the way. Fitch spent six years wandering through the East, garnering knowledge of the countries he passed

against Portuguese attacks. Now English expansion began in earnest. An English factory had been established in Masulipatam on the east coast in 1611, and in 1639, Francis Day founded St. George—present-day Madras. Bombay came under English rule in the 1660's, and in 1690 Calcutta was founded.

By the late 1600's, the Moguls were no longer all-powerful, and the English were forced to take measures to protect themselves. They chose direct rule as the best means to secure their interests. So successful were they that until the mid-1800's, it seemed they had achieved their aim of "English dominion in India for all time to come".

5 The Conquistadors

When the Great Age of Discovery drew to its close, the Portuguese had gained a foothold in the countries of the East. In the west, however, it was the Spanish who had firmly staked their claim. At first they displayed little interest in their new American lands, because Spain, like Portugal, still looked on a share in the spice trade as the goal of exploration, and the islands of the Caribbean yielded nothing to compare with the riches of the East.

As time passed, however, Spanish interest in the Caribbean region gradually increased. Why should those strange and distant lands not hold a way to riches and to fame? The Spanish sailed west to make their fortunes, and to gain honor for themselves, hoping that in so doing they would win new lands for the Spanish crown. These first emigrants were hardy adventurers, as they had every need to be, for the early colonies in the Caribbean afforded little but hard work and disease. In time, however, the search for gold and glory led to the Spanish west from the Caribbean to the American mainland shores. There, in Mexico and Peru, they found the treasure that they sought.

These bold adventurers earned the name *conquistadors,* for they conquered while they explored. The time that they held sway in the Americas was one of turbulence and romance, for these small bands of European adventurers brought mighty empires under Spanish rule. The conquistadors made themselves vast fortunes, sent immense treasure back to Spain, and in so doing, opened up the Americas from southern North America and Mexico in the north to Chile in the south. As they conquered, they paved the way to nearly 300 years of Spanish colonial rule.

The means used by the conquistadors have been questioned, for they were ruthless and cruel, and the Spanish conquest destroyed not just civilizations, but decimated whole peoples as well. But the Spanish had reasons other than gold lust for the methods that they used. They were vigorous and determined Christians who used the sword to spread God's word, feeling that any means were justified to stamp out the heathen practices that they found. Fear, too, made them terrible, for they were stranded far from home. Deep among hostile peoples, they chose terror as the best means to establish their power and thus to ensure their safety.

The rule of the conquistadors was a short one, for their conquests were soon complete. Alone, they had founded their empires under the distant control of Spain. But as peace descended on the Americas, their star began to decline. The Spanish government, determined to maintain its grip on its rich new colonies, preferred to place their government in other hands. The conquistadors were not the type of men to make good administrators, and besides, such warlike conquerors might well seize power for themselves. Gradually, the place of the conquistadors was taken by bureaucrats from Spain.

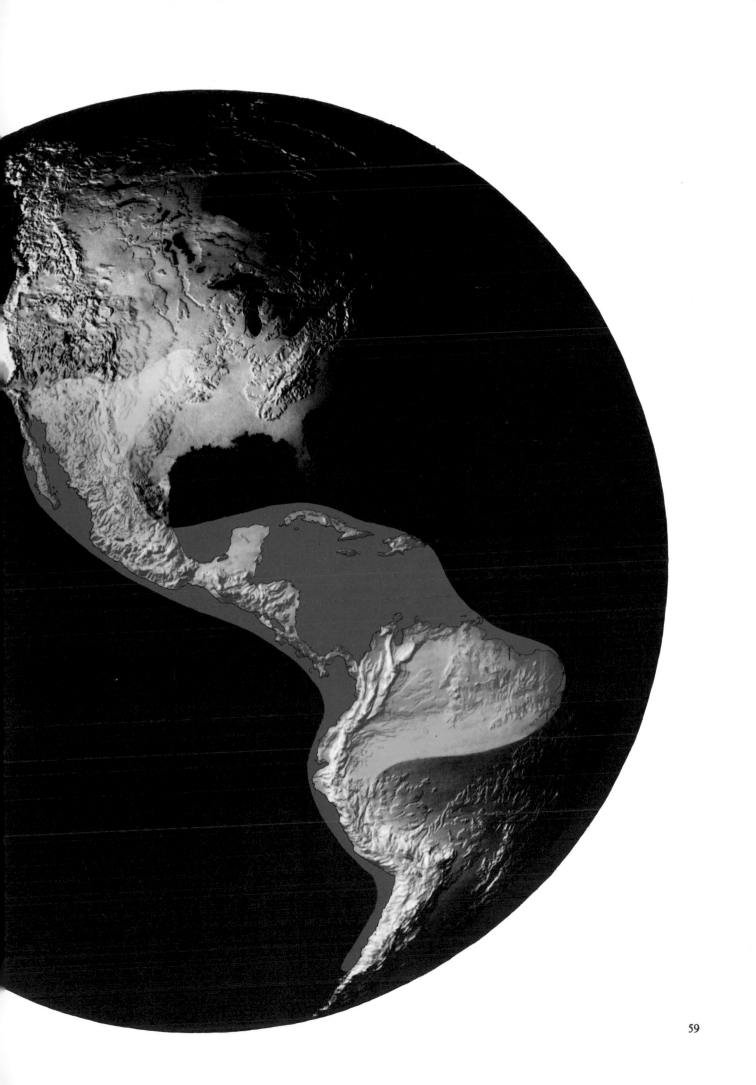

The Taking of Mexico

In the year Ce Acatl, so the Aztec legend ran, the god Quetzalcoatl would return. Strange portents foretold his coming in the Ce Acatl year 1519. In the event, however, it was the Spanish conquistador Hernando Cortes, not Quetzalcoatl, who came to the Aztec lands.

According to Aztec legend, Quetzalcoatl had been driven from Mexico by his rival Huitzilopochtli, but, on leaving his lands, he had promised to come back. Small wonder the Aztec, who knew nothing

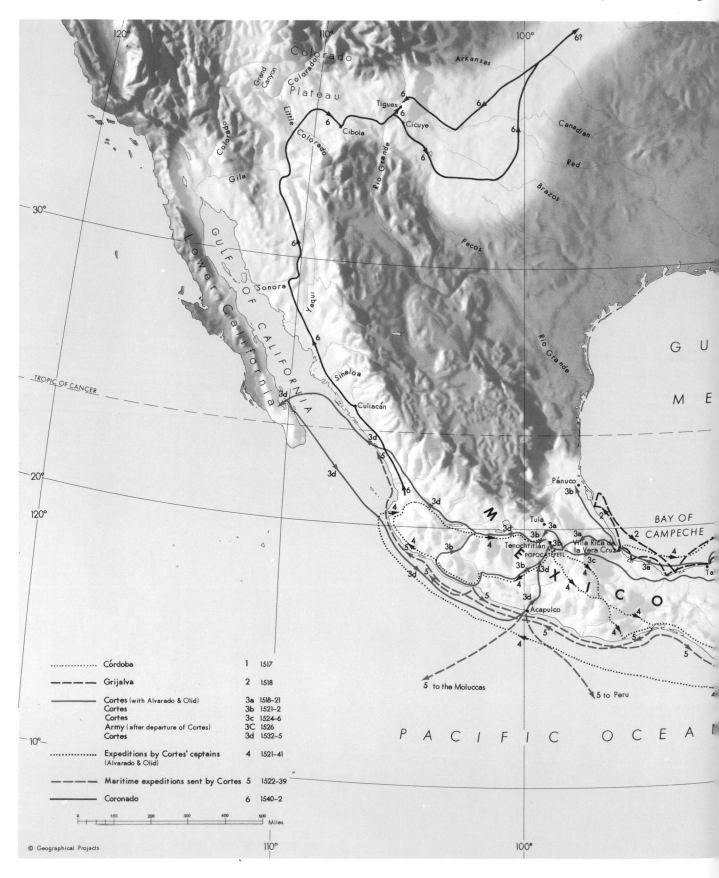

....	Córdoba	1	1517
– – – – –	Grijalva	2	1518
────────	Cortes (with Alvarado & Olid)	3a	1518–21
	Cortes	3b	1521–2
	Cortes	3c	1524–6
	Army (after departure of Cortes)	3C	1526
	Cortes	3d	1532–5
···········	Expeditions by Cortes' captains (Alvarado & Olid)	4	1521–41
– – – – –	Maritime expeditions sent by Cortes	5	1522–39
────────	Coronado	6	1540–2

0 100 200 300 400 500 Miles

of Europeans, thought **Hernando Cortes** (1485-1547) was their god.

When Cortes set out on his expedition, the Spanish knew little of the lands west of their Caribbean bases. To the south, Vasco Núñez de Balboa had founded a colony on the Isthmus of Panama, and in 1513, had crossed the isthmus to the Pacific; but to the west **Francisco Fernández de Córdoba** (?-1518) and **Juan de Grijalva** (1489?-1527) had merely coasted Central America, discovering the Yucatan Peninsula, and finding traces of a great civilization there. Gold especially appeared to be plentiful, and in Mexico, Grijalva heard of greater treasure inland.

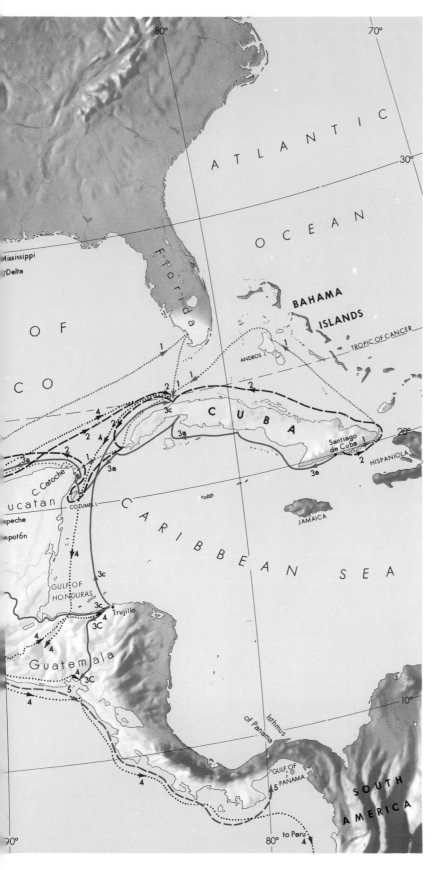

▲ *Cortes, by an Indian artist.*

Seeking that treasure, Cortes set sail. With **Pedro dc Alvarado** (1495?-1541) and **Cristóbal de Olid** (1492?-1524), he disembarked at Villa Rica de la Vera Cruz, near present-day Veracruz, on Friday, 22 April 1519. This was the day the legend had named for Quetzalcoatl's return.

Emissaries from the Aztec emperor Montezuma met Cortes at the coast, but the rich gifts they gave him only increased his desire for gold. Determined to see Montezuma himself, Cortes set out for the Aztec capital Tenochtitlán. There, he was received as befitted a god.

The friendship between Aztec and Spaniard did not last long. Cortes saw that his life and those of his men were in Montezuma's hands, and he decided to act. He arrested the Aztec emperor, hoping to make him a puppet ruler under the king of Spain.

At this critical moment, Cortes was forced to leave Alvarado in charge at Tenochtitlán, while he returned to the coast. On arriving in Mexico, he had declared himself responsible only to his king, thus usurping the authority—and possible profits—of the governor of Cuba, sponsor of his expedition. Keen to keep control of an undertaking of such potential, the governor sent troops to bring Cortes to heel. Their threat was easily disposed of, but Cortes' absence from Tenochtitlán led to a crisis. During a religious festival, Alvarado massacred thousands of Aztec, and Cortes returned in 1520 to find the city hostile. Soon after his return, the Indians attacked.

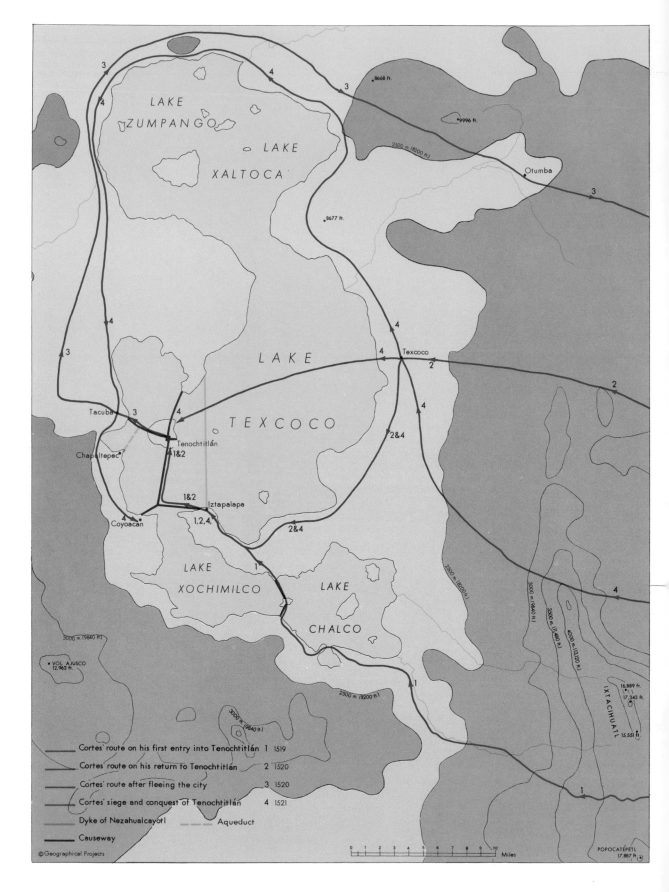

LAKE ZUMPANGO

LAKE XALTOCA

8668 ft.

•9996 ft.

2500 m. (8200 ft)

Otumba

8677 ft.

3

LAKE TEXCOCO

Texcoco

2

2

2&4

4

4

Tacuba

3

4

Chapultepec

Tenochtitlán

1&2

1&2

Iztapalapa

Coyoacán

4

1,2,4.

2&4

LAKE XOCHIMILCO

1

LAKE CHALCO

2500 m. (8000 ft)

3000 m. (9840 ft.)

• VOL AJUSCO
12,962 ft.

3000 m. (9840 ft.)

2500 m. (8200 ft.)

3000 m. (9840 ft)

3500 m. (11,480 ft.)

4000 m. (13,120 ft.)

16,889 ft.
17,343 ft.

IXTACCIHUATL

15,551 ft.

_____ Cortes' route on his first entry into Tenochtitlán   1   1519

_____ Cortes' route on his return to Tenochtitlán   2   1520

_____ Cortes' route after fleeing the city   3   1520

_____ Cortes' siege and conquest of Tenochtitlán   4   1521

_____ Dyke of Nezahualcayotl   _ _ _ _ Aqueduct

_____ Causeway

©Geographical Projects

0 1 2 3 4 5 6 7 8 9 10   Miles

POPOCATÉPETL
17,887 ft.

The Aztec capital, Tenochtitlán, was called by the Spanish the "Venice of the New World". Built on an island in Lake Texcoco, it was joined to the mainland by wide stone causeways, and a stone aqueduct brought drinking water from the springs of Chapultepec, some three miles away. The city, with its fine stone buildings and beautiful chinampas (floating gardens), was razed almost to the ground during Cortes' siege of 1521. It was not long to remain in ruins, however, for on its site the Spanish built Mexico City as the capital of New Spain.

During the fighting, Montezuma was killed when, at Cortes' request, he tried to persuade the Aztec to allow the Spanish to leave unharmed. Now, as the Spanish were in great

When the Spanish reached mainland America, they were faced with a surprise. Here were no primitive tribesmen, such as those who inhabited the islands of the Caribbean. Instead, mighty, civilized empires held sway over the land.

▲ *Mexico City in the 1500's.*

danger, Cortes attempted to break from the island city to the nearby mainland. Although he succeeded, nearly two-thirds of the Spanish soldiers were killed. It took the conquistadors nearly a year to prepare another attack, and not until May 1521 did Tenochtitlán come under Spanish siege. Then, the Aztec held out for 80 grueling days, surrendering to the Spanish only when their leader was captured.

After the fall of Tenochtitlán, Cortes began to consolidate Spanish authority in his colony of New Spain and, within three years, the land was at peace. Mexico City was built as capital of the Spanish domains, and Cortes arranged expeditions outside Mexico. Alvarado marched into Guatemala, while Olid traveled in the west and then, via Cuba, to the coast of the Gulf of Honduras. There, he rebelled against the authority of Cortes.

Cortes himself made a punitive expedition to the Pánuco River in the north, and marched east across southern Yucatan against Olid. In 1522-4, he arranged voyages along the Pacific coast to search for a strait to the Atlantic, and in 1527 sent a fleet to the Moluccas. He tried, unsuccessfully, to colonize Lower California in 1532-5, and in 1536, sent ships to the aid of Pizarro in Peru. But it was after his time that **Francisco Vásquez de Coronado** (1510-1554) carried his gold lust north and, in so doing, explored much of what is now the southern United States.

The most ancient of these empires, and one which, at the arrival of the Spanish, was in the final stages of decline, was that of the **Maya** in Guatemala, Honduras, and the peninsula of Yucatan. Between the A.D. 300's and 800's, when Europe was sunk in darkness, Maya civilization reached its height. In the 900's, however, it suffered a period of decay and, although a later revival did take place, the Maya never regained their former greatness.

To the west of the Maya homelands, in what is now Mexico, lay the empire of the **Aztec.** The Aztec were a warrior people, and their men were constantly fighting to enlarge the boundaries of their empire, or to bring new tribes under their rule. As befitted such a fierce people, the religion around which their life centered was bloodthirsty, too. They believed that disaster could only be averted by offering Huitzilopochtli, the chief of their gods, the most valuable of all gifts—life. In Aztec religious ceremonies, thousands of

people were slain. Yet for all this, the Aztec were no uncivilized barbarians, but a highly cultured race. Their legends told of a gentle god, Quetzalcoatl, patron of learning and the priesthood, he for whom Cortes was mistaken. Although these same legends recounted how the fierce Huitzilopochtli had driven Quetzalcoatl out, still, under Aztec rule, science and art flourished, and beautiful temples and palaces were built.

According to an old saying, while the Maya dreamed and the Aztec worshiped, the **Inca** built, and the land of the Inca in what is now Peru bears splendid testimony to this. Houses, palaces, and irrigation projects—to all these they lent their hands. In the 1400's, they conquered a vast area stretching from Peru north into Ecuador, and south into Bolivia and Chile. Throughout this empire, they set up a magnificent network of roads. The Inca were a farming people and theirs was a community, rather than an individual, way of life.

Aztec Empire at time of Conquest
Maya Empire at time of Conquest
Inca Empire at its greatest extent

© Geographical Projects

The Conquest of Peru

From the Spanish colony of Panama, the conquistadors sent their ships sailing south. In 1522, under *Pascual de Andagoya* (1495?-1548), the first government survey was made. It brought back tales of a rich kingdom, which Indians called Birú. Probably from this word developed the name by which the Spanish knew the country—Peru.

Andagoya's report aroused interest in the south, and soon a group of Spaniards had applied to the governor of Panama for the right to explore. In 1524, **Francisco Pizarro** (1475-1541) sailed south, followed by **Diego de Almagro** (1475?-1538). Most of their capital was provided by a priest, Fernando de Luque, who helped plan the expedition, but who did not actually take part.

This first Spanish venture met with little success. Although the adventurers explored part of the coast north of the equator, their hopes of gold were unfounded, and they had to return to Panama when their supplies ran out. But this did not deter them from making a second expedition. This time, they sailed with a pilot, **Bartolome de la Ruiz** (dates unknown), a sea captain who was to become the first Spaniard to meet the Inca people of Peru. On this expedition, the Spaniards reached the city of Tumbes, confirming for themselves earlier reports of Inca wealth, and sailed south to the Santa Pau River.

Despite this new proof of Peru's riches, the government of Panama proved unwilling to sponsor further exploration to the south. Pizarro therefore took his case to the king of Spain, who at length agreed to back an expedition, and created Pizarro governor and captain-general of any lands he might subdue. In 1531, accompanied by his four half brothers **Hernando** (1475?-1578), **Gonzalo** (1506?-1548), and **Juan Pizarro** (1500?-1536), and **Martin de Alcántara** (dates unknown), Pizarro set out.

The Spanish adventurer could not have chosen a better moment to embark on his quest. For five years, civil war had raged in Peru between Huáscar, the legitimate Inca emperor, and his half brother Atahualpa, to whom Huáscar's father had left one-fifth of his kingdom. Although in the year 1532 the war ended, and Atahualpa ruled, dissent still filled the Inca lands.

Pizarro and his men landed at San Mateo Bay, from which they advanced overland to Tumbes. Since Pizarro's last visit, the civil war had reached Tumbes, and the city had been sacked and stripped of many of its treasures. Now, Pizarro remained there only long enough for reinforcements to reach him. Then, leaving a small garrison at Tumbes, he advanced south. On the edge of the Sechura Desert, he founded San Miguel, where he and his men stayed for several months. From the Indians, they learned that Atahualpa was not at Cusco, his capital far to the south, but at Cajamarca, little more than a quarter as long a journey away. In September 1532, the Spanish set out for Cajamarca. From the burning desert, their route led through the snow-capped mountains of the Andes and, so hard was the way that, had the Inca attacked, the Spaniards might never have reached their goal. But Atahualpa had determined to receive the invaders as friends. Secure in his strength as Inca ruler, he saw no threat in the tiny Spanish force.

The Spanish expedition reached Cajamarca on 15 November 1532. Pizarro, determined to strike his blow against the Inca quickly, chose his first meeting with Atahualpa as the occasion for his coup. When the Inca ruler and his unarmed bodyguard arrived for the meeting, the Spaniards were lying in wait. Taking Atahualpa prisoner, they slew his followers.

Atahualpa hoped the conquistador's greed might secure his release, and he promised Pizarro a huge ransom—enough gold to fill a room 22 feet long by 17 feet wide, as high

The rival Inca emperors, Atahualpa (left) and his half brother Huáscar. ▼

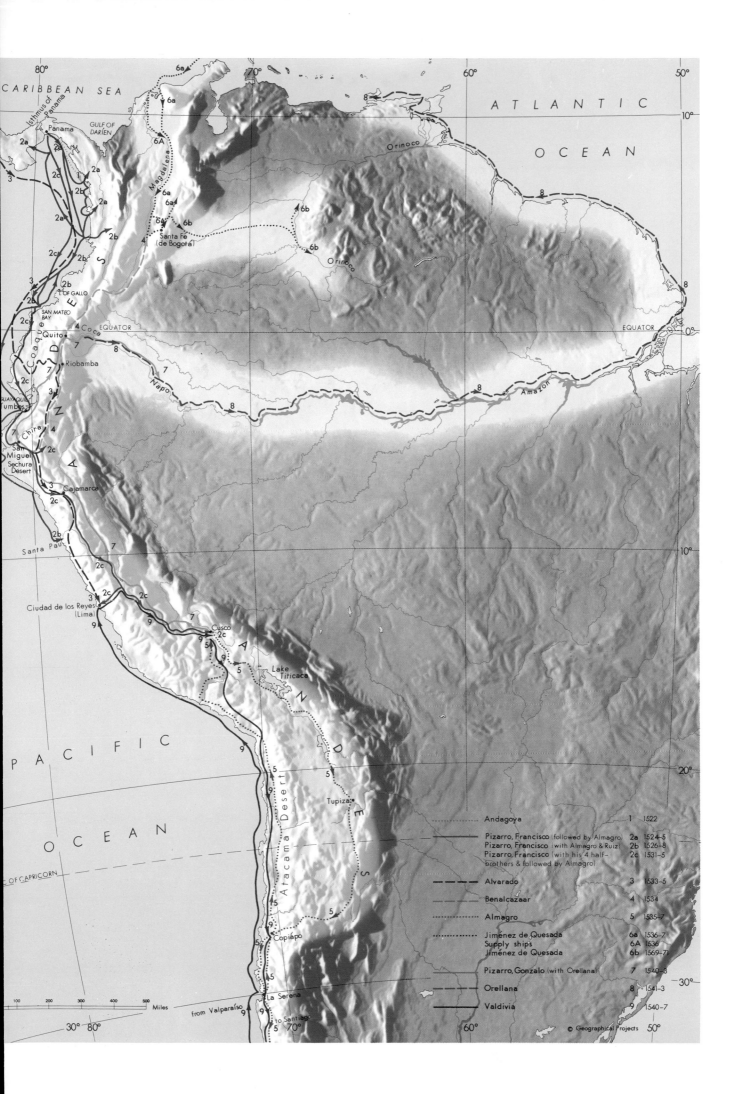

CARIBBEAN SEA

ATLANTIC

OCEAN

PACIFIC

OCEAN

Panama

GULF OF DARIEN

Isthmus of Panama

Orinoco

Orinoco

Magdalena

Santa Fe (de Bogotá)

I. OF GALLO

SAN MATEO BAY

Quito

Coca

EQUATOR

EQUATOR

Riobamba

Napo

Amazon

GUAYAQUIL

Tumbes

Chira

San Miguel

Sechura Desert

Cajamarca

Santa

Pau

Ciudad de los Reyes (Lima)

Cusco

Lake Titicaca

Atacama Desert

Tupiza

Copiapó

OF CAPRICORN

La Serena

from Valparaíso

to Santiago

....	Andagoya	1	1522
────────	Pizarro, Francisco (followed by Almagro)	2a	1524-5
	Pizarro, Francisco (with Almagro & Ruiz)	2b	1526-8
	Pizarro, Francisco (with his 4 half-brothers & followed by Almagro)	2c	1531-5
── ── ──	Alvarado	3	1533-5
────────	Benalcazaar	4	1534
....	Almagro	5	1535-7
....	Jiménez de Quesada	6a	1536-7
	Supply ships	6A	1536
	Jiménez de Quesada	6b	1569-71
── ── ──	Pizarro, Gonzalo (with Orellana)	7	1540-3
── ── ──	Orellana	8	1541-3
────────	Valdivia	9	1540-7

© Geographical Projects

100 200 300 400 500

Miles

as the emperor could reach (some seven feet). But even when the treasure was assembled, Pizarro dared not let the Inca ruler go. He had him tried for treason, and strangled.

From Cajamarca, Pizarro continued to the Inca capital Cusco. There, the Spanish soldiers ran wild. They plundered temples, looted houses and palaces, raped, and generally debauched. Eventually, Pizarro managed to restore order and gain a firm grip on the city but, nevertheless, he was never to have the same control of Peru that Cortes had of Mexico. He founded Lima—which he named *Ciudad de los Reyes* (the City of the Kings)—as capital of the Spanish domains, and appointed Manco Capac, half brother of Huáscar and Atahualpa, Inca ruler under the Spanish king. At first, the Inca accepted the conquest almost without resistance; but, among Pizarro's own followers, dissatisfaction and jealousy were rife.

Pizarro's position was first threatened even before the founding of Lima, and from outside, rather than from within, Peru. In 1533, **Pedro de Alvarado,** Cortes' captain, sailed from New Spain for South America, and marched on the kingdom of Quito, where he thought he would find great wealth. He was forestalled, however, by **Sebastian de Benalcazaar** (1495?-1550?), governor of San Miguel, who had already captured Quito when he heard of the approach of Almagro, sent to put down Alvarado. He joined Almagro at Riobamba, and there they were able to buy Alvarado's departure without a fight. Alvarado even visited Pizarro before traveling north again. Benalcazaar himself was appointed governor of Quito, and extended Spanish rule north, beyond what had been the Inca's northern frontier.

Almagro, as a reward for his services, was created governor of a province in the south, stretching for 500 miles beyond Pizarro's land. In July 1535, he left Cusco on a tour of his new domain. Although he claimed the lands as far south as present-day Santiago for the Spanish king, he returned to Peru a bitterly disillusioned man. In his province, there were no riches to rival the Inca wealth, and he saw little hope that his governorship would bring him the reward he felt was his due.

In 1537, Almagro arrived back in Cusco to find the Inca had rebelled. The situation seemed serious, for the Indians, unlike the Spanish, were accustomed to fighting in mountain territory, and had managed to lay siege to Cusco, and to prevent the relief parties sent from Lima by Pizarro from reaching the city. Almagro defeated their army; but then he turned rebel himself. Claiming that Cusco lay within his territory, and not Pizarro's, he seized the city. In 1538, he was defeated and executed but, three years later, his followers were revenged. In 1541, they murdered Francisco Pizarro, the conqueror of Peru.

The conquistadors, in their search for gold, traveled far beyond Peru's frontiers, and thus opened up much of South America. **Gonzalo Jiménez de Quesada** (1497?-1579?) traveled in the northwest, and, on the plateau of Bogotá he conquered the Chibcha, the last of the wealthy Indian peoples. Pizarro's brother Gonzalo, meanwhile, made an expedition with **Francisco de Orellana** (1500?-1550?) that led to Orellana making the first voyage down the Amazon River. **Pedro de Valdivia** (1500?-1553) established a colony in Chile, and founded both Santiago—today the capital of the country—and Valparaíso.

▼ *Battle between the Inca and Spanish.*

AMERICAE SIVE QVARTAE ORBIS PARTIS NOVA ET EXACTISSIMA DESCRIPTIO.

This map of the Americas in the years after the Spanish conquest was drawn by Diego Gutiérrez (?-1554) and engraved posthumously by Hieronymus Cock in Antwerp in 1562. Gutiérrez was a cosmographer —an expert in the science dealing with the general appearance and structure of the earth—at the Casa de la Contratación de Las Indias (the House of Trade for the Indies) in Seville, Spain. This establishment, founded in 1503, had as its first head Amerigo Vespucci, and from 1518 to 1548 it was under the direction of Sebastian Cabot.

Gutiérrez' map concentrates chiefly on the Atlantic seaboard, and on Central and South America. For the latter regions, he was able to take into account discoveries made by the Portuguese in the east of the continent, as well as those of the Spanish in the west, Pizarro and his followers in Peru, and Cortes in Mexico. The most important feature of his map of South America is the Amazon River, which Orellana's voyage enabled him to place. However, he had little idea of its true course, and based his sinuous portrayal on Sebastian Cabot's map of 1554. The Paraná and Uruguay rivers, which flow into the Rio de la Plata, he greatly exaggerated in size, and Tierra del Fuego, which he called Tierra de Magallanes —the land of Magellan—he extended southward, making it part of a great continental land.

Although the coastline of the Americas, like that of Africa, was already reasonably well known, Gutiérrez was almost completely ignorant of the interior. In compensation, the continents team with life, as do the seas. In Africa, Gutiérrez shows an elephant, a rhinoceros, and a lion, and he peoples South America with imaginary natives. Cannibals carry out their horrible practices in Brazil; to the south, in Patagonia, giants are shown. Ever since Magellan's expedition had nicknamed the inhabitants of this region *Patagonians* —which in Spanish means "big feet" —the belief had grown in Europe that this area was populated by a race of enormous people. The life of the seas is even more fabulous than that of the land. And, amidst weird gods and monsters, the ships of Europe ply their way over the newly known seas.

67

6 A New World No Longer

It is difficult to imagine a time when North America was hardly known, much less explored, when Europeans could not trace the continent's outline, nor guess at its extent. Yet, for the first explorers to reach there, America was indeed a "new world". The great continent stretched before them, unknown, mysterious, no one knew how far. In its vastness were hidden deserts and mountains, great rivers and rolling plains. There were furs there for the trader, and land for the farmer. Above all, in the unknown, there was adventure for the brave.

When Christopher Columbus sailed the Atlantic, his goal was not the Americas—indeed, he did not even know of the existence of such a land. Like many of the mariners who would follow him, he sought a new route to the Orient, and it was by these seekers after Eastern treasure that the first western landfalls were made. The sailors were followed by the gold-seekers, who made the first journeys into the interior, but it was not until the arrival of traders and colonists that North American exploration really began. For, in the pursuit of their own interests, these pioneers set out westward, gradually extending their knowledge far beyond the Atlantic shores.

To the pioneers, this magnificent country lay open for the taking, despite the fact that they found an indigenous people already there. With the Eskimos of the far north, the European settlers had little contact, but they encountered the Indian inhabitants of the rest of the continent at every step they took. At first, the Indians often helped the European settlers, but although friendly relations were maintained in the north, in what is now Canada, the situation soon changed farther south. When the colonists became self-sufficient, they regarded the Indians as obstacles to the expansion of white rule. The struggle between invaders and natives was to be long and bitter, but eventually the Indians were driven from their homelands in the face of the white advance.

The traders and settlers who set out into the American interior were the spearhead of a continuing drive by the white man toward the West. After 1783, when the United States came into being, there was a sense among the pioneers that their advance was inevitable, that it was their nation's true destiny to expand to the Pacific shores. In 1845, this sense of destiny was put into words when John L. Sullivan wrote in a New York City newspaper, "It is our manifest destiny to overspread and possess the whole of the continent which Providence has given us". Soon the phrase "Manifest Destiny" was being used whenever westward expansion was talked of, yet this was only the voicing of a belief that every pioneer held. First through trade, then through this sense of the inevitability of the push to the westward, North America was explored.

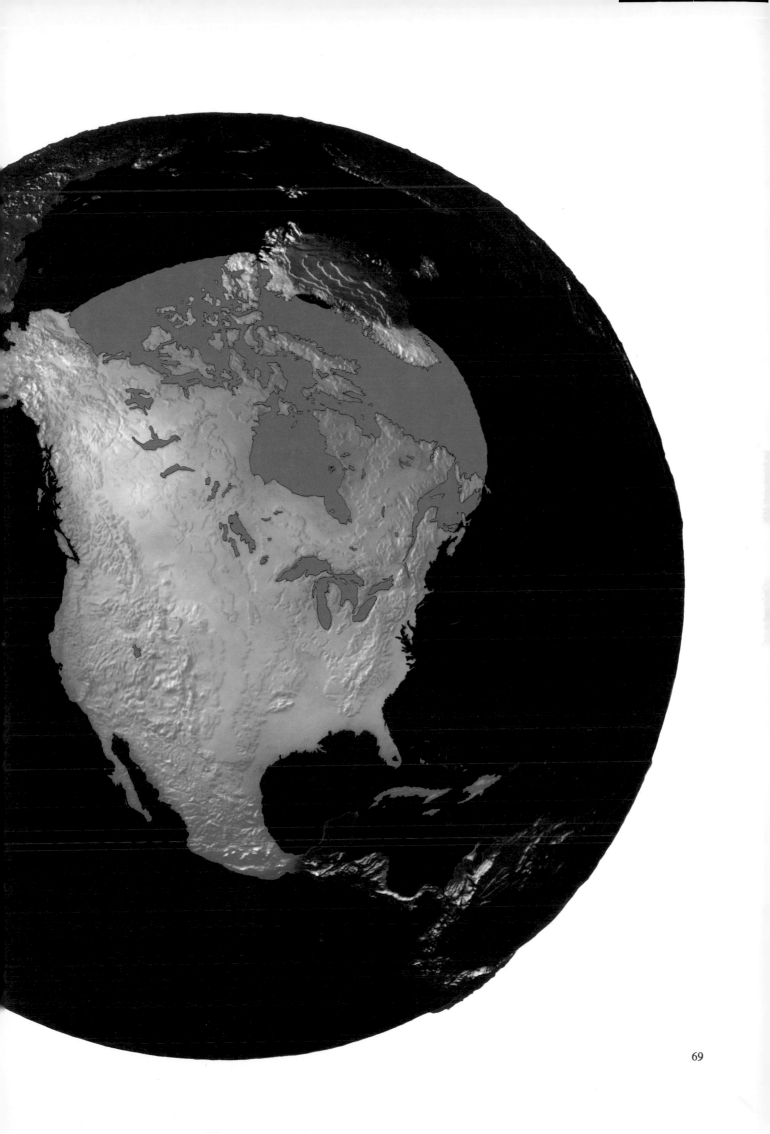

The Conquistadors Push Northward

Restless, and greedy for glory and for gold, the Spanish left their homelands to sail to the American shores. They looked not for new lands to discover, but for treasure, conquest, and honor for God and Spain. For many of these conquistadors, the reward was to be small.

Juan Ponce de León (1460?-1521), who had sailed on Columbus' second expedition, set out not for love of gold, but seeking a fountain whose waters he believed would give eternal youth. Although he never found it, he discovered Florida, which he thought was a great new island. He named it after the day he sighted it— *Pascua Florida* (Easter Sunday).

In 1527, **Pánfilo de Narváez** (1478?-1528) left Spain to conquer and colonize Florida, but his overland march there revealed none of the gold he longed for, so he resolved to rejoin his ships and continue to New Spain. When he reached the coast, however, he found that his ships had sailed without him, and his men had to build boats for the voyage around the Gulf of Mexico. After passing the Mississippi delta, they were caught in a storm. Narváez' boat was blown out to sea, and the conquistador was never seen again.

Only one of the other four boats, and the crew of a second, survived. Then, after the men had landed, many died, or were enslaved by Indians. But **Álvar Núñez Cabeza de Vaca** (1490?-1557?) was lucky enough to fall in with a friendly tribe, whose nomadic existence he shared for nearly six years. At last, with three companions, he managed to escape, and in April 1536, after a grueling journey, the four men were found by Spanish cavalrymen on the frontiers of New Spain.

Although the Indians De Vaca had lived with had been poor, from them he had heard of rich tribes farther north. A reconnaissance expedition sent from New Spain to investigate his story glowingly confirmed the Indians' report. The men even

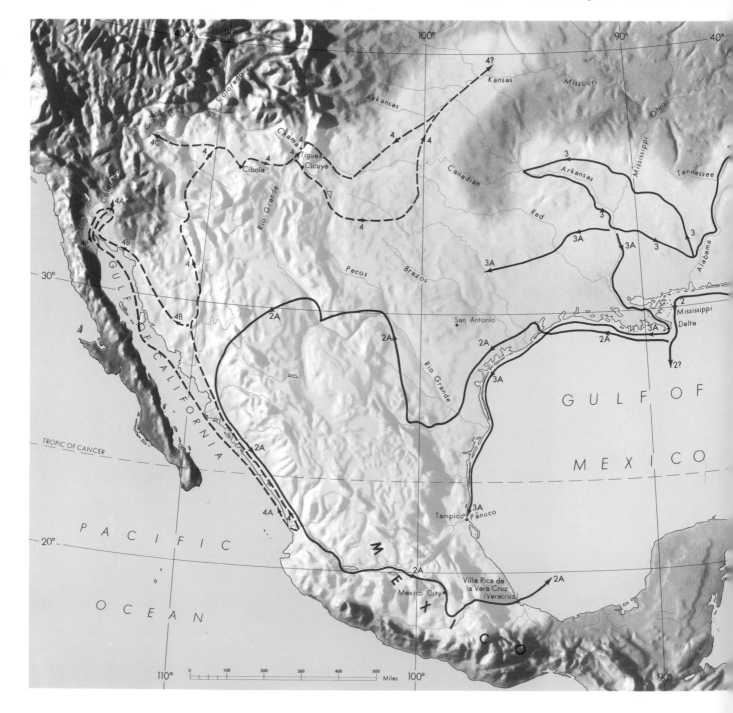

claimed to have seen the fabled Seven Cities of Cibola, reputedly one of the world's greatest sources of riches. In 1540, therefore, the viceroy of Mexico dispatched an expedition to capture the Seven Cities' wealth.

While **Francisco Vásquez de Coronado** led a large force from New Spain northward, **Hernando de Alarcón** (dates unknown) sailed with two ships up the Gulf of California, carrying supplies. His voyage was to prove that California was a peninsula, not an island as had previously been conjectured, and he discovered the mouth of the Colorado River, and traveled up it a little way. He never met up with Coronado, and sailed for home alone.

Coronado himself reached Cibola, to find that it was only a poor Indian village. He sent **Melchior Diaz** (dates unknown) to find Alarcón and get supplies, but at the mouth of the Colorado, Diaz discovered a message from Alarcón saying he had left for home. Other parties were sent to search for richer lands and one, led by **García López de Cárdenas** (dates unknown), traveled a short way down the Colorado, and discovered the Grand Canyon. Coronado himself, continuing to Cicuye and Tiguex, heard of a rich land called Quivira to the north. Seeking Quivira, he pushed north and across the Arkansas, but the legendary kingdom never materialized. Disillusioned, Coronado led his men back to New Spain. The expedition had made many discoveries and reported on the Indians and their customs. But because they had discovered no treasure, Coronado found himself in disgrace.

While Coronado sought the Seven Cities in southwestern North America, **Hernando de Soto** (1500?-1542) was seeking them in the southeast. As a reward for his part in the conquest of the Inca, De Soto had been appointed governor of Cuba, and given the right to conquer Florida. He reached Tampa Bay in May 1539, and set out overland. Pushing north past the Savannah River, he crossed the Appalachians, turning south, then west. In 1541, he arrived at the Mississippi. Although he pushed far to the west of that river, his hopes of gold proved ill-founded. In 1542, sick and exhausted, he died on the Mississippi's banks. His successor, **Luis de Moscoso** (dates unknown), buried him in the river, then turned west on another unsuccessful quest. At last, abandoning his search for gold, he sailed down the Mississippi and around the coast to New Spain.

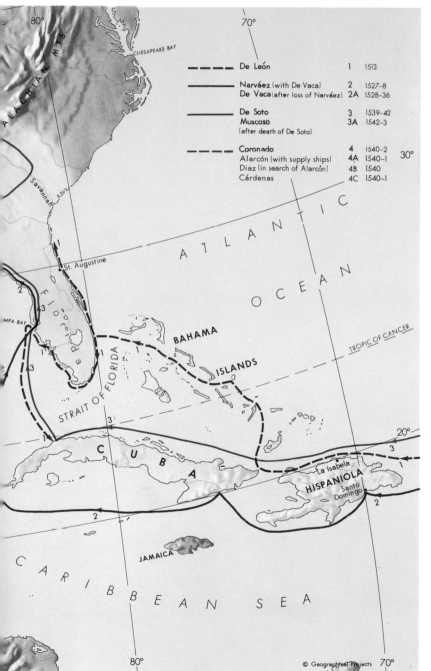

De León 1 1513
Narváez (with De Vaca) 2 1527-8
De Vaca (after loss of Narváez) 2A 1528-36
De Soto 3 1539-42
Muscoso 3A 1542-3
(after death of De Soto)
Coronado 4 1540-2
Alarcón (with supply ships) 4A 1540-1
Diaz (in search of Alarcón) 4B 1540
Cárdenas 4C 1540-1

© Geographical Projects

A "New Description of America"

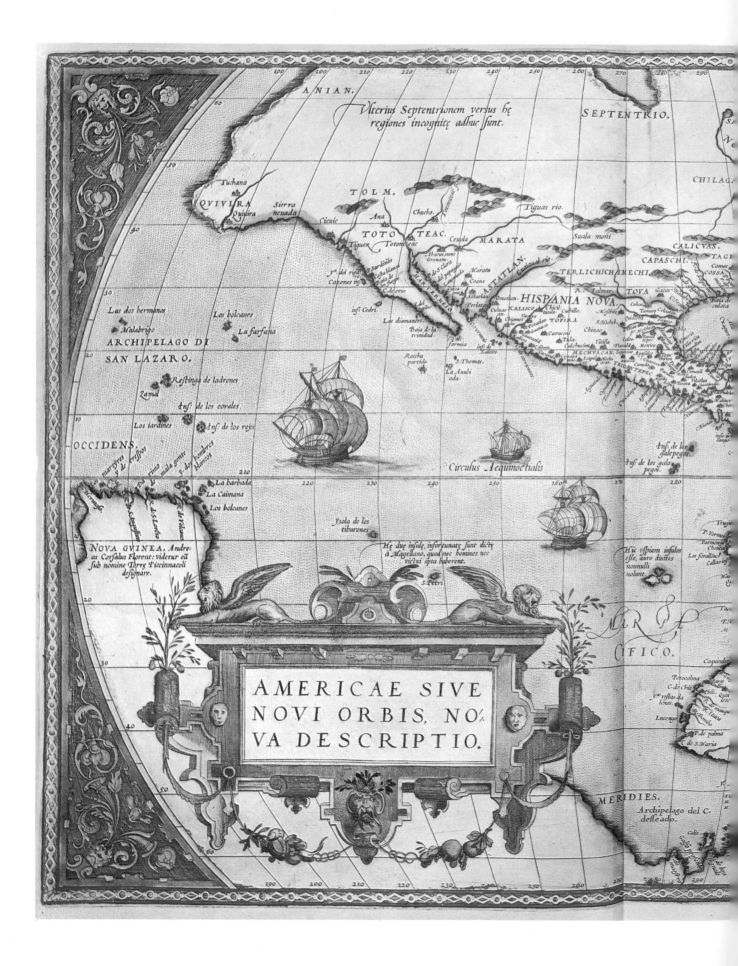

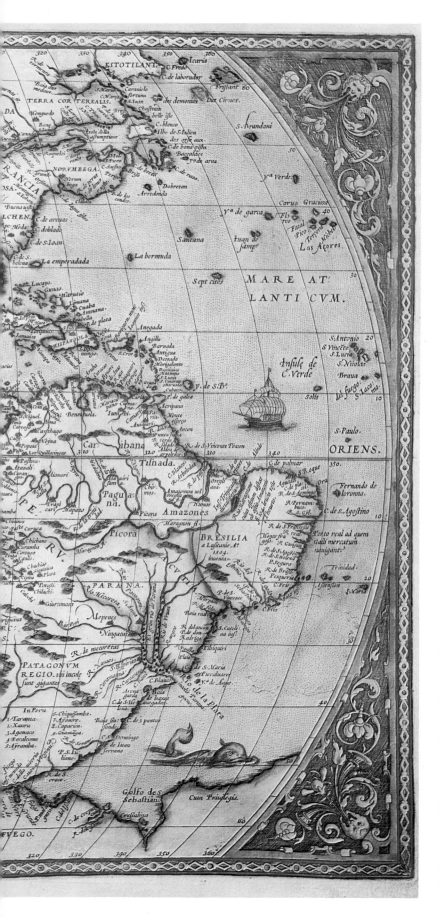

In 1570, Abraham Ortelius (1527-1598), an Antwerp cartographer and map publisher, produced the first edition of his atlas *Theatrum Orbis Terrarum* (theater of the world). This work is generally considered to be the first modern atlas, for although collections of maps had been issued earlier, they were made up of existing maps of varying sizes, and by different cartographers, whereas every one of the 70 maps in Ortelius' atlas was especially engraved for the occasion. After 1570, the atlas went through numerous editions, and for many of them new maps were added. By 1601, there were 121 in the body of the atlas, besides 40 in a supplement that was devoted to historical maps.

In the first edition of his atlas, Ortelius included only one map of the Americas, and another was not added until 1579. This first map—the "New Description of America, or the New World"—showed both North and South America, and also a large portion of the imaginary southern continent (usually known as *Terra Australis Incognita*—the unknown southern land), which was then supposed to cover the southern part of the earth. Surprisingly, the outline of South America is less accurate than in Gutiérrez' map published eight years earlier but, even so, Ortelius knew more of South America than of the north.

Ortelius' North America is easily recognizable, but its proportions are far from the truth. The Gulf of Mexico coastline is too short, and the distance from Florida to Cape Breton too small. In mapping the southern part of the continent, Ortelius could draw on his knowledge of the Spanish expeditions northward, and he marks Tiguex and Quivira, but far from the area of Coronado's search. For the St. Lawrence region, he had the journeys of Jacques Cartier, made between 1534 and 1542, to help him. Elsewhere, his knowledge was so limited that he simply left his map blank, with the exception, that is, of a few mountain ranges dotted about the interior, and a legend to the effect that the northwest was unknown. It seems odd that he did know of the existence of Hudson Bay, even though his map was drawn 40 years before Hudson's ill-fated voyage there. Generally, however, the impression his map leaves is of just how much remained for the explorers of North America to reveal.

73

The French Explore

As the Spanish pushed northward from Mexico, another nation began to explore farther north. In 1534, searching for a westward passage to Asia, **Jacques Cartier** (1491-1557) reached the Gaspé Peninsula. A year later, he discovered the St. Lawrence River, and sailed up it to Hochelaga, on the site of Montreal. But he was prevented by the Lachine rapids from going farther, and his 1541-2 voyage added nothing to knowledge of "New France".

Jacques Cartier. ▼

Cartier certainly did not reach Asia, but he paved France's way to America. In his wake, French fishermen regularly visited the fishing grounds off Newfoundland, and fur trade with the Indians was also opened up.

The man whose travels laid the foundations of French Canada first traveled there on behalf of the fur trade monopoly. His name was **Samuel de Champlain** (1567?-1635), and he made his first expedition up the St. Lawrence in 1603. The year after, he explored the North American coast, sailing south beyond Cape Cod, and helped to found Port Royal, Nova Scotia, the first French colony in the New World. In 1608, he was again on the St. Lawrence, and established Quebec as a base for the fur trade. He made friends with the Huron Indians, and agreed to fight with them against the Iroquois tribes,

who were their enemies. With a Huron war party, in 1609 he discovered Lake Champlain.

In 1610, Champlain met a youth named **Etienne Brulé** (1592?-1633), who wanted to live with an Indian tribe to learn its language. To Champlain, anxious to find out more about the interior, this seemed an excellent idea. On Brulé's return, Champlain was able to learn about the region Brulé had visited, and about Georgian Bay, which Brulé was the first white man to see. From another Frenchman, **Nicolas Vigneau** (dates unknown), Champlain heard that north of the Ottawa River there lay a great sea, and in 1613 he set out to find it. Some way up the Ottawa, however, it became clear that Vigneau was lying, and Champlain turned back.

In 1615, Champlain promised to join the Hurons in an attack on an

Iroquois stronghold near Lake Oneida, but he missed their rendezvous at the Lachine rapids, and had to travel to Georgian Bay to catch up. Then Brulé, who had accompanied Champlain, left the main force to take part in a separate attack. When he arrived, the battle was over, and Champlain and the Hurons had been defeated. Brulé then traveled south down the Susquehanna to Chesapeake Bay.

Five years after his journey down the Susquehanna, Brulé made another expedition. He traveled west, and may perhaps have reached Chequamegon Bay. During his career of exploration, he had discovered four of the five Great Lakes. In 1634, **Jean Nicolet** (1598-1642), another of Champlain's protégés, reached the watershed between the Fox and Mississippi rivers, and did much to clarify the Great Lakes' geography.

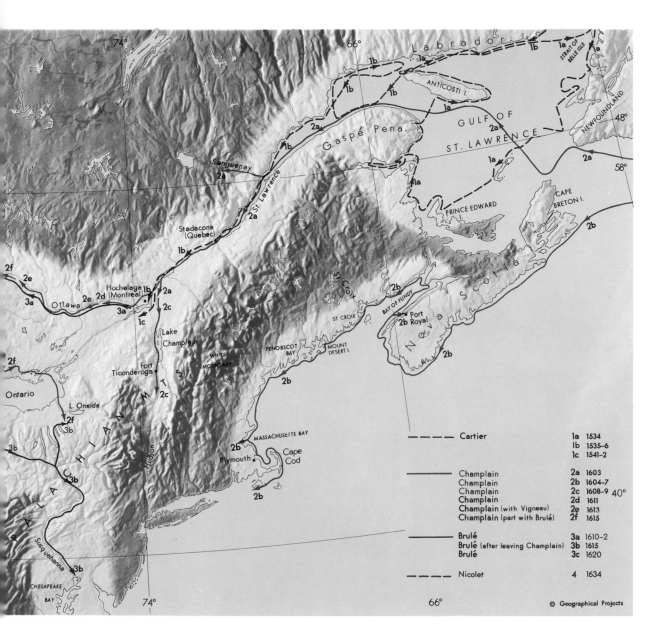

The work of Champlain and his followers was continued by two brothers-in-law, **Médart Chouart, Sieur de Groseilliers** (1625?-1697) and **Pierre Esprit Radisson** (1636?-1710?). Groseilliers and Radisson were traders who ranged through the Great Lakes in search of furs. Their travels finally established the relationship between Lake Superior and Hudson Bay—the "sea" Champlain had searched for in the north—and the trading missions that they carried out for England from about 1668 drew English attention to the Hudson Bay area. Through this new interest, the Hudson's Bay Company was formed in 1670.

To the west of Lake Michigan lie the headwaters of the Mississippi, North America's greatest river. In 1634, during his travels, Nicolet had heard Indians talk of this waterway, and in 1673 **Louis Joliet** (1645-1700)

was sent to find and explore it. In May, Joliet left the Strait of Mackinac accompanied by **Father Jacques Marquette** (1637-1675), a Jesuit priest. The two men traveled via Green Bay and the Fox and Wisconsin rivers to the Mississippi, and paddled far enough down that river to be almost sure that it flowed into the Gulf of Mexico. Then, afraid of being captured by Indians or by the Spanish, they set out again upstream. Father Marquette later founded a mission among the Illinois Indians, working with them until his death.

Although Joliet and Marquette were the first to travel down the Mississippi, the river is linked above all with another man. **Robert Cavelier, Sieur de la Salle** (1643-1687), a French nobleman, had emigrated to Canada hoping to make his fortune in the fur trade. In 1669, he discovered the Ohio River, and followed it to

what is now Louisville, Kentucky. In 1678, on the Niagara, he built a ship, *Le Griffon,* to collect furs from Indians around the Great Lakes. One of his companions, **Louis Hennepin** (1640-1701?) first described Niagara Falls.

Le Griffon sailed as far as Green Bay, Lake Michigan, and then La Salle disembarked and sent the ship to take its cargo of furs to the Niagara, and to collect supplies. Continuing south, he founded Fort St. Joseph, Fort Miami, and Fort Crèvecoeur (Fort Heartbreak); but when after three months there was no sign of *Le Griffon,* La Salle traveled east to the Niagara for news, then returned to Montreal. The ship was never heard of again and, while La Salle was away, the Fort Crèvecoeur garrison mutinied and drove out their leader, **Henri de Tonti** (1650-1704). La Salle took time to find his friend, so it was not until 1681 that he was able to

75

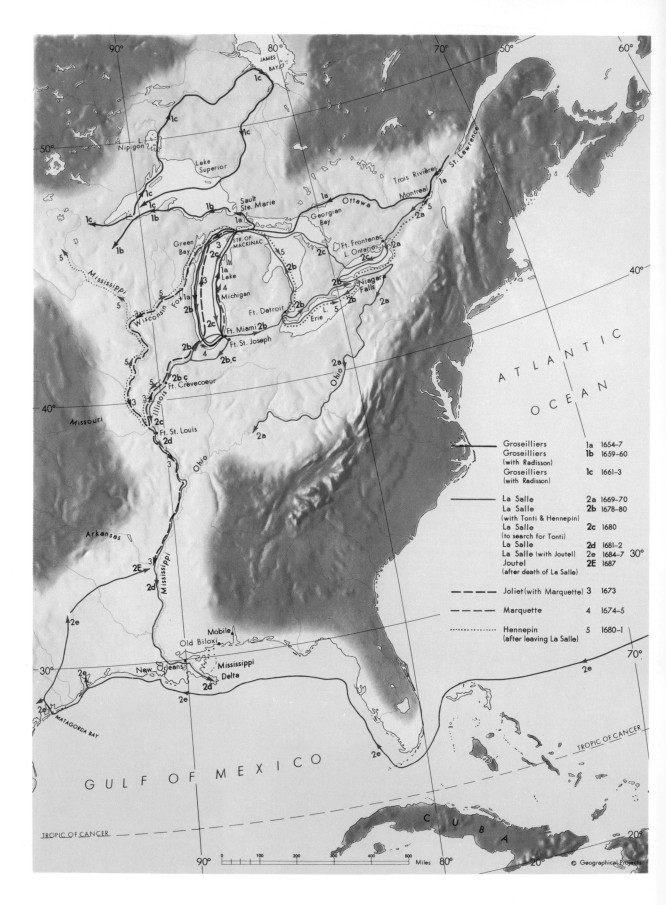

JAMES BAY

1c

L. Nipigon

Lake Superior

50°

Sault Ste. Marie

Green Bay

STR OF MACKINAC

Lake Michigan

Ottawa

Georgian Bay

Montreal

Trois Rivières

St. Lawrence

Ft. Frontenac

L. Ontario

Niagara Falls

Mississippi

Wisconsin

Ft. Detroit

Ft. Miami

Ft. St. Joseph

Erie

L.

Ohio

40°

ATLANTIC

OCEAN

Illinois

Ft. Crevecoeur

Missouri

Ft. St. Louis

Ohio

Arkansas

Mississippi

Groseilliers	1a	1654-7
Groseilliers (with Radisson)	1b	1659-60
Groseilliers (with Radisson)	1c	1661-3
La Salle	2a	1669-70
La Salle (with Tonti & Hennepin)	2b	1678-80
La Salle (to search for Tonti)	2c	1680
La Salle	2d	1681-2
La Salle (with Joutel)	2e	1684-7
Joutel (after death of La Salle)	2E	1687
Joliet (with Marquette)	3	1673
Marquette	4	1674-5
Hennepin (after leaving La Salle)	5	1680-1

30°

Mobile

Old Biloxi

New Orleans

Mississippi Delta

30°

TROPIC OF CANCER

MATAGORDA BAY

2e

GULF OF MEXICO

70°

CUBA

TROPIC OF CANCER

20°

20°

80°

90°

0 100 200 300 400 500 Miles

© Geographical Projects

start his long-planned journey down the Mississippi River.

In 1681-2, La Salle traveled down the Mississippi to the Gulf of Mexico, taking possession of the valley of the Mississippi for France, and calling it Louisiana after the French king. Then, seeking backing for a perma-

nent Gulf coast colony, La Salle

returned north, and made his way to France. In 1684, he set out on the ill-fated journey that has been recounted by **Henri Joutel** (dates unknown), his aide. La Salle's ships missed the mouth of the Mississippi altogether, and every attempt to find the river failed. At last, La Salle was murdered by his own men. Joutel, however, did

eventually reach the Mississippi, and there met Tonti, who had established a post to await La Salle.

Meanwhile, in 1680-1, Father Hennepin had made an independent expedition to the upper Mississippi. Taken prisoner by Indians, he joined their wanderings and only escaped when Sieur Duluth arrived.

When Columbus reached the Bahamas, he thought he was in the East. Identifying the islands with the East Indies, he called their people "Indians". In time, the name was applied to the inhabitants of the American mainland too.

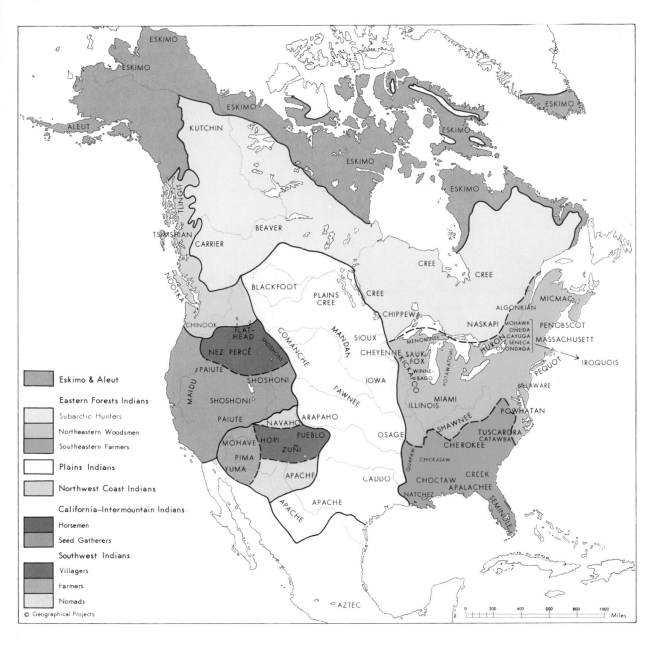

At the time of Columbus' landing, there were more than 600 Indian tribes in North America, speaking at least 200 separate languages, and following widely differing ways of life. Everywhere the white man traveled, he encountered the Indians, and although some were helpful, others did all they could to hinder the European advance. As the white man spread his dominion ever farther, the Indians were driven from the lands that were their home.

When the first Europeans reached America, the Indians, apart from the northern Eskimo, could be divided into five main regional groups. In the north and east lived the **Eastern Forests Indians**—Subarctic Hunters, Northeastern Woodsmen, and South-eastern Farmers. The Subarctic Hunters were nomads, who followed the herds of caribou and moose, but the Northeastern Woodsmen were farmers, though they lived from hunting and fishing as well. The Southeastern Farmers also farmed, hunted, and fished.

To the west, in the center of the continent, lived the **Plains Indians.** Some tribes were originally farmers, but others were nomads, following the herds of buffalo around. After the coming of the white man, however, the Plains Indians acquired horses and guns, and buffalo hunting became their normal way of life.

The **Northwest Coast Indians** were fishermen, whereas their southerly neighbors—the **California-Intermoun-tain Indians,** who lived between the plains and the Pacific coast—were divided into two groups, the Seed Gatherers and the Horsemen. The former were nomads, who gathered seeds, nuts, and berries as they ripened; the latter also gathered seeds, but combined this with hunting and riding, learned from the Indians of the plains.

The **Southwest Indians,** like those of the Eastern Forests, comprised three groups. All—save one tribe of Nomads, the Apache, who lived by raiding their more peaceful neighbors —lived from farming, although the Farmers were seminomadic too. Generally speaking, the culture of the Southwest Indians was the most stable and highly developed of all.

77

Charting the Eastern Seaboard

As ship followed ship across the Atlantic, the outline of North America began at last to take shape. Still searching for a Northwest Passage by way of which they might reach the Indies, mariners sailed north of mainland Canada, while colonists, in settling, opened up the east coast.

▲ *Hudson lands on Manhattan Island.*

It was **Sir Humphrey Gilbert** (1539?-1583) who reawakened in England an interest in the Northwest Passage, for he believed that America was the legendary island of Atlantis, and that a northern passage around it must exist. To find this passage, **Martin Frobisher** (1535?-1594) set sail in 1576. He rediscovered Greenland, and discovered Baffin Island, sailing into Frobisher Bay, which he thought was the strait. In England, however, greater interest was aroused by "gold" ore he discovered, and in search of this he sailed in 1577 and 1578. The "gold" was found to be worthless, and his 1578 colonizing attempt failed, but he did reach the entrance to Hudson Strait.

Frobisher's sight of Hudson Strait convinced him that this, not Frobisher Bay, was the Northwest Passage. Nevertheless, he did not explore it. That was left to the man after whom it is named. **Henry Hudson** (1550?-1611) made his first voyages in search of a North*east* Passage to China, and it was northeast that he set his course when he sailed for the Dutch East India Company in 1609. After rounding northernmost Norway, however, he turned west, and crossed the Atlantic. On this first voyage westward, he discovered and explored the Hudson River, and landed on Manhattan Island, where he and his crew were welcomed by the Indians. It was clear that the Hudson River could not be the strait he was seeking, but his voyage did draw Dutch attention to America. Soon enterprising Dutch traders were traveling there to deal in furs.

One of these explorer-traders was **Adriaen Block** (dates unknown), who in 1614 discovered the waterway that the Indians called the *Quinnitukut*— the Connecticut River. Block sailed some 50 miles up the river, and was so impressed with the surrounding country that he urged the Dutch to colonize the area. However, it was around the Hudson that they settled, and to that region that the name New Netherland came to apply. The first settlement on Manhattan Island, on the site of present-day New York, was made by the Dutch, and called New Amsterdam.

In 1610, Henry Hudson made a second voyage to America, this time in English service. His route now lay to the northward, through Hudson Strait and into Hudson Bay. Throughout the voyage his crew was mutinous and, after a terrible winter, rebellion broke out. Hudson, his son, and seven other men were cast adrift in an open boat. The mutineers then sailed for England, and the ship, under the command of **Robert Bylot** (dates unknown), arrived home safely; but Hudson and his companions were never seen again.

Hudson's fate in no way lessened interest in the Northwest Passage—indeed, from Bylot's report, some concluded that the passage had been found. The groups of businessmen and merchants who then sponsored voyages of discovery for trading purposes continued commissioning expeditions. A number were briefed to trade with Asia via the strait some thought Hudson had discovered; others, with more skeptical sponsors, to find a northwest strait.

In 1615, Robert Bylot sailed to find the Northwest Passage, with **William Baffin** (1584-1622). The expedition sailed through Hudson Strait to Foxe Basin, and from his observations, Baffin concluded that that route did not lead to a Northwest Passage. Although on their second voyage, in 1616, Bylot and Baffin made many valuable discoveries, they never managed to find the passage that was their goal. They did, however, explore Baffin Bay thoroughly, discovering the entrances to both Jones and Lancaster sounds.

One of the first English attempts to colonize North America was made by the same Sir Humphrey Gilbert who had argued that a Northwest Passage did exist. In 1583, he tried to settle Newfoundland, but his expedition met with nothing but ill luck. On the outward voyage one ship deserted, at Newfoundland another had to be abandoned as unseaworthy, and the largest of Gilbert's three remaining vessels ran aground on Cape Breton Island. With two tiny ships—one, the flagship, of only 10 tons—Gilbert set out to sail back to England. But during the voyage his frail flagship sank, and he was drowned. His Newfoundland colony did not long survive his death.

Farther south, **Walter Raleigh** (1552?-1618), Gilbert's half brother, organized three expeditions to the New World. The first, led by **Arthur Barlow** (1550?-1620?) and **Philip Amadas** (1550-1618), was a voyage of reconnaissance. The queen of England was so pleased at its glowing reports of the region, named Virginia after her, that she knighted Raleigh. A party of settlers was sent to Virginia the following year under **Sir Richard Grenville** (1541?-1591). Expeditions were made inland but, once the colony was established, Grenville returned to England. The settlement he left on Roanoke Island, under the direction of **Ralph Lane** (1530?-1603), had trouble with the Indians, and soon ran short of supplies. When, in 1586, Drake's fleet stopped at Roanoke Island, the colonists were only too glad to leave for home.

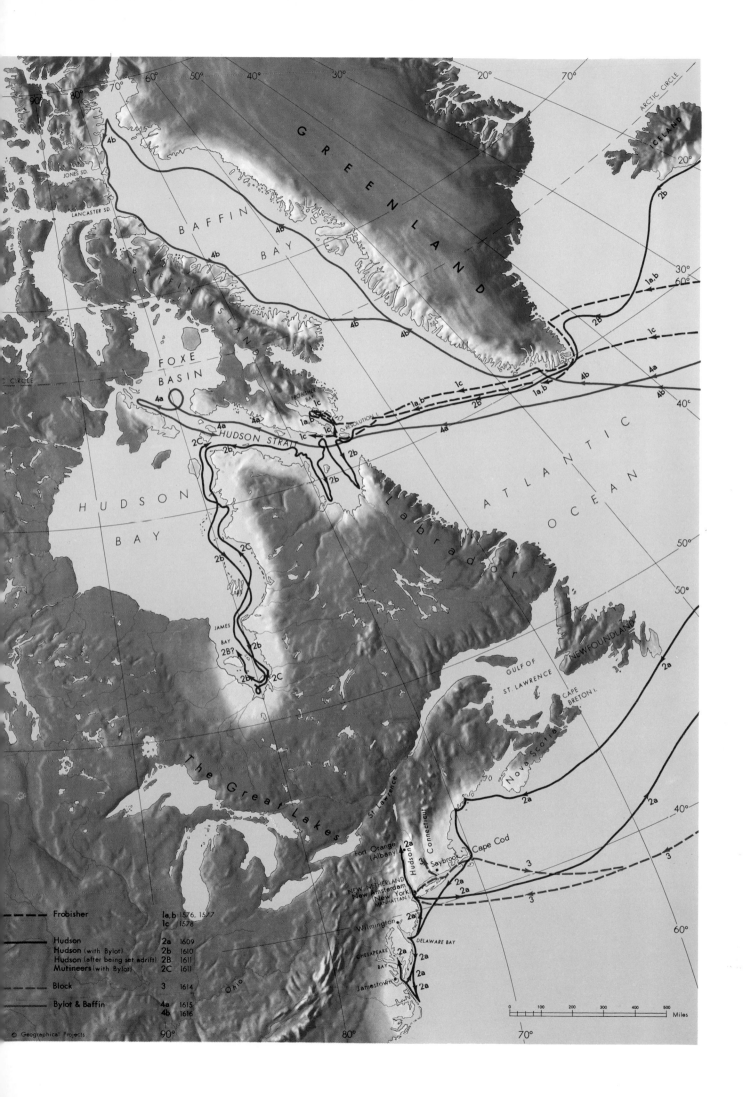

ARCTIC CIRCLE

G R E E N L A N D

ICELAND

BAFFIN BAY

B A F F I N I S L A N D

FOXE
BASIN

HUDSON STRAIT

FROBISHER
BAY

RESOLUTION

L a b r a d o r

A T L A N T I C   O C E A N

JONES SD.

LANCASTER SD.

HUDSON

BAY

JAMES
BAY

The Great Lakes

NEWFOUNDLAND

GULF OF
ST. LAWRENCE

CAPE
BRETON I.

St. Lawrence

Nova Scotia

Cape Cod

Fort Orange
(Albany)

NEW NETHERLAND
New Amsterdam
(New York)
(MANHATTAN)

Hudson

Connecticut

Saybrook

Wilmington

DELAWARE BAY

CHESAPEAKE
BAY

Jamestown

Ohio

Frobisher   1a,b 1576, 1577
                   1c   1578

Hudson   2a   1609
Hudson (with Bylot) 2b   1610
Hudson (after being set adrift) 2B 1611
Mutineers (with Bylot) 2C 1611

Block   3   1614

Bylot & Baffin   4a   1615
                   4b   1616

© Geographical Projects

0   100   200   300   400   500
                              Miles

The following appears on the map:

HUDSON BAY

NEWFOUNDLAND

GULF OF ST. LAWRENCE

NOVA SCOTIA

The Great Lakes

APPALACHIAN MTS.

Mississippi

Ohio

St. Lawrence

Hudson

James

Virginia

New England

Connecticut

Kennebec

PENOBSCOT BAY

SABLE I.

Salem
Boston
Plymouth
Providence
RHODE I.

MASSACHUSETTS BAY
Cape Cod
NANTUCKET
ELIZABETH IS.
MARTHA'S VINEYARD
LONG I.

DELAWARE B.
CHESAPEAKE BAY

Williamsburg
Jamestown
Roanoke
ROANOKE I.
PAMLICO SD.
C. Hatteras

ATLANTIC OCEAN

0 100 200 300 400 500 Miles

Ⓖ Geographical Projects

Legend:

		Gilbert	1	1583
Raleigh's expeditions under:				
	Barlow (with Amadas)	2a	1584
	Grenville (with Lane & White)	2b	1585–6
	White	2c	1587
	Gosnold	3	1602
	Waymouth	4	1605
	Smith (for the London Company)	5a	1606–9
	Smith (for the Plymouth Company)	5b	1614

Raleigh's third expedition was led by **John White** (dates unknown), who had already visited the New World with Grenville and Lane. It, too, ended in disaster for, while White was back in England obtaining supplies, all the settlers disappeared. Their fate remains a mystery, for the only trace found of them was the name "Croatoan" carved on a tree.

In 1602, **Bartholomew Gosnold** (?-1607), on a voyage to collect sassafras, a medicinal plant, discovered and named Cape Cod, and in 1605 **George Waymouth** (dates unknown), while investigating the possibilities of colonizing the northeast, discovered the Kennebec River,

and explored it and Penobscot Bay. Such coastal expeditions marked the limits of English exploration, for, although a few expeditions had been made from the Roanoke colonies, the English at this stage never penetrated far inland.

In 1606, two companies were granted patents by King James I of England to colonize North America. The Plymouth Company was to settle a northern area—roughly between Penobscot Bay and Chesapeake Bay —and the London Company a region stretching south from the Hudson River. In the service of the London Company, **John Smith** (1580-1631) set sail for America in 1606. His ex-

pedition founded Jamestown, which was named after the king of England and, largely due to Smith's efforts, the colony survived. In 1609, an accident forced him to return to England, but before that he explored Chesapeake Bay, and made several expeditions into Virginia, opening the way for the colony to expand. Smith never, however, tried to cross the mountains in the west.

In the year 1614, for the Plymouth Company, Smith surveyed the North American coast from Cape Cod to Penobscot Bay. He made a map of the region, which he called "New England", a name that is still used to describe the area today.

As the European explorers pushed into America, each claimed his discoveries for his country and king. By 1700, three nations were established in North America, each believing it had indisputable rights to the land.

On the east coast, the British had set up their colonies, and they also claimed the region around Hudson Bay. They knew this area as Rupert's Land, after Prince Rupert, cousin of England's King Charles II, who was the Hudson's Bay Company's first governor. Between the British claims lay New France, stretching from the St. Lawrence Valley through the Great Lakes—the area that Champlain and his successors had explored. After La Salle's 1681-2 journey, France also laid claim to the Mississippi basin, which La Salle had named Louisiana. To the west of Louisiana lay New Spain, whose frontiers had been pushed northward past San Francisco.

Britain and France had long been in dispute over their territories, and it eventually became clear that only war would settle their rival claims. After 1689, there was almost constant fighting between them, but from the first the British held the upper hand. Not only were there far more British than French settlers, but the British were more willing to fight. They regarded America as their home, whereas the French were mainly interested in trade.

The wars Britain and France fought in North America were offshoots of their struggle in Europe—fighting in Europe gave rise in 1689 in North America to the so-called King William's War, which lasted until 1697. The War of the Spanish Succession, Queen Anne's War in America, in 1713 won Britain recognition of her claim to Hudson Bay, Newfoundland, and Nova Scotia, and the War of the Austrian Succession (1740-8) was fought in North America under the name of King George's War. After King George's War, to strengthen their position, the French built forts around the British colonies. Some were in the Ohio Valley, to which the French laid claim, but in which Britain was greatly interested. In the Ohio Valley conflict, the final struggle for dominion was born.

The French and Indian War—the Seven Years' War (1756-63) in Europe—saw New France finally won for Britain by the capture of Quebec in 1759. Britain's gain was confirmed by the Treaty of Paris of 1763. By this, Britain also gained French possessions east of the Mississippi, except New Orleans, which was ceded to Spain. Spain also received French land west of the Mississippi, but had to give Britain Florida in return. Thus, in 1763, Britain became supreme in the east of the North American continent, while Spain still ruled in the west.

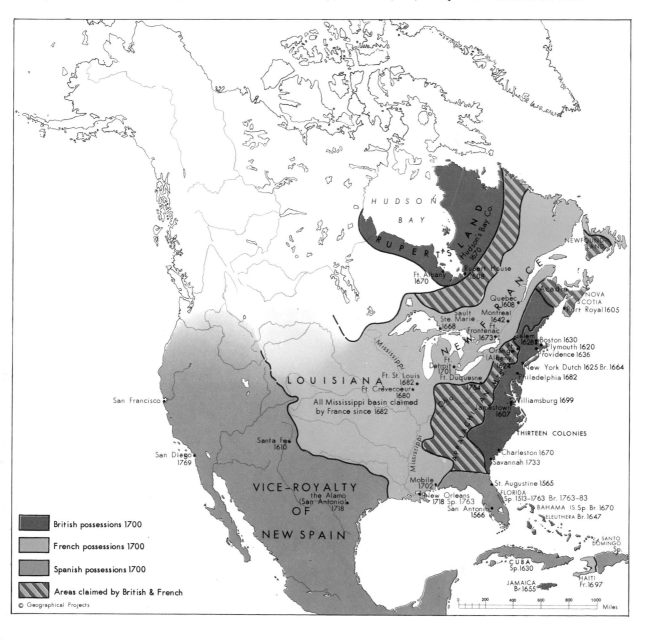

British possessions 1700

French possessions 1700

Spanish possessions 1700

Areas claimed by British & French

© Geographical Projects

Traders in the Northwest

In 1670, the Hudson's Bay Company was founded in England to further trade with British North America, and to promote discovery and the search for the Northwest Passage. It was the servants of this company, and—later—their rivals, who opened up the Northwest.

At first, the Hudson's Bay Company depended for trade on furs the Indians brought to the coast, and initially none of its servants penetrated far inland. Not until 1690 was a serious attempt made at exploration. Then, **Henry Kelsey** (1670?-?) traveled inland to try to persuade more Indians to come to Hudson Bay with furs. His was the first journey

into the Northwest since that of Groseilliers and Radisson, and it was to be the last until 1754. In that year, **Anthony Henday** (dates unknown) left York Factory to explore, and to try to increase the company's trade. He ranged through the region between the North and South Saskatchewan rivers, and wintered with the Blackfoot Indians before returning to Hudson Bay.

Despite the company's interest in trading, the search for the Northwest Passage was not forgotten, and in 1769 **Samuel Hearne** (1745-1792) was sent to see whether a waterway linked the Pacific to Hudson Bay. He was also to follow up reports of a river in

which copper abounded. Hearne, an inexperienced traveler, did not get far on his first attempt. A year later, however, he explored much previously unknown country, on his return journey meeting an Indian named Matonabbee, who promised to lead him to a so-called copper "mine".

Hearne set out again from Churchill in December 1770 and, thanks to Matonabbee's guidance, he reached the Coppermine River, and followed it to the sea. But the ocean he reached was the Arctic, not the Pacific, and although he found some copper, the quantity was small. He did, however, prove that those regions held little hope for trade.

After Britain took over New France in the mid-1700's, a new type of trader began to appear in the Northwest. These men, backed by Montreal trading companies, tried to circle Hudson Bay, thus preventing the Indians and their furs from reaching the coast. The Hudson's Bay Company scornfully called the traders "Pedlars", but their threat was nevertheless real. Their trading activities were in time to force the Hudson's Bay Company to send its men inland.

One of these independent traders, **Peter Pond** (1740-1807), set out in 1778 on behalf of a group of Saskatchewan merchants to find a new source of furs. From Lake Winnipegosis, he traveled to the southern shores of Lake Athabasca, where he built a trading post. It was a great success, for the Indians could now trade without making the journey to Hudson Bay.

Pond was convinced that a water route existed to the Pacific, and in 1789 **Alexander Mackenzie** (1764-1820) left Fort Chipewyan to test the truth of this theory. His expedition was made for the Northwest Company, an organization formed in 1783, made up of the various independent traders. His route led to the Great Slave Lake, then down the Mackenzie River. Soon, however, it

Samuel Hearne. ▲

became clear that the Mackenzie led to the Arctic Ocean, but all the same Mackenzie followed it to that point.

In 1792, Mackenzie set out again for the Pacific, following the Peace River to the fork of the Finlay and Parsnip, where he turned south. Soon, he reached another great river (the Fraser). He thought this was the Columbia, but when he was told it was unnavigable, he turned north. Crossing to the Dean, he followed it to the Pacific Ocean. His was the first crossing of the continent since that of Cabeza de Vaca, more than 250 years before.

In 1808, **Simon Fraser** (1776-1862) proved that Mackenzie's unnavigable river was not the Columbia when he traveled down it to the sea. This new river was named the Fraser after him. Soon, the course of the Columbia itself was traced. **David Thompson** (1770-1857), its explorer, was a fur trader, a brilliant surveyor, and one of the most important of all North American travelers. Between 1790 and 1811, Thompson covered vast areas of the Northwest—and his achievement is particularly impressive inasmuch as his first duty was to trade. In 1790, for the Hudson's Bay Company, he surveyed the Saskatchewan River, and in 1792-7, the area between the Nelson River and Lake Athabasca. In 1797, he transferred to the Northwest Company. For them, he traveled widely between 1797 and 1802. Then, in 1807-11, he explored around the headwaters of the Columbia, and followed that river to its mouth. He had proved that, with only short overland treks, traders could travel by water from the St. Lawrence Valley to the Pacific coast.

83

Fulfilling the American Destiny

In 1776, the 13 British colonies in America declared themselves independent and Britain, to defend her possessions, went to war. But the Americans won the struggle, and in 1783 the colonies became the first 13 "united states".

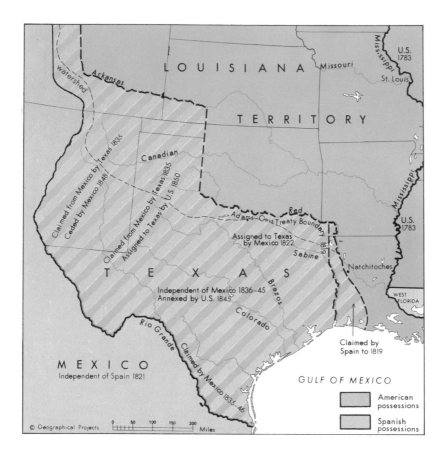

On their return journey, Lewis left ▶ *Clark in the Bitterroot Range in order to look for a more direct route.*

Even before the United States had become owner of Louisiana, President Jefferson planned an expedition west. Led by **Meriwether Lewis** (1774-1809) and **William Clark** (1770-1838), its purpose was to find a water route to the Pacific coast.

Lewis and Clark left St. Louis only five months after Louisiana became part of the United States. They traveled up the Missouri, and on its banks built Fort Mandan, where they wintered. There, they obtained the services of a reliable Indian guide. She led them through the Rocky Mountains, and in November 1805, they arrived at the Pacific. In December, they made a short voyage out to sea before preparing for the winter. Not until March 1806 did they start their journey home.

On 23 September 1806, the explorers arrived back in St. Louis. They had opened the way for future transcontinental journeys, and had shown United States fur traders the potential of the West. They were careful and systematic explorers, and as such they marked the beginning of a new era of exploration.

Lewis and Clark left St. Louis on 14 May 1804, and reached the Pacific coast 18 months later. ▼

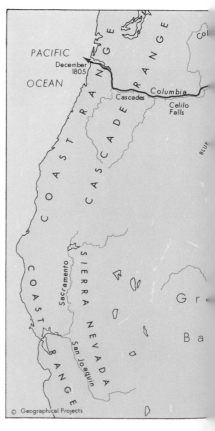

The new American nation ruled all the territories east of the Mississippi, that had belonged to Britain since 1763. Louisiana—now taken to refer only to the land west of the Mississippi—had from the same date been a Spanish possession but in 1801, by a secret treaty, Spain ceded the whole area to France. For the newly formed United States, this was an undesirable change. The France of Napoleon Bonaparte was aggressive and warlike, very different from weak Spain. Besides, Spain had allowed the United States to use New Orleans, a strategic southern port. Fearing that France might close this vital outlet to United States shipping, President Jefferson sent an envoy to Paris to try to buy New Orleans. Imagine his surprise when Napoleon offered to sell him all of Louisiana.

In 1803, for a price of some 15 million dollars, Louisiana Territory became part of the United States. The acquisition of such a vast area of land doubled the size of the American nation and, in one giant step, its frontiers were pushed

west. At first, however, these western frontiers were not clearly defined. According to the Spanish rulers of Mexico, the boundary lay on the Red River, while the United States believed that it ran along the Rio Grande, which would add a strip of land some 500 miles wide to the United States. This disputed area included Texas—whose boundaries differed from those of present-day Texas—which sought to break free from Mexican rule.

As the dispute continued, United States explorers pushed into what the Spanish regarded as their territory and, in retaliation, the Spanish clapped them in jail. And indeed, in 1819, the Adams-Onis Treaty substantiated the Spanish claim to the region by fixing the boundary line along the Red River.

In 1821, Mexico—including Texas—became independent of Spain, and over the next years, many Americans went there to live. In 1835, the Texas Americans revolted against Mexico, and Texas became an independent republic the following year. In 1845, the republic of Texas became part of the United States.

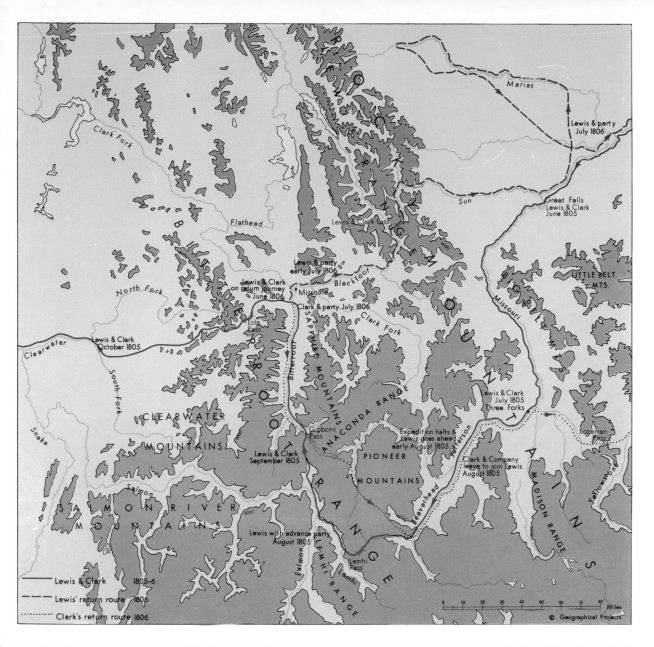

Clark Fork
Marias
Lewis & party
July 1806
Sun
Great Falls
Lewis & Clark
June 1805
Flathead
Lewis & Clark Pass
LITTLE BELT
MTS.
Lewis & party
early July 1806
Lewis & Clark on return journey June 1806
Blackfoot
Missoula
North Fork
Clark & party July 1806
Missouri
Lola
Pass
Clark Fork
Clearwater
Lewis & Clark
October 1805
South Fork
Lewis & Clark
July 1805
Three Forks
Bozeman
Pass
Snake
CLEARWATER
MOUNTAINS
Gibbons
Pass
ANACONDA RANGE
Expedition halts &
Lewis goes ahead
early August 1805
Lewis & Clark
September 1805
PIONEER
MOUNTAINS
Jefferson
Clark & Company
leave to join Lewis
August 1805
MADISON RANGE
Yellowstone
Salmon
SALMON RIVER
MOUNTAINS
6000
Beaverhead
Lewis with advance party
August 1805
Salmon
LEMHI RANGE
Lemhi
Pass
Lemhi

Lewis & Clark   1805-6
Lewis' return route   1806
Clark's return route 1806

0 10 20 30 40 50 60 70 80
Miles
© Geographical Projects

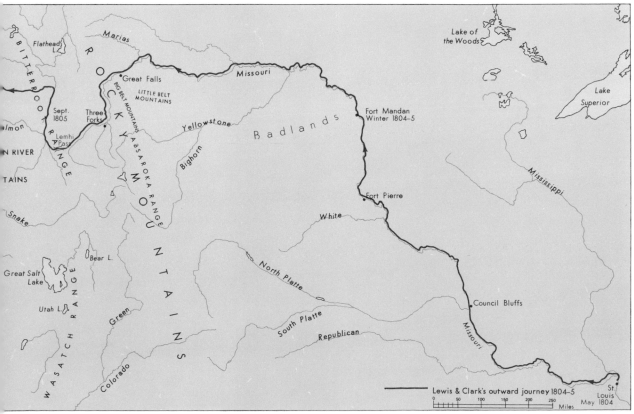

BITTERROOT
Flathead
L.
Marias
Lake of
the Woods
ROCKY
Great Falls
Missouri
LITTLE BELT
MOUNTAINS
Lake
Superior
Sept.
1805
Three
Forks
BIG BELT MOUNTAINS
ABSAROKA RANGE
Yellowstone
Badlands
Fort Mandan
Winter 1804-5
Salmon
Lemhi
Pass
N RIVER
TAINS
Bighorn
Fort Pierre
Snake
MOUNTAINS
White
Bear L.
Great Salt
Lake
North Platte
Council Bluffs
Utah L.
WASATCH RANGE
Green
South Platte
Colorado
Republican
Missouri
St.
Louis
May 1804

Lewis & Clark's outward journey 1804-5
0 50 100 150 200 250
Miles

Following the United States purchase of Louisiana, explorers began to penetrate the American Southwest. In 1806, **Zebulon Pike** (1779-1813), an army officer, was sent to investigate the headwaters of the Arkansas and Red rivers, and to make peace between two warring Indian tribes. This was not his first journey of exploration, for in 1805-6 he had traveled up the Mississippi to Leech Lake, establishing the United States in the area in the face of infiltration south from British North America.

Pike's official orders for his 1806 journey forbade him to enter Spanish territory, but his party became lost among the foothills of the Rockies, and mistook the headwaters of the Rio Grande for those of the Red. Following the Rio Grande, the explorers found themselves in Spanish country, and they were arrested and taken to Santa Fe. Their records were confiscated, and they themselves were sent on to Chihuahua, from which they were deported through Texas to the United States.

Pike was the first American to travel those regions and, despite the loss of his notes, he wrote a very detailed report. His work opened the way for other explorers and traders, but hardly encouraged settlers, for he deemed the Arkansas River region unfit for farming. From his account arose a belief that the central plains were a desert.

Pike's theory about the plains was supported some 12 years later by another army officer, **Stephen Long** (1784-1864). Their adverse reports led pioneers to settle the Far West before the plains. Long's journey was made after the signing of the Adams-Onis Treaty, to obtain detailed knowledge of the new boundary area. His party traveled along the Platte to the Rocky Mountains. Then Long attempted to return down the Red, which formed part of the Adams-Onis frontier. But the river he followed turned out to be the Canadian, and his expedition brought back little information of any worth.

Meanwhile, farther north, fur traders had moved westward after Lewis and Clark's expedition, and fur companies were to play an important part in opening up those lands. Manuel Lisa founded the Missouri Fur Company in 1807, and John Jacob Astor, a New York merchant, established the Pacific Fur Company in 1810. He sent an expedition by sea to build Fort Astoria at the mouth of the Columbia, and another overland.

Astor's overland expedition was led by **Wilson Price Hunt** (1782?-1842), whose party endured a gruel-

ing journey only to find that David Thompson had already claimed the Columbia region for Britain. To inform Astor of this development, a party under **Robert Stuart** (1785-1848) set out east. The War of 1812 broke out before they reached Astor, and Fort Astoria passed into British hands. But Stuart's journey was not altogether wasted, for he discovered South Pass, a 20-mile-wide gap in the Rockies, which could be used by settlers going west.

Another fur trader, **Peter Skene Ogden** (1794-1854), was to do much to open up the northwest United States. In 1824-5, he traveled across the Blue Mountains to the Snake River, then north to the Bitterroot Range, and south to the Great Salt Lake. From Fort Vancouver, in 1826 he traveled up the Deschutes, then turned west

to discover the Klamath. A year later, traveling from Malheur Lake, Ogden discovered the Humboldt, which he called the Unknown. He went on to the Great Salt Lake, returned to Malheur Lake, and pushed north to the John Day River. In 1829-30, he journeyed to the Colorado, becoming the first white man to cross the West from north to south.

Another, almost legendary, pioneer was **Jedediah Smith** (1798-1831). In 1826-7, Smith traveled via the Great Salt Lake to San Gabriel (today the city of Los Angeles), becoming the first American to reach California overland. This territory was part of the newly independent land of Mexico, and the Mexican officials at San Gabriel made Smith appear before the governor at San Diego before he could continue his journey.

Pike   1a 1805-6
                              1b 1806-7
Astorians (Hunt & Stuart) 2 1811-3
Long   3 1819-20
Frémont (with Nicollet)   4a 1838-40
Frémont   4b 1841
                           4c 1842
                           4d 1843-4
                           4e 1845-7
Frémont (after resigning   4f 1848-9
from Army)   4g 1853-4

Then, skirting San Gabriel and turning inland, he crossed the mountains via the Tehachapi Pass, and passed north into the San Joaquin Valley. Turning east, he crossed the Sierra Nevada and the Great Basin—the great desert of Nevada—to the Great Salt Lake and Bear Lake. That same year, he journeyed via San Gabriel to Monterey, where he was arrested. After his release, Smith took a ship to San Francisco Bay, then made his way up the Sacramento, and down the Willamette to Fort Vancouver, where the Canadian fur traders welcomed him. Pushing up the Columbia, he crossed to Flathead Post, from which he traveled south through the Bitterroot Range, then turned east.

Smith's first journey had helped to fix the route of the Old Spanish Trail, although later, owing to Indian hostility, it had to be changed. Yet another important link in communications with the West was discovered by **Joseph Reddeford Walker** (1798-1876), who in 1832 joined a fur-trading and scientific expedition led by Benjamin Bonneville. In 1833, Walker was commissioned to explore the Great Salt Lake and its surroundings, and from there he followed the Humboldt River, crossing the Sierra Nevada to Monterey. His return journey led him around the southern end of the Sierra Nevada, and it was then that he discovered Walker Pass.

By the time of Walker's journey, Americans were already settling in the extreme West. In California, they obtained land grants from Mexico and, in the Sacramento Valley,

one American, John Sutter, built Sutter's Fort. In 1822, the first wagons were seen on the Midwestern plains when William Becknell led a wagon train along the trail he had blazed to Santa Fe. Soon, long lines of covered wagons became a familiar sight on the plains, as settlers pushed northwest along the California and Oregon trails, or followed Becknell's route southwest to Santa Fe. From Santa Fe, the pioneers either moved southwest along the Gila Trail, or turned northwest along the Old Spanish Trail. Part of the Mormon Trail was carved out in 1846-7 by Brigham Young and the Mormons in their trek to the Great Salt Lake, and soon others were using this trail to cross from the Oregon to the Old Spanish trails. The trails gave the settlers a measure of safety, but the dangers

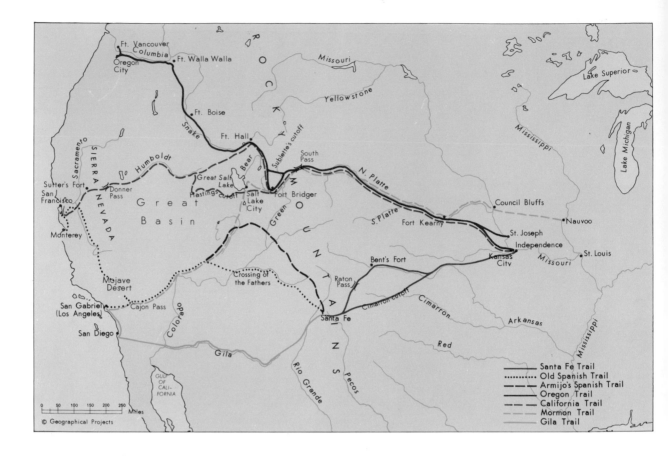

▲ Trails the settlers followed west.

were still numerous, and many died from hardship, or in Indian attacks.

In 1848, gold was discovered at Sutter's Fort, and immediately there was a rush of prospectors to the West. They were known as "Forty-Niners", from the year the first party arrived in California. They were interested in wealth, not exploration, and the discoveries they made were few, but they greatly increased California's population—in one year some 80,000 migrants reached the West.

In 1838, the United States Army Reorganization Act set up a Corps of Topographical Engineers to make a scientific investigation of the American Far West. One of its members, **John Charles Frémont** (1813-1890), earned the nickname "Pathfinder", so detailed were his explorations. Frémont's career began in 1838-40, when he surveyed the Missouri-Mississippi area with **J. N. Nicollet** (1786-1843). In 1841, he made a survey of the Des Moines River, and his next expedition, in 1842, disproved Pike's theory of a "Great American Desert". By showing that the land west of the Mississippi was good for cultivation, he inspired pioneers to settle the plains. In 1843-4, he examined the area from the Columbia south to Mexico and east to the Great Salt Lake. His investigation of California fostered

interest in the area and fully awakened the spirit of Manifest Destiny in the United States.

By the mid-1840's, tension was high between the United States and Mexico, and when Frémont set out on his next journey, he was also equipped to fight. When he heard that war had broken out, he rallied the Californian Americans, and managed to gain complete control of northern California. Frémont retired from the army not long afterward, but he continued his exploits as an explorer. Later, he made two independent expeditions, seeking a route for a railroad to the West.

Wagon train attacked by Indians. ▼

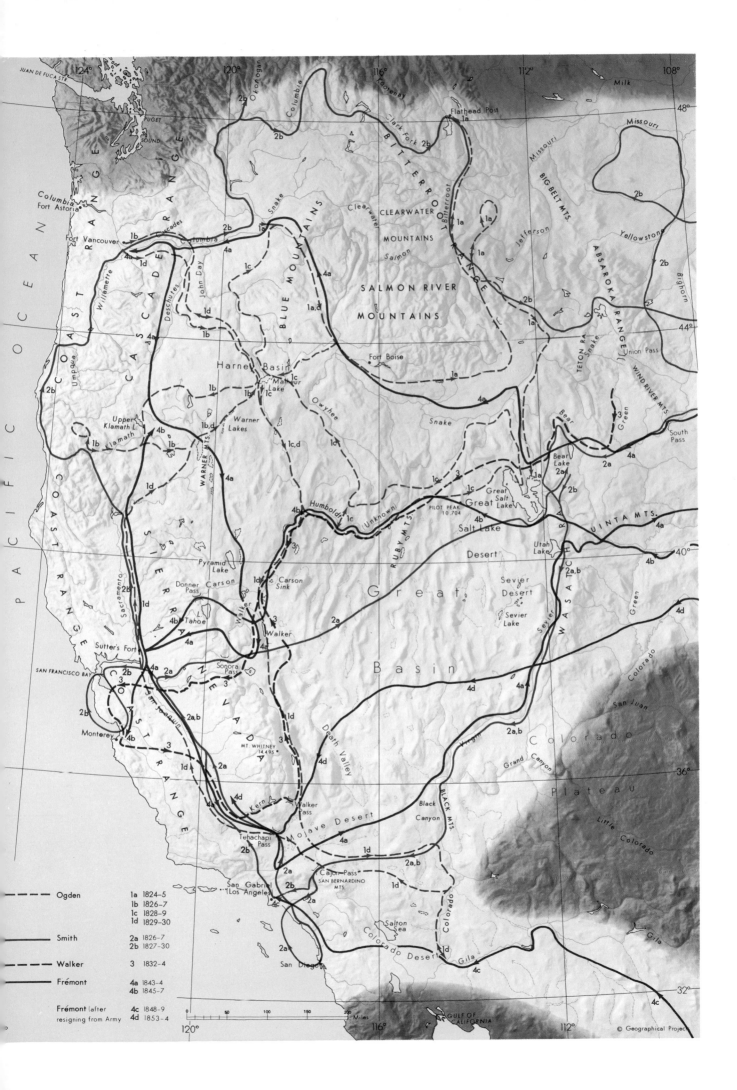

The Continent Revealed

After the expeditions of John Charles Frémont, few major geographical discoveries remained to be made in North America. From his time on, the story of the West was that of the pioneer, the man traveling in search of land and opportunity, the man through whose efforts the American West would be tamed. But before extensive settlement could take place, detailed scientific knowledge of the southern and western United States was necessary. Such information would pinpoint the best regions to settle, and pave the way for the building of railroads.

The army in particular sent out a series of surveying expeditions. In the mid-1850's, **Gouverneur Kemble Warren** (1830-1882) examined the region between the North Platte and the Missouri, and followed the Yellowstone for some of its course. In part, his expedition was conceived to find routes for military expeditions against the Sioux Indians. The map of the area that he completed in 1857 was the most accurate and comprehensive to be made of the region at that time.

In 1857, **Joseph Ives** (1828-1868) traveled up the Colorado to find how far it was navigable, and succeeded in reaching the Black Canyon by boat. Retracing his steps, he crossed to the Grand Canyon, then continued to Fort Union. **James Hervey Simpson** (1813-1883) twice crossed the Great Basin during reconnaissance for a wagon road, and explored the region of the Great Salt Lake. **John M. Macomb** (dates unknown) worked in the country northwest of Santa Fe, gaining the first clear idea of the area's river system. **William F. Raynolds** (dates unknown) crossed from the Cheyenne to the Powder River, and followed the Yellowstone and the Bighorn rivers. He crossed the watershed to the Snake, then recrossed it to reach the Missouri at Three Forks. From Three Forks, he continued down the Missouri to St. Louis.

By the mid-1860's, the surveyors' work had resulted in a number of railroads being built in the Midwest. In 1862, work was started on the first transcontinental railroad, and seven years later the link between California and the east coast was complete. At last, the dream of Manifest Destiny was fulfilled.

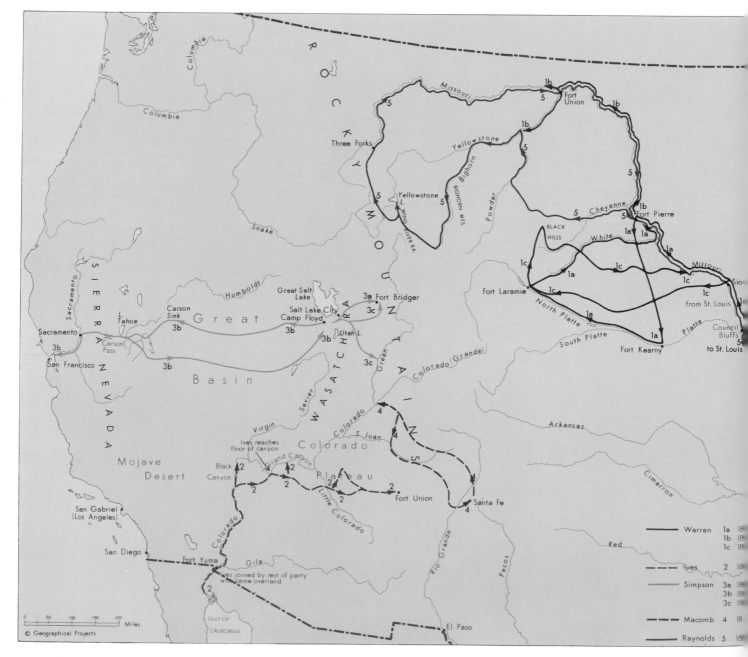

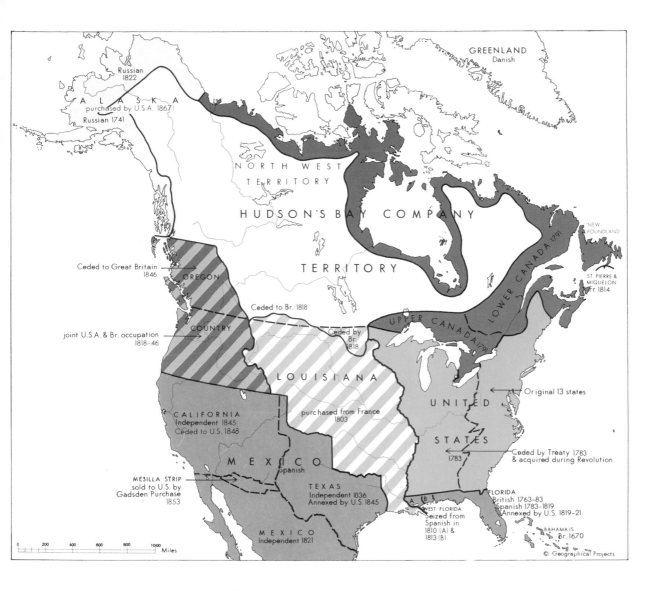

On the map:

GREENLAND Danish

Russian 1822

A L A S K A
purchased by U.S.A. 1867
Russian 1741

NORTH WEST TERRITORY

HUDSON'S BAY COMPANY

TERRITORY

NEW-FOUNDLAND

LOWER CANADA 1791

ST. PIERRE & MIQUELON Fr. 1814

Ceded to Great Britain 1846

OREGON

Ceded to Br. 1818

joint U.S.A. & Br. occupation 1818-46

COUNTRY

Ceded by Br. 1818

UPPER CANADA 1791

L O U I S I A N A

Original 13 states

purchased from France 1803

U N I T E D

CALIFORNIA
Independent 1845
Ceded to U.S. 1848

S T A T E S

1783

Ceded by Treaty 1783 & acquired during Revolution

M E X I C O
Spanish

MESILLA STRIP
sold to U.S. by Gadsden Purchase 1853

TEXAS
Independent 1836
Annexed by U.S. 1845

FLORIDA
British 1763-83
Spanish 1783-1819
Annexed by U.S. 1819-21

[A] [B]
WEST FLORIDA
Seized from Spanish in 1810 (A) & 1813 (B)

BAHAMA IS.
Br. 1670

M E X I C O
Independent 1821

0 200 400 600 800 1000 Miles

© Geographical Projects

By the mid-1800's, from the vast lands of North America, two great transcontinental nations had been forged. One, it is true, was still closely linked to Britain, but the other had been independent since 1783. These same two nations still rule North America today.

The United States grew from the original Thirteen Colonies, to which were added British lands east of the Mississippi, and Louisiana, which had been bought from France. At first, Louisiana's northern boundary was disputed with Britain, but in 1818 the 49th parallel was established as that territory's frontier. United States lands north of this line were ceded to Britain, and British lands south of it to the United States. Florida, retaken by the Spanish during the American Revolution, was bought from Spain for five million dollars in 1819, and passed formally to the United States in 1821.

To the northwest of Louisiana lay the region known from the early 1800's as Oregon Country. At that time, Russia and Spain also laid claim to Oregon, but by 1825 both had relinquished their claim to Britain and the United States. In

1818, the United States and Britain signed a treaty allowing the citizens of both countries to trade and settle in Oregon; but by 1846 so many Americans had entered the region that a firm frontier had become imperative. In that year, the 49th parallel was fixed as the boundary of Oregon, making it even with that of Louisiana Territory.

Texas, the region to the southwest of Louisiana, had become independent of Mexico in 1836, and was admitted to the United States in 1845. A dispute over the new state's exact frontiers led to the outbreak of war with Mexico, but by the 1848 treaty ending the war, all Mexican territories west to, and including, California, became part of the United States. In 1853, to settle the southern boundary—which was still a disputed area—James Gadsden purchased the Mesilla strip from Mexico for the United States.

The extreme northwestern tip of North America—Alaska—had been claimed by Russia since 1741, for in that year, the Russian navigator Vitus Bering had landed there. After 1799, the region was governed by the Russian-American trading company.

In treaties made in 1824 and 1825 with the United States and Great Britain, Russia's southern frontier in America was recognized as 54°40'. In 1867, Alaska was sold to the United States for more than seven million dollars.

After Britain gained control of New France in 1763, the region became known as the Province of Quebec. In 1791, the Province was divided into two parts, Upper and Lower Canada. In Upper Canada lived Americans who, loyal to Britain, had fled to Canada during the American Revolution, whereas Lower Canada was populated by the Canadian French. The region west of these provinces was still ruled by the Hudson's Bay Company. In 1867, the Dominion of Canada was formed. Upper Canada became the province of Ontario, and Lower Canada the province of Quebec. Two other provinces, New Brunswick and Nova Scotia, also joined the dominion, and, as time passed, others were carved out of the Hudson's Bay Company lands. Thus, in less than 400 years after America's discovery, from a vast unknown continent, two great and prosperous nations had been formed.

91

7 South America Unveiled

Southward from the Isthmus of Panama stretches the second great continent of the New World. From its northernmost point in Colombia, some 830 miles north of the equator, it spans more than 40° of latitude to its southernmost point—Cape Horn. This vast land mass encompasses many regional types, mountains, deserts, and pampas (grasslands). In the selvas of the Amazon basin, it holds the largest continuous area of low-lying tropical forest in the world.

With the exception of the pampas, these widely contrasting regions have one outstanding characteristic—their impenetrability to man. Explorers could enter the selvas up the Amazon River and its tributaries, but once on land, travel became impossible. The jungles are so dense that a path cannot be cleared, torrential rain frequently turns the land into a sea of mud, and incessant damp rots supplies. The Andes, with their rugged passes and harsh climate, formed a barrier to exploration in the western part of the continent, and the near-desert that covered much of the south proved an obstacle too. Even in the pampas— the temperate grasslands—of southern South America, little exploration took place.

The difficulties of terrain and climate were not the only obstacles in the way of explorers in South America. The inhabitants—both human and animal—were no more welcoming than the land. The Indians—the continent's original peoples—struggled for self-survival, and were fiercely and bitterly resentful of the Europeans. Vicious insects, wild animals, and poisonous snakes abounded. Even the shortest journey was a hazardous undertaking.

Nevertheless, from the time of the conquistadors to the present century, explorers have found that the fascination of South America outweighs the dangers it holds. Some, such as the buccaneers of the 1500's and 1600's, traveled there in search of gold, but others have sought a different treasure— the scientific data that can be obtained nowhere else in the world. In their journeys, the explorers outlined and then opened up South America, sailing its rivers and climbing its mountain peaks; but the country's hostility to intruders remains implacable, and vast stretches are still to be explored. So dense are the jungles, and so quickly do they grow, that they can soon mask the features, and change the appearance of the land. Perhaps somewhere, remains of an ancient civilization rivaling that of the Inca may be hidden, for certainly unexpected riches have already been found. In 1911, high in the Andes, Hiram Bingham discovered the ruins of the ancient city of Machu Picchu, perhaps the last stronghold of the Inca. The sacred city of Chavin de Hauntar, built in the 700's, was discovered by Julio C. Tello in 1943. In a continent that holds some of the last stretches of land in the world to remain unexplored, who can tell what strange and fascinating discoveries may still be made.

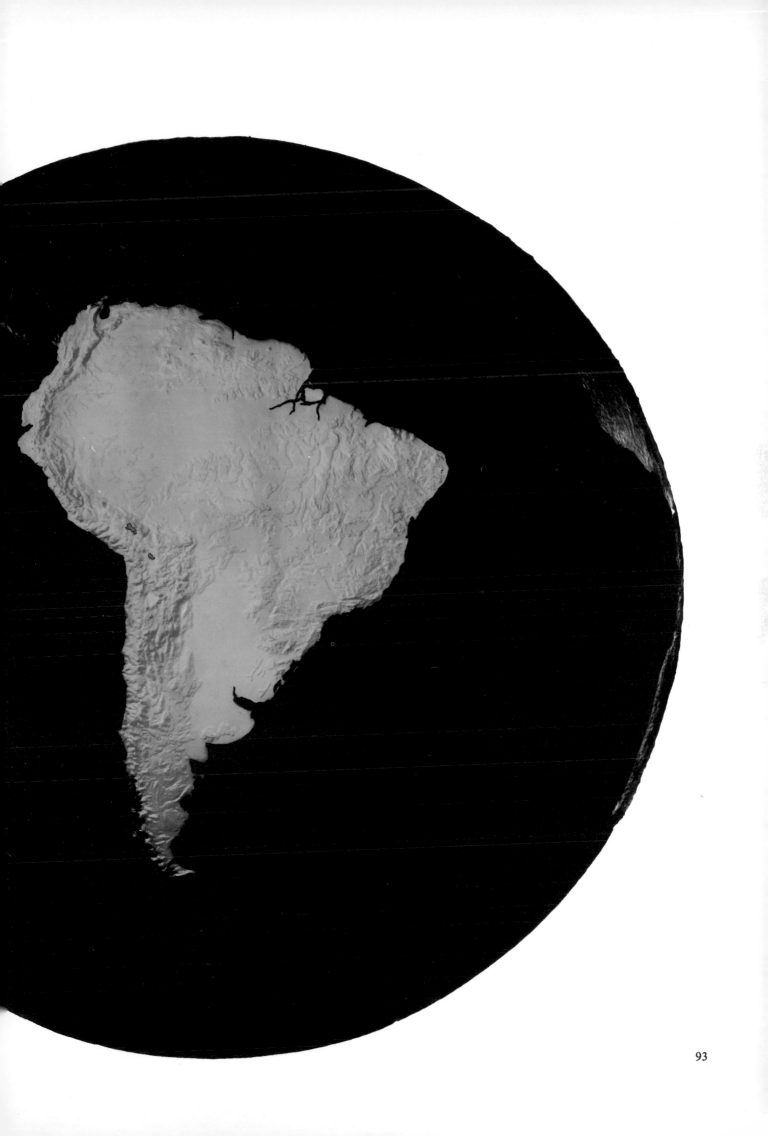

The Search for El Dorado

Even before the Spanish had conquered the Inca Indians, their hearts began to beat faster at a new and exciting tale. Somewhere in South America, they heard, lay yet another fabulous kingdom. Its monarch was known as El Dorado—the "gilded one"—because each day he dusted his body with gold. At a time when every explorer's dream was treasure, no story could have attracted adventurers more.

The seekers for El Dorado were doomed to disappointment, for no such monarch existed. But their quest led to the exploration of much of northern South America, and to the conquest of the last of the rich Indian kingdoms there. This was the land of the Chibcha Indians on the plateau of Bogotá.

In 1536, **Gonzalo Jiménez de Quesada** led an expedition south from the Caribbean coast in search of El Dorado's kingdom. While the main part of his force marched overland, ships sailed up the Magdalena River carrying supplies. The voyage was difficult, and one ship partially wrecked, but the survivors did eventually meet the land force, and they continued south together. On the plateau of Bogotá, Jiménez de Quesada founded the town of Santa Fé. Later called Santa Fé de Bogotá, and then simply Bogotá, it is today the capital of Colombia.

In that region, Jiménez de Quesada made contact with the Chibcha, and abandoned his search for El Dorado to plunder their wealth. His expedition amassed vast treasure, besides opening much previously unknown country, but his only reward was, in the 1560's, to be appointed councilor at Santa Fé de Bogotá. He took up his post in 1565 and, in 1569-71, made another expedition, reaching the Orinoco River.

Gonzalo Pizarro was the next Spaniard to search for El Dorado, during an expedition whose principal object was to find a land where the valuable cinnamon spice grew. Such a country was supposed to lie to the east of Quito, and from Quito, Gonzalo had to travel across the snowbound Andes, then through the densely forested Amazon basin with its numerous streams and swamps. The hardships of travel were considerable but, worse, supplies ran short, and Gonzalo delegated **Francisco de Orellana** to sail down the Coca River to find food. Orellana did not reappear, and although Gonzalo and his men struggled some way down the river after him, they could not find him, and eventually had to turn back. They arrived in

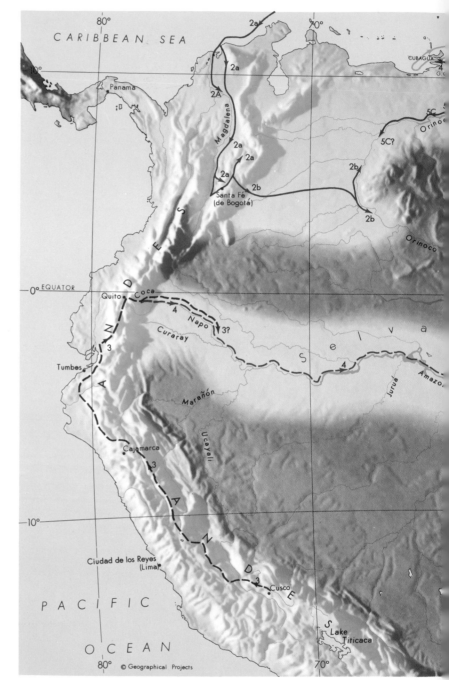

Quito, a sadly ragged and depleted force, early in June 1542, and branded Orellana a deserter.

According to Orellana, however, his boat had been swept down the Coca River, and into the Napo. Then, when he had found food, the current had been too strong for him to return upstream. He had therefore followed the only course open to him—to continue his voyage east. In February 1541, he reached the point where the Napo flows into the Amazon River.

Orellana was not the first European to see the Amazon. On a voyage to South America in 1499-1500, **Vicente Pinzón**, who had cap-

tained the *Niña* on Columbus' first voyage, had discovered the river's mouth, and named it Rio Santa Maria de la Mar Dulce. But when Orellana sailed down the Amazon from its confluence with the Napo, he became the first white man to explore the river's course. His adventurous voyage was recorded by a companion, **Gaspar de Carvajal** (dates unknown), a Dominican friar. Of all De Carvajal's tales, the one that most intrigued Europe was that of an encounter with warrior women, reminiscent of the Amazons of classical legend. It was after these mythical beings—the Amazons—that the river was named.

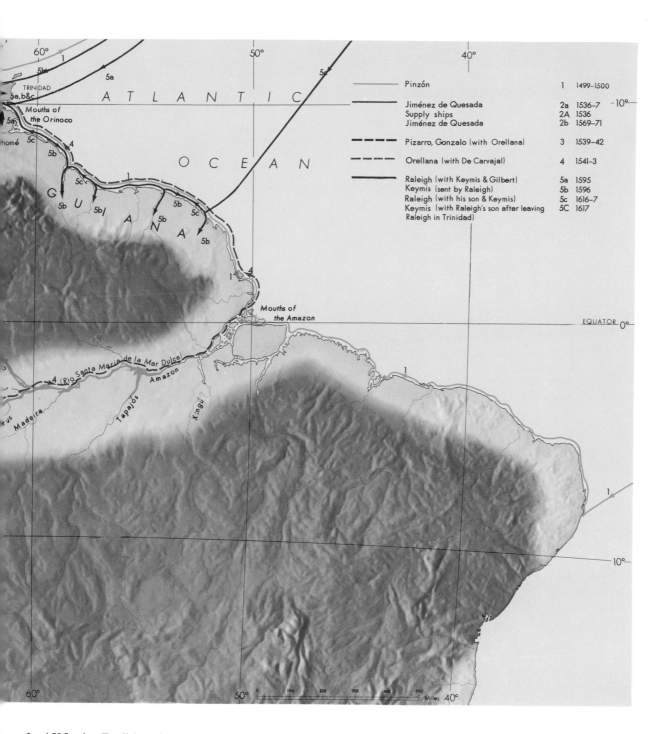

In 1595, the English adventurer **Walter Raleigh,** pioneer of the Virginia colonies, joined the search for El Dorado's kingdom. He hoped that if he discovered it he could restore himself to the good graces of Queen Elizabeth I, whose favor he had forfeited by his marriage to one of the queen's ladies-in-waiting. Raleigh sailed from Plymouth, England, accompanied by his nephew, **John Gilbert** (dates unknown), and **Lawrence Keymis** (?-1617), a friend from Oxford University. Their goal was the Orinoco River, where Raleigh believed the land of El Dorado lay. Although they sailed up the river to its junction with

the Caroní, and then up the Caroní, they found no trace of El Dorado. The following year, however, when Keymis was sent back to South America, he brought back a report of a lake named Parime, situated on the way to the city of the golden king.

Twenty years passed before Raleigh could test the truth of Keymis' report. In 1603, Queen Elizabeth died, and her successor, King James I, cordially disliked the gallant adventurer. Raleigh was arrested on a trumped-up charge of treason, and imprisoned in the Tower of London until 1616. In that year, however, King James himself became interested in El Dorado, and he promised

Raleigh that if he found the kingdom, a free pardon should be his. But this new venture, led by Raleigh, his son **Walter** (1592?-1617), and Keymis, was ill-fated from the start. Raleigh was stricken by fever, and had to wait in Trinidad, and Keymis, although he explored some way up the Orinoco, ruined the expedition's chances of a happy outcome by attacking the Spanish town of San Thomé. Raleigh's son was killed and Keymis, filled with remorse, committed suicide. When Raleigh returned to England after his disastrous expedition, the old charge of treason was revived. In October 1618, Raleigh was beheaded.

95

Blaeu Maps the Americas

The sea pioneers, the conquistadors and pirates, the searchers for El Dorado, all played their part in making South America known to the world. By soon after 1630, when Willem Blaeu (1571-1638) probably made his map of the Americas, the outline of the continent had already been established, and parts of the interior had also been explored. Explorers had made their way into North America too, and Blaeu had at his disposal far more information than Ortelius did in 1570. His superior knowledge is evident in the increased detail and accuracy of his map.

The line of demarcation laid down by the 1494 Treaty of Tordesillas between the territories of Spain and Portugal gave Spain claim to most of South America. The eastern bulge of Brazil, however, fell within the Portuguese sphere. From both Spain and Portugal, throughout the 1500's and 1600's, settlers poured into South America, setting up ranches and plantations in the accessible coastal lands. Blaeu's map clearly divides these known coastlands from the vast, unexplored interior. For those regions, he had to rely on a combination of hearsay and imagination to fill in the blanks on his map. He shows Keymis' Lake Parime as a vast inland sea straddling the equator in Guiana, and the strange peoples of rumor and wild tales also found their way onto the map.

Blaeu depicts Tierra del Fuego as an island, and not as part of the southern continent, even though Terra Australis Incognita does appear on his map. The name Terra Australis is given, however, to a strangely indeterminate region, whose boundaries are not defined. The Amazon River is no longer formally serpentine, and Blaeu's picture of its course is close to reality, but the Paraná River, which flows into the Rio de la Plata, is still exaggerated in size.

On the side margins of his map, Blaeu shows the peoples of the Americas—the inhabitants of the north are pictured in the left-hand margin, while the peoples of South America are shown to the right. Along the top, vignettes depict the towns of America, and it is interesting that, although colonization of North America had already started, all those shown are in the center or in South America.

96

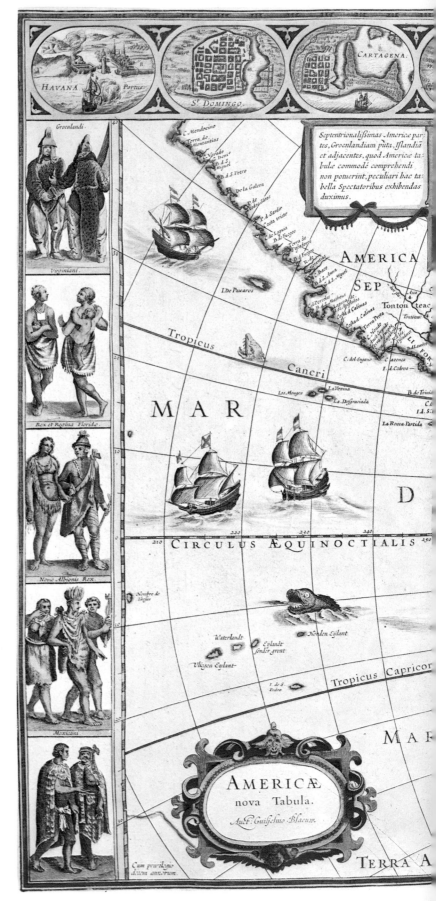

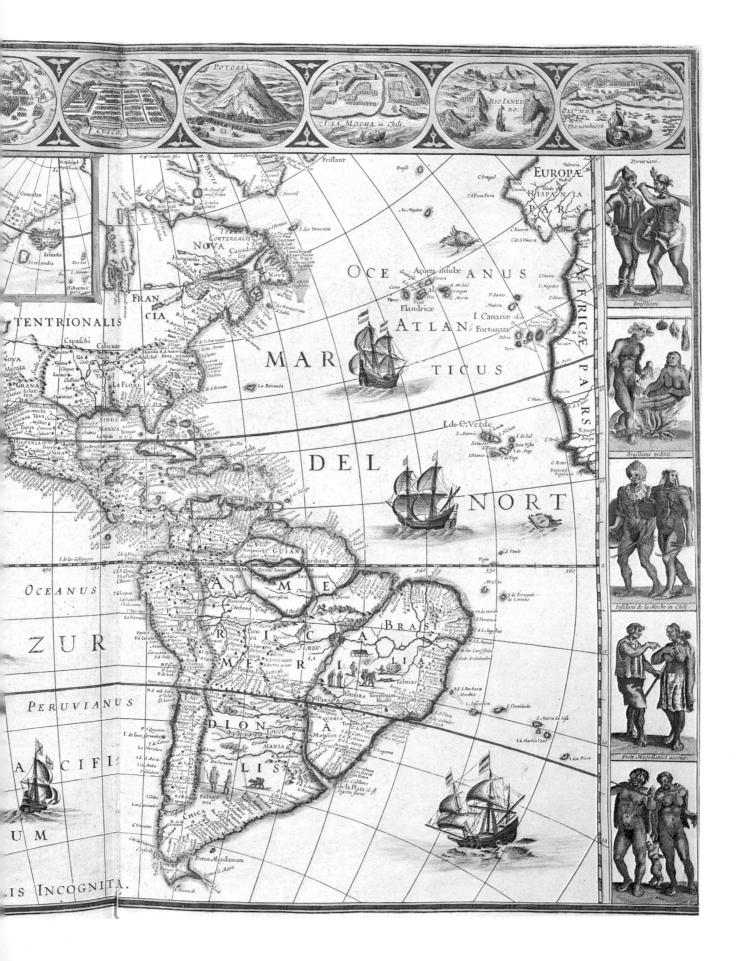

Peruviani.

Brasiliani.

Brasiliani milites.

Insulani de la Moche in Chili.

Freti Magellanici accolæ.

EUROPÆ HISPANIA PARS

OCEANUS ATLANTICUS

MAR DEL NORT

AFRICÆ PARS

Açores insulæ

I. de C. Verde

I. Canariæ olim Fortunatæ

AMERICA SEPTENTRIONALIS

FRANCIA

NOVA

TERRÆ CORTEREALIS

NOVA Canadeles

Honguedo

Ienni Nova

Capaschi Calicuas

NOVA Marata

GRANADA

HISPANIA NOVA

MEXICANUS SINUS

La Florida

Virginia

La Bermuda

Spanniola

Cuba

OCEANUS

ZUR

PERUVIANUS

PACIFICUM

AMERICA MERIDIONALIS

GUIANA Caribana

Amazones

BRASILIA

PERU

CHARCAS

CHILI

PARAGUAI

TOUCUMANIA

Patagones

CHICA

Fretum Magellanicum

Fretum le Maire

IS INCOGNITA

The Scientist-Adventurers

In the year 1734, the French Academy of Sciences commissioned two expeditions to take measurements that would determine once and for all the exact shape of the earth. One party of scientists was to carry out its work in Lapland, the other in the Pichincha province of Ecuador, which straddles the equator. The expedition to Pichincha was led by **Charles Marie de la Condamine** (1701-1774), a French nobleman who was also a distinguished scientist.

La Condamine's party consisted of 10 men, including an astronomer, **Louis Godin des Odonais** (1704-1760), and a mathematician, **Pierre Bouguer** (1698-1758), as well as a draftsman, a botanist, and a doctor. They sailed from La Rochelle, France, in May 1735, and traveled via Cartagena, Colombia, and Panama to Manta, Ecuador. Then, while the others continued to Pichincha by the usual

but they soon found that they were harassed by government officials who found scientific procedures incomprehensible, and thought the Frenchmen were searching for Inca treasure. Only by visiting Lima could La Condamine obtain an order allowing them to work in peace. Although his journey meant an eight-month delay in the project, it enabled him to see more of South America than he had ever dreamed.

Battling with extremes of climate, difficult terrain, and a hostile people, not until 1743, near Cuenca, did La Condamine take his last measurement. By then, his survey was unnecessary, for the Lapland party had obtained the necessary proofs. Their mission over, La Condamine and Maldonado sailed down the Amazon River, the first time that a trained scientist had traveled its waters.

The South American llanos. ▼

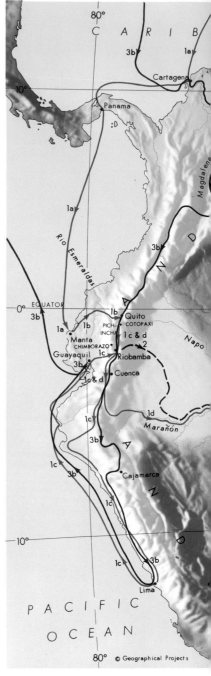

route through Guayaquil, La Condamine and Bouguer stayed on the coast to take their first measurements. There, they met **Pedro Vincente Maldonado** (1704-1748?), a keen amateur scientist, who volunteered to lead La Condamine to Pichincha via the little-used Rio Esmeraldas route. On the journey, La Condamine made many observations preparatory to the start of his survey, and viewed with fascination the strange tropical world. He discovered rubber, which, although known to the Spanish, had never been seen in Europe, and the precious metal platinum.

In Quito, capital of Pichincha, the scientists began their survey,

After La Condamine's journey, the South American interior was no longer totally unknown and mysterious. Vast areas did, however, remain to be explored. His expedition was to have one amazing sequel—the journey of **Isabela Godin des Odonais** (1729?-?), the wife of Louis Godin des Odonais. In 1769, she set out down the Amazon to join her husband who was then on the Atlantic coast, but her journey was a catalog of disasters. All Madame Godin des Odonais' companions died, and it was only with the help of friendly Indians that she managed to reach the river mouth to be reunited with her husband at last.

La Condamine's work was to be continued by a German scientist, **Alexander von Humboldt** (1769-1859). Accompanied by the doctor and botanist **Aimé Bonpland** (1773-1858), Humboldt sailed for South America in 1799. Their journey was made under the protection of the king of Spain, who gave them official permission to travel anywhere on the continent—still mainly under Spanish rule—in return for a report on mineral deposits and special metals there.

Humboldt first set himself to investigate the possibility of a water link between the Orinoco and the Amazon river system, which had been reported by La Condamine, but

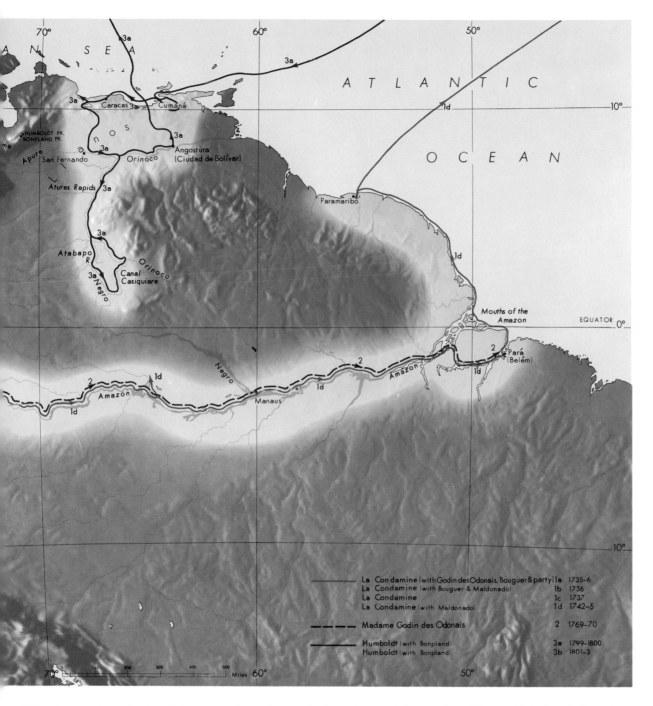

SEA

70°   3a   60°   3a   50°

ATLANTIC

3a

Caracas 3a ~ Cumaná   1d   10°

HUMBOLDT PK.   OCEAN
BONPLAND PK.
ma   3a
Apure   San Fernando   Orinoco   Angostura
                                    (Ciudad de Bolívar)
Atures Rapids 3a
                                    Paramaribo
              3a   1d
Atabapo
R   Orinoco
3a   Canal
Negro   Casiquiare
                                    Mouths of the
                                    Amazon   EQUATOR   0°

              Negro   2 Pará
                                                          (Belém)
        2   1d   2   Amazon   1d
        Amazon   1d   1d
1d   Manaus

                                                            10°

```
                    La Condamine (with Godin des Odonais, Bouguer & party) 1a  1735-6
                    La Condamine (with Bouguer & Maldonado)                 1b  1736
                    La Condamine                                           1c  1737
                    La Condamine (with Maldonado)                          1d  1742-5

- - - - - - - - -   Madame Godin des Odonais                               2   1769-70

―――――――――         Humboldt (with Bonpland)                                3a  1799-1800
                    Humboldt (with Bonpland)                               3b  1801-3
```

70°   0   100   200   300   400   500   Miles 60°   50°

which that explorer had not been able to check. Humboldt and Bonpland crossed the llanos, the dry tropical grasslands of northern South America, to the Apure, then sailed up the Orinoco. As they went, they made observations and collected botanical specimens, few of which survived the damp and the voracious insects. From the Atabapo River, they crossed to the Negro, sailing down it as far as the Casiquiare, which proved to be the link they sought. Then, they headed back down the Orinoco to Angostura, and recrossed the plains to the coast.

Their first task completed, Humboldt and Bonpland sailed for Cuba,

where they packed up the surviving botanical specimens. Of the three almost identical collections, one remained in Cuba, while the other two were shipped to Europe. Luckily, the two collections were dispatched separately, for the ship carrying one was wrecked, and the hard-won specimens lost.

In 1801, the scientists returned to South America. This time their goal was the Andes, for Humboldt wanted to gather information in northwestern South America that would enable him to map accurately the entire continent north of the Amazon. The two men traveled from Cartagena, Colombia, to the Magda-

lena River, which they followed upstream into the Andes. They then journeyed south through the mountains, descending to the coastal plain north of Lima, Peru, constantly observing and recording all they saw. They climbed high up Mount Chimborazo, and visited the Inca city of Cajamarca. They witnessed an eruption of Cotopaxi, and realized the value of guano as a fertilizer. Their work continued magnificently the researches of La Condamine, opening northern South America to the world. Now, realizing the treasures that lay hidden in the continent, countless scientists and explorers would travel there in their wake.

Naturalists and Explorers

In 1859, Britain was rocked by a new publication, which suggested that the Biblical story of the Creation was untrue. Its author was *Charles Darwin* (1809-1882), a naturalist—and in his youth a keen and adventurous explorer as well.

▲ *H.M.S.* Beagle *at anchor in Sydney Harbour, Australia.*

Darwin called his book *On the Origin of Species by Means of Natural Selection, or the Preservation of Favoured Races in the Struggle for Life.* In it, he propounded the theory of evolution by means of natural selection—that is, the gradual change and development of plants and animals by means of which they survive. Darwin's theory implied that the earth and life on it had developed slowly, instead of being created in seven days, as the Bible affirms, and as most people then believed.

Darwin gathered his evidence on natural selection during the 1830's, when he acted as honorary naturalist on H.M.S. *Beagle* during a voyage to complete a survey, which had been begun in 1826, of the coasts of Patagonia and Tierra del Fuego. The *Beagle* was to extend the survey up the west coast to include Chile, Peru, and some Pacific islands. The *Beagle* sailed from England on 27 December 1831, and from Bahia, Brazil, continued via Rio de Janeiro to the Rio de la Plata. Then, for nearly three years, the ship tacked backward and forward along the coasts of southernmost South America, and around the bleak shores of Tierra del Fuego, surveying as it went. During the trips out to sea to take measurements, Darwin would remain on land. To him, South America was a new world, untamed and unknown, and he experienced its life to the full. With a gaucho (cowboy) guide, he traveled from Bahía Blanca to Buenos Aires across the pampas, and at Valdivia he felt the tremors of an earthquake that de-vastated Concepción and other towns. He studied the plants, animals, and people of South America, and made geological observations. On these, Darwin's first surmise of how the world had evolved was based. Important as his South American studies were, however, they were only the prelude to his greatest work. On the Galápagos Islands, in the Pacific Ocean, actual evidence for natural selection was found.

Another naturalist, **Alfred Wallace** (1823-1913), conceived the principle of natural selection quite independently of Darwin. His idea was based on observations he made in the forests of Southeast Asia but, like Darwin, he had previously traveled in South America, arriving there in 1848 with **Henry Bates** (1825-1892). Both men were entomologists—naturalists specializing in insect life. They made their first expeditions to collect specimens in the country around Pará (present-day Belém) and up the Tocantins River; then in September 1848, they went their separate ways. Bates remained in Pará, while Wallace made an expedition to the mouths of the Amazon. For part of the time, he was accompanied by an orchid collector named **Yates** (dates unknown). Then Wallace, accompanied by his brother **Herbert** (?-1851), who had just arrived in South America, and by **Richard Spruce** (1817-1893), a botanist, set out up the Amazon. At that time, the river basin was almost a virgin field for collectors, for La Condamine had returned with few specimens, and Humboldt and Bonpland had worked farther north.

The Wallace brothers made their base at Santarém. Then, after spending several months in and around the town, they continued without Spruce to Manaus. There, in 1850, they were rejoined by Bates, who went on to collect in the region of Ega. Meanwhile, Herbert Wallace had tired of collecting, and started back down the Amazon on the first stage of his journey home. He was, however, never to reach England, for he died of yellow fever in Pará while awaiting a ship. With him when he died was Henry Bates, who had been forced to return to Pará when his money was stolen.

From Manaus, Alfred Wallace had sailed up the Negro River, and there, and on the Uaupés, he spent two years studying insect life. Only on his return to Manaus did he hear of Herbert's death. That tragedy, coupled with persistent attacks of fever, made him decide to leave for home. But he was not deterred from making the expedition to Southeast Asia, during which his theory of natural selection evolved.

Bates, meanwhile, had traveled back up the Amazon to Santarém, and there he made his base until 1855, when he returned to Ega for a further four years. On his first trip up the Amazon, he had collected hundreds of formerly unknown insects, and dozens of birds, and this score increased progressively during this later expedition. The collection he took back to England in 1859 included more than 14,000 species of animals, 8000 of which were formerly unknown.

Spruce, attracted by Wallace's reports of the rich botanical harvest to be garnered on the Negro River, set out for it in 1851. He completed Wallace's work on the Negro and Uaupés rivers, and in 1854, he returned to Manaus. From there he traveled up the Amazon and made his way to the Andes, where he spent several adventurous years, crossing the mountains, and working among the western foothills and on the coast. Eventually, he was forced by ill health to return to England, but although he brought back 30,000 plant specimens, he never received the credit that was his due. His pension was minute, and the only recognition of his invaluable work—an honorary doctorate of philosophy—came from a German institution. Yet it was he who had opened the upper Amazon region to the world.

TROPIC OF CAPRICORN

70°   60°   50°

TROPIC OF CAPRICORN

1h
to Peru &
Galápagos Is.

1a
from Rio de Janeiro

30°

Paraná

2n Copiapó
2n
1h
2n

Coquimbo

Paraná

Santa Fe 2e

Uruguay

2n
1h 2j 2m
Valparaíso 2j 2m
2m Santiago
1f 2j
2m
1g

Negro
2f
2b
2f

2e

2e

2e Montevideo
1a Maldonado
1a

1d

1g

Buenos
2d Aires
Salado
1b & c

1d

PACIFIC OCEAN

1g

Talcahuano
Concepción

SA DE LA
VENTANA
Bahía Blanca
2c
1b

2d

1e

ATLANTIC

1b,c & d

40°

1g

1g

Valdivia

Negro 2c

1c & d

1f

1g

1d

OCEAN

1c

1g

I. DE
CHILOÉ
2K

1e

CHONOS
ARCHO.
1f

Puerto
Deseado
1e

Darwin's voyage on the Beagle:

1a 27 December 1831 – 26 July 1832
1b 19 August – 2 November 1832
1c 26 November 1832 – 28 April 1833
1d 23 July – 3 August 1833
1e 6 December 1833 – 13 April 1834
1f 12 May – 23 July 1834
1g 10 November 1834 – 11 March 1835
1h 27 June 1835 (Beagle picks up Darwin on 5 July 1835)

1c & e

1g

2h 2h

1e

1e

FALKLAND
ISLANDS

1c & e

50°

1c,e & f

2g

STR OF MAGELLAN

Darwin's expeditions:

2a 19 January – 7 February 1833 (with small boats)
2b mid 1833
2c 11–17 August 1833 (on horseback)
2d 8 – 20 September 1833 (on horseback)
2e 27 September – 7(?) November 1833 (on horseback
     and in small boat)
2f 14 – 28 November 1833 (on horseback)
2g 16–19 March 1834
2h 18 April – 8 May 1834 (with small boats)
2j 14 August – 27 September 1834
2k 22–28 January 1835
2m 13 March – 10 April 1835
2n 27 April – 4 July 1835

STR. OF
MAGELLAN

1e

1f

TIERRA

1e

DEL
FUEGO
1e 1c

1c & e

STATEN I.

1f

2a

2a & 1e 1e

100 200 300 400 500
Miles 70°

2a 2a

1c 1c

Cape Horn
60°

50°

© Geographical Projects

So vast was South America that, even early in the 20th century, much remained unknown. The unexplored regions were the subject of much speculation, and rumors abounded of "lost" tribes of fair-skinned Indians, and strange cities no white man had seen. While exploring the jungle country south of the Amazon, **Percy Fawcett** (1867-1925?) came into possession of a document about one such city, and resolved that he would find it. Fawcett called this undiscovered city "Ƶ".

With his son **Jack** (?-1925?) and **Raleigh Rimell** (?-1925?), Fawcett set out in 1925 in search of Z. He was well qualified to lead such an expedition, for his knowledge of South America was extensive. After 1906, he had carried out four surveys in unknown country to determine the boundaries of Peru, Bolivia, and Brazil. He had also made other expeditions into the vast, unexplored heart of the continent. Fawcett believed that Z was situated between the Tocantins and São Francisco rivers, and in that direction his proposed route for the journey lay. But, somewhere near the Xingú River, Fawcett disappeared. Neither he nor his companions were ever seen again.

To the west of the area where the Fawcett expedition disappeared lies a region called Rondonia, named after **Candido Rondon** (dates unknown), a Brazilian explorer. There, in 1909, some explorers located the source of a previously unknown river which they called the Rio Duvido—the "River of Doubt" —because they knew nothing of its course. When Rondon heard that a former President of the United States, **Theodore Roosevelt** (1858-1919), was planning an expedition to South America, he suggested that they should join forces to investigate this stream. The party, which also included Roosevelt's son **Kermit** (1889-1943), traveled up the Paraguay River, then across highland country to the Rio Duvido's source. In seven dugout canoes, they set out to sail down the river, but this was much easier to plan than to accomplish. The upper course of the river was broken by numerous rapids, and in nearly three weeks the expedition covered barely 70 miles, and lost four canoes. They built more, however, and continued to struggle onward, passing from the Duvido onto the Aripuanã, and following the Aripuanã to its junction with the Madeira. Soon they were at the Amazon itself. They had put a totally new river on the map of South America, a river that was renamed the Theodore Roosevelt after the man whose journey meant that it could no longer be called the "River of Doubt".

Wallace & Bates	1a	1848
Wallace (with Yates)	1b	1848-9
Wallace (with Herbert Wallace & Spruce)	1c	1849
Wallace (with Herbert Wallace)	1d	1849
Wallace (after meeting Bates in Manaus & after Herbert Wallace's return to Pará)	1e	1850-2
Bates	2a	1849-50
Bates (after meeting Wallace brothers in Manaus)	2b	1850-1
Bates (based at Santarém)	2c	1851-5
Bates (based at Ega)	2d	1855-9
Spruce	3a	1850
Spruce	3b	1851-4
Spruce	3c	1855-61
Fawcett	4a	1906-7
	4b	1908-9
	4c	1910
	4d	1911
	4e	1913
	4f	1913-4
	4g	1920
	4h	1921
Fawcett (with his son & Rimell)	4j	1925-?
Fawcett's projected route	4k	
Roosevelt (with his son & Rondon)	5	1913-14

© Geographical Projects

ATLANTIC

OCEAN

EQUATOR 0°

Mouths of the
1b Amazon

I. DE MARAJÓ

Pará
(Belém)

2a & c

1a & 1c

3b

Manaus
1d
1e

Amazon
1c

Santarém

1d
1c

2a & c

1a

azon

3c

3a

2a & d

2b & d

Madeira

Xingú

Tapajós
2c

2c

2c

Tocantins

Aripuana

Theodore Roosevelt (Rio Duvido)

O I A

Araguaia

Z?

4j?   4k

4k

4k

Dead Horse Camp

São Francisco

10°

4f

4b & f

5

4g
& j
4j

Planalto

4f
4b

4b

do Mato

Salvador

4k

4h

4h

4b
& f

4b

4g & j

Grosso

4b, g & j

5

4h

4h

4h

4b

4g & j

5

Parana

5

20°

Paraguay

Rio de Janeiro

4g & j

TROPIC OF CAPRICORN

Parana

Uruguay

5

4b

5   to
Montevideo

B R A Z I L I A N   H I G H L A N D S

0   100   200   300   400   500

Miles

60°

50°

40° 30°

30°

8 The Exploration of Asia

For Europeans in the 1500's, the continent of Asia was no new world to be discovered, but a land whose history through the ages had been intertwined with theirs. It was in Asia—in the Fertile Crescent, in China, and in the valley of the Indus River—that the world's first civilizations had developed, and it was in Asia too that all the world's great religions had been born. Since the very earliest times, there had been intercourse between Europe and Asia, whether caused by the ebb and flow of peoples, or by the necessity for trade. In the days of the Roman Empire, Chinese silk was imported to Europe, as was incense from Arabia, while in the 1200's European envoys traveled east to the Mongol rulers, in an attempt to save Europe from the all-conquering Mongol hordes. When the Portuguese rounded southern Africa, the goal of their journeys was Asia, for they longed to share the treasures that they knew came from Asia's rich and fabled lands.

Although in the 1500's, Asia had long been known to Europe, hundreds of years were to pass before the land mass was fully explored. One reason for this was its size, for at more than 17 million square miles in area Asia is the largest of the world's continents. Within this huge area, too, lies some of the world's most hostile terrain. The northern coastlands of Asia lie north of the Arctic Circle and are cold, desolate, and uninviting. In central Asia, great deserts stretch for mile upon mile—barren areas, noted for their extremes of cold and heat. The deserts are broken and enclosed by forbidding mountain ranges, which can be crossed only by treacherous passes, and which include some of the world's highest peaks. The Middle East—southwest Asia—is another desert region: the Arabian Peninsula in particular is one of the world's most barren lands.

The lands of Asia were hostile to foreigners, and so were many of the Asian peoples. In Arabia, for example, after the birth of the Islamic religion in the A.D. 600's, religious fanaticism was so pronounced that any Christian traveler risked death. And, for long periods in the country's history, no foreigner was permitted to enter Tibet. From the 1500's on, however, the exploration of Asia went forward—the first steps were taken by Cossack adventurers, by traders, by envoys, and by Jesuit priests. In the 1800's, the opening of central Asia became a political matter as the great powers, Britain and Russia, struggled for influence, and later it was the lure of Asia's past that led archeologists there. Not until the present century was the puzzle at last completed, and then the newly known lands would not remain open for long. For communism was soon to envelop much of Asia and, as the iron curtain descended, the gates to the heartland closed.

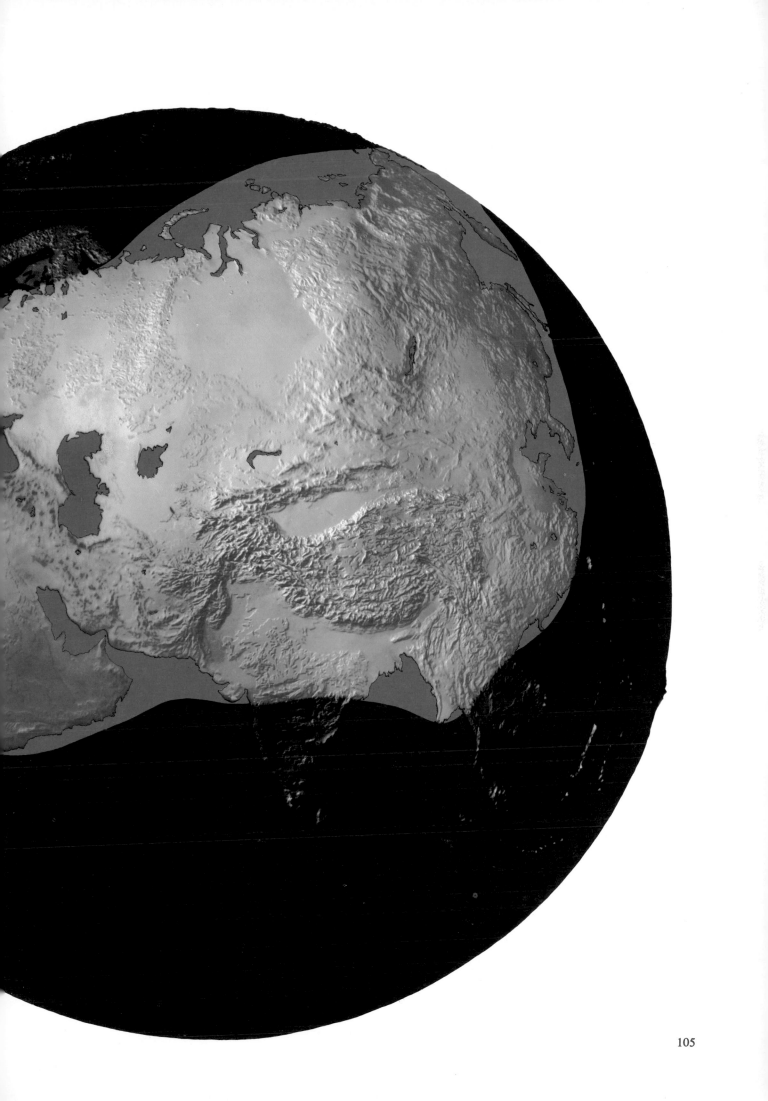

A New Map of Asia

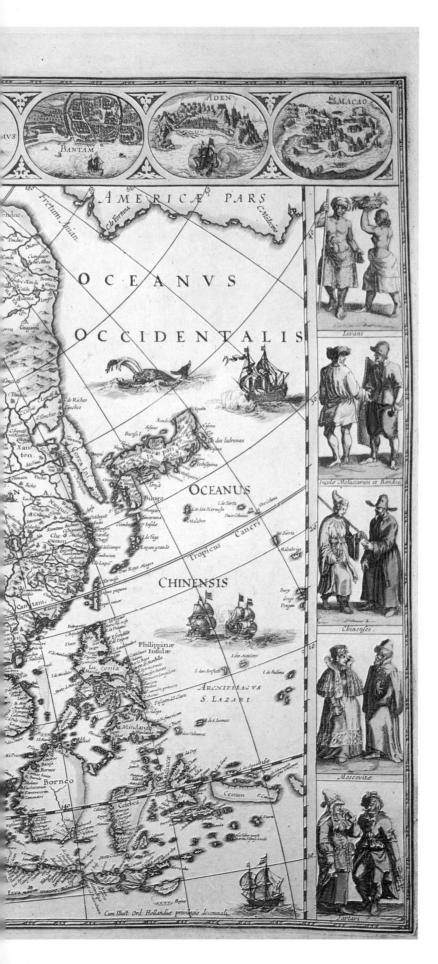

The atlas that Abraham Ortelius had published in 1570 under the title *Theatrum Orbis Terrarum* was the forerunner of other, similar collections of maps. Each gave an updated, and progressively more realistic, picture of the world. In 1585, the Flemish cartographer, Gerardus Mercator (1512-1594), published the first part of his atlas, and four years later a second section appeared. In 1595, some months after Mercator's death, his son Rumold published a third section and the same year saw the appearance of the complete atlas of 107 maps.

Only two editions of this complete atlas were ever published, however, in 1595 and 1602. Then, in 1604, the plates were bought by the Flemish cartographer Jodocus Hondius (1563-1612). Over the next 60 years new editions appeared, published by Hondius, his son Henricus, and Henricus' brother-in-law. The atlas was frequently revised, and new maps added.

This map of Asia was included for the first time in the 1623 edition of the Mercator-Hondius atlas to replace an earlier, less accurate map. It was drawn by Willem Blaeu, who until 1619 signed his work with his patronymic Janszoon, and was first published by itself about 1617. Like the map Blaeu later drew of the Americas, the margins of his map of Asia are decorated with vignettes of Asian peoples and towns.

By the time Blaeu drew his map, the outline of the Asian continent had been established, apart from the Arctic coastline and the extreme northeast. There, Blaeu shows a strait, which he calls Anian, dividing northeastern Asia from Alaska. Such a strait, the Bering Strait, does indeed exist. It was not until 1644-9, however, that the Bering Strait was discovered, and not until nearly a hundred years later that its existence was generally acknowledged. Farther south, Korea (Corea) is shown as an island, and India appears narrower than it does on present-day maps.

Early in the 1600's, little more was known about the interior of Asia than in the days of Marco Polo, and Blaeu's map combines hearsay and legend, as did most maps of his time. Overtones of classical geography linger on in the names "Arabia Felix" and "Arabia Deserta" on the Arabian Peninsula, and Marco Polo had written of the "desert of Lop". And Blaeu drew the Caspian Sea oriented east-west, exactly as Herodotus had described it more than 2000 years before.

The Advance to Siberia

In May 1553, three ships sailed from Deptford, England. Commanded by **Sir Hugh Willoughby** (?-1554), and with **Richard Chancellor** (?-1556) as pilot-major, their mission was to find a Northeast Passage to China. From Deptford, the ships steered north, but north of the Lofoten Islands they were separated in a storm. Willoughby and his crew landed on the Scandinavian coast in the region of Vardö, where they had arranged to meet Chancellor, then sailed on, probably to Novaya Zemlya. Returning, the ship was wrecked off Vardö and all were drowned.

The second of the expedition's three ships disappeared completely,

Mongol ruler turned him back. On his second journey, Jenkinson reached Qazvin, Persia, returning to Moskva with trading goods.

Prior to the journeys of Chancellor and Jenkinson, the land of Muscovy had been virtually unknown. For centuries, it had formed part of the Mongol Empire, and only in 1480 had the Russians overthrown the Golden Horde. Even in the 1500's, the country was wild and lawless. Western Muscovy was roamed by bands of warrior brigands—the Cossacks—while Siberia, east of the Urals, was a strange, hostile land.

It was the Cossacks who pushed the frontiers of Russia east into

Semen Ivanov Deshnef (1605?-1673), founding what is now Nizhiye Kolymsk on the river's bank.

From the mouth of the Kolyma, Deshnef's party took to the sea, and sailed south around the coast, discovering the Bering Strait, which divides Siberia from Alaska. Deshnef's discovery of Bering Strait was, however, never generally known. To the south, **Vasily Danilovich Poyarkov** (dates unknown) discovered the Amur River and traveled down it to its mouth. A shorter, easier route to the Amur from Yakutsk was found by **Khabarov** (dates unknown).

In 1689, Czar Peter I came to the throne of Russia. He set about mod-

▲ *The battle between Cossacks and Mongols that decided Sibir's fate.*

and Richard Chancellor sailed alone around northern Scandinavia, and into the White Sea. At Colmagro (present-day Archangel) he landed to find that he was in Muscovy—as Russia was then called.

Abandoning the search for the Northeast Passage, Chancellor set out for Moskva (Moscow), the capital. In Moskva, he met the Russian czar Ivan, and opened the way for Anglo-Russian trade. So pleased were the English at Chancellor's achievement that in 1555 they sent him to Moskva again. He secured from Ivan a trade monopoly in the White Sea for the Muscovy Company.

In the year 1557, **Antony Jenkinson** (?-1611), chief factor of the Muscovy Company, visited Moskva and was well received by Czar Ivan who gave him letters of introduction to help him travel farther afield. On his first journey, Jenkinson reached Bukhara whence he had hoped to continue to China. At Bukhara, however, the

Siberia. In 1579, **Yermak Timofeyev** (1540-1584?) entered the employ of a fur trader in the Ural Mountains. His mission was to drive back the Mongol raiders who had cut off fur supplies from the east. In 1581, Yermak took the Mongol capital Sibir, then sent a messenger to lay this newly conquered region at the feet of the czar. Ivan, delighted, made the Cossack his representative in Siberia but, before the news could reach him, Yermak had been killed.

In 1587, Yermak's followers built Tobolsk near the site of Sibir, then gradually they fanned out to the east. They traveled to the mouth of the Ob River, and discovered the Yenisei and the Lena rivers. Eventually, in 1638, they reached the Sea of Okhotsk. **Elisei Busa** (dates unknown) discovered the Olenek and the Yana rivers, while **Ivanov Postnik** (dates unknown) traced the course of the Indigirka. In 1641-4, **Mikhailo Stadukhin** (dates unknown) traveled from Yakutsk to the Kolyma River. In 1644, Stadukhin repeated his journey down the Kolyma with

ernizing its cumbersome and primitive society, and pushed Russia's frontiers west to the Baltic Sea. There, he built St. Petersburg (present-day Leningrad) as the new capital of his domains. More important from the point of view of exploration, he prompted the first scientific surveys of Siberia.

In 1719, the Prussian naturalist **Messerschmidt** (?-1735) left St. Petersburg to travel in the region of the Ob, Yenisei, and Amur rivers. For part of his journey, he was accompanied by the Swede **Strahlenberg** (dates unknown), by which title Philipp Tabbert was generally known. Messerschmidt traveled widely, collecting much valuable information, but on his return to St. Petersburg his achievements were hardly noticed. He therefore set out for his native Danzig, hoping to find recognition there. But again he failed and he returned to Russia where, in 1735, he died in poverty.

In Czar Peter's time, little was known of Deshnef's voyage, and such information as did exist was disputed. The czar was still uncertain whether Asia and America were joined. In his possession, however, he had a map, which marked a strait dividing Siberia from Alaska, and in 1725 he commissioned the Danish navigator **Vitus Bering** (1680-1741) to discover whether such a strait did exist. All the supplies for Bering's expedition were taken overland from St. Petersburg, and one ship was built at Okhotsk, and another on the east coast of Kamchatka before the voyage began. It was 1728 when Bering, with his lieutenants **Alexei Chirikov** (dates unknown) and **Martin Spanberg** (dates unknown), set out north. They sailed through Bering Strait—named after Bering— to the point where the coast bears west. There, Bering turned back, rightly convinced that he had passed northernmost Asia. But, because he had not sighted America, the strait's existence was not truly proved.

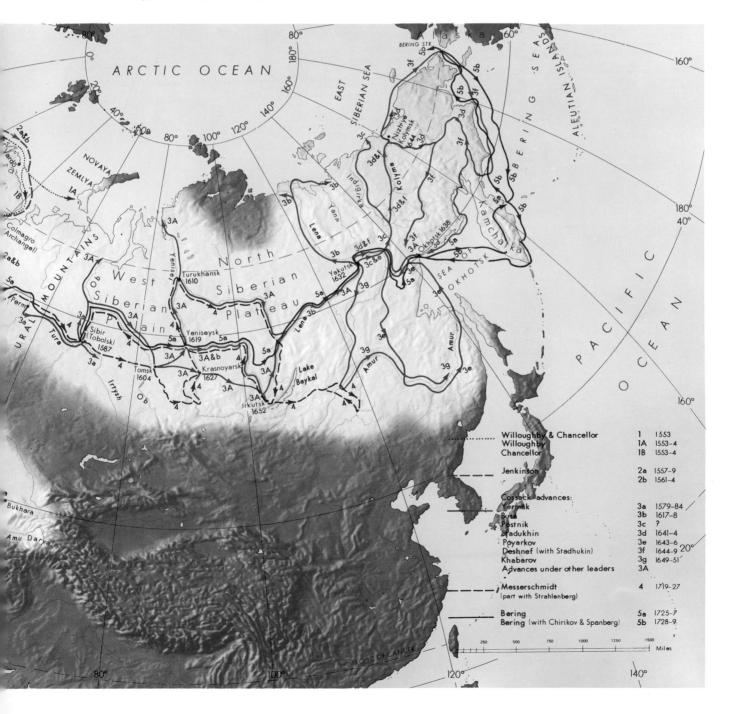

Willoughby & Chancellor	1	1553
Willoughby	1A	1553-4
Chancellor	1B	1553-4
Jenkinson	2a	1557-9
	2b	1561-4
Cossack advances:		
Yermak	3a	1579-84
Busa	3b	1617-8
Postnik	3c	?
Stadukhin	3d	1641-4
Poyarkov	3e	1643-6
Deshnef (with Stadhukin)	3f	1644-9
Khabarov	3g	1649-51
Advances under other leaders	3A	
Messerschmidt (part with Strahlenberg)	4	1719-27
Bering	5a	1725-7
Bering (with Chirikov & Spanberg)	5b	1728-9

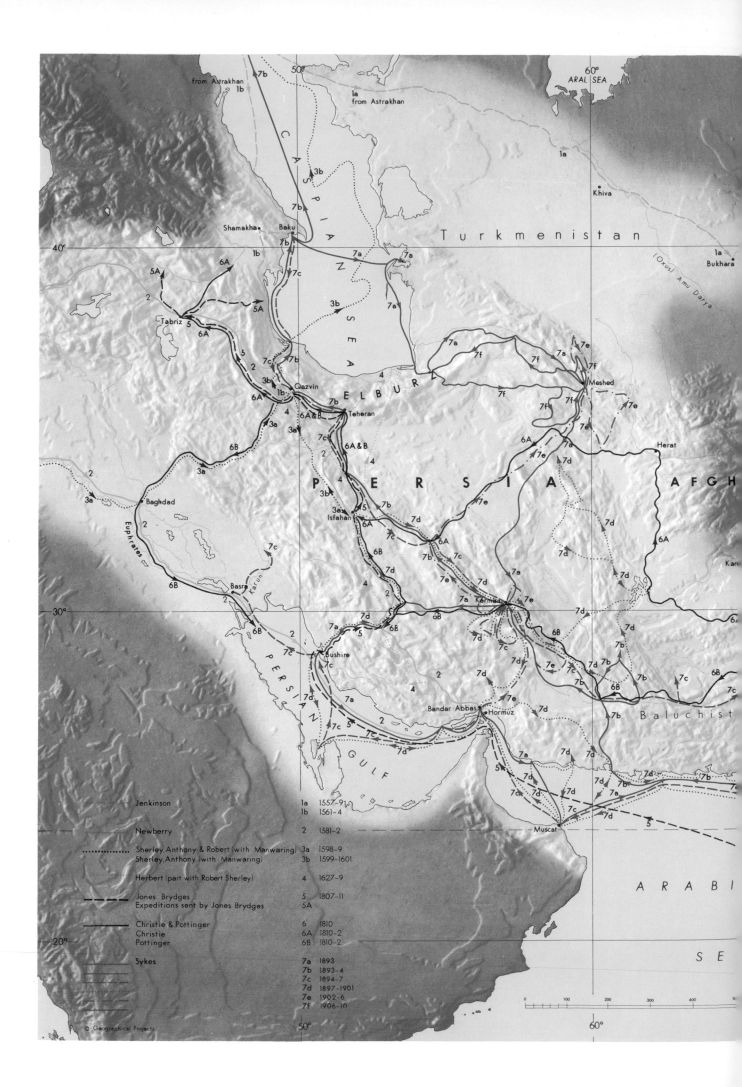

ARAL SEA

Khiva

Turkmenistan

(Oxus) Amu Darya

1a

Bukhara

from Astrakhan
1b

1a
from Astrakhan

Shamakha

Baku

CASPIAN SEA

Tabriz

ELBURZ

Qazvin

Teheran

Meshed

Herat

AFGH

PERSIA

Baghdad

Euphrates

Isfahan

Karun

Basra

Kermān

Kan

6A

30°

PERSIAN

Bushire

Bandar Abbas

Hormuz

Baluchist

GULF

Muscat

ARABI

SE

Jenkinson	1a	1557–91
	1b	1561–4
Newberry	2	1581–2
Sherley, Anthony & Robert (with Manwaring)	3a	1598–9
Sherley, Anthony (with Manwaring)	3b	1599–1601
Herbert (part with Robert Sherley)	4	1627–9
Jones Brydges	5	1807–11
Expeditions sent by Jones Brydges	5A	
Christie & Pottinger	6	1810
Christie	6A	1810–2
Pottinger	6B	1810–2
Sykes	7a	1893
	7b	1893–4
	7c	1894–7
	7d	1897–1901
	7e	1902–6
	7f	1906–10

40°

20°

30°

50°

60°

0   100   200   300   400   5

The Kingdom of Persia

To the Portuguese, Afonso d'Albuquerque's capture of Hormuz was important because the city was a vital link in the trade routes with the East. It showed Europe that the Moslem monopolies could be challenged, and it focused attention on the country at whose gateway Hormuz lay. That was the kingdom of Persia, a rich and fabulous land.

The first European to visit Persia was the English trader **Antony Jenkinson** and, indeed, it was almost exclusively by the English that Persia was explored. But the route Jenkinson had followed was a long one, and dangerous, and, although other travelers did attempt it, they were few. In 1581, however, **John Newberry,** a merchant, was encouraged by the Levant Company to reopen the ancient caravan route leading from the Mediterranean to the Persian Gulf. Newberry made the journey safely, then sailed from the head of the gulf to Hormuz. He returned through Persia, becoming the first Englishman to cross that country. In 1583, he was to lead a party to India using, and finding out more about, this overland route.

In 1598, **Sir Anthony Sherley** (1565-1635?) and his brother **Robert** (1581?-1628) traveled with **John Manwaring** (dates unknown) to Persia in search of adventure. At Qazvin, they entered the service of the Shah of Persia, helping him to reorganize his army to fight his enemies, the Turks. In 1599, Anthony Sherley was sent as ambassador to Europe and left Persia with Manwaring. Some 10 years later, Robert Sherley too became an ambassador for the shah. Despite all his efforts to seek allies for Persia, when he returned there for the last time in 1627 he was coldly received.

The party with which Robert Sherley returned to Persia in 1627 included another Englishman, **Thomas Herbert** (dates unknown). Herbert spent more than a year in the country and wrote a popular account of it. During the 1600's, merchants also visited Persia, but they contributed little to exploration and, in England's race for the treasures of India, the country was almost forgotten. It was, however, because of India that English interest in Persia revived.

Early in the 1800's, India, the British Empire's most valued possession, was seriously threatened by Russian expansion. Persia, with Afghanistan and Kashmir farther east, provided a buffer between India and Russia, and Britain therefore wanted to extend its influence there. Russia, too, tried to gain power in the area. The struggle between the two was nicknamed the "Great Game".

In those years Britain sent a number of diplomatic missions to Persia, one of them led by **Sir Harford Jones Brydges** (dates unknown), who was received by the shah in 1809. Jones Brydges traveled north to Tabriz and sent expeditions still farther north, and to the Caspian Sea. Britain also commissioned the exploration of unknown parts of Persia and Afghanistan, and much valuable information was acquired by **Charles Christie** (?-1812) and **Henry Pottinger** (1789-1856) in 1810-2. The two men set out from Bombay, and traveled into Baluchistan disguised as horse dealers. At Nushki, they separated, Christie to travel by a northerly route through Herat, and Pottinger to make his westing farther south. From Isfahan, they journeyed together to Qazvin, then, while Christie pushed north, Pottinger continued to the Persian Gulf.

It was 100 years after Christie and Pottinger's journey before the last blanks were filled in on the map of Persia. This was achieved by the explorations of **Percy Sykes** (1867-1945). In 1893, Sykes traveled from Baku on the Caspian to Meshed, then south to Kermān and Bushire. That year and the next, he explored Persian Baluchistan, continuing to Astrakhan via Kermān and Teheran. His next journey started at Baku in 1894, and in 1896 he served on the Perso-Baluch boundary commission, subsequently investigating a political dispute in the Karun valley in southwest Persia. The following year, he was again in Baluchistan, surveying much unexplored country, and in 1898 he pioneered a route for the Central Persian Telegraph Line. He then explored south of Kermān and, from 1902 to 1906, in the regions of Kermān and Meshed, finally spending four more years traveling in the northeast, between Meshed and the Caspian Sea. In 1907, just after he had started this final phase of exploration, the "Great Game" ended in Persia when Britain and Russia divided the country into three. In the north was a Russian zone, divided from southwest Persia, Britain's province, by a neutral central area. The country remained divided until after World War I.

111

Into the Heartland

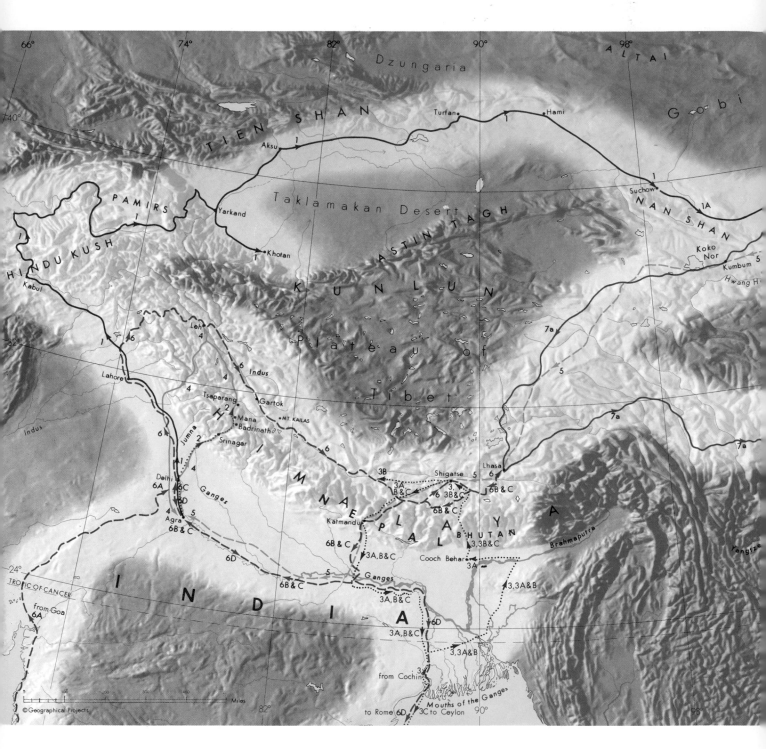

The Portuguese had sailed east-ward and had established trade with China, Marco Polo had traveled overland to a country he called Cathay. In the 1600's, when geographical knowledge of Asia was limited, Europeans were unsure whether these two places were the same. In 1603, therefore, **Bento de Goes** (1562-1607) was sent overland from India to try to reach Cathay. He traveled as a Moslem merchant, and journeyed through Kabul and Yarkand. While waiting for a caravan from Yarkand to Suchow, he visited the jade mines at Khotan.

When De Goes reached Suchow, Cathay's westernmost limit, he sent a messenger to Matteo Ricci, head of the Jesuit mission in Peking. From Ricci, De Goes learned that Cathay was indeed the same place as China. No sooner had the message reached De Goes than he died. His was the first overland journey to China since the 1300's, and it helped fix the country's position on the map.

De Goes had had to travel by a roundabout way to China, for no caravan route crossed the Himalaya, the vast mountain range guarding India's northern frontier. North of

these great mountains, severed by them from the Indian subcontinent, lies Tibet, one of the most inaccessible countries in the world. Tibet contains some of earth's most deso-late regions and highest mountain peaks. It was this inhospitable land that the Jesuits would next try to reach. Rumors had penetrated India that there were Christians in Tibet, and in 1624 **Antonio de Andrade** (1580?-1634) set out to see whether this was true.

Andrade, disguised as a Hindu on a pilgrimage, traveled to Badrinath, then struggled over the 18,000-foot

112

De Goes | 1 | 1603-5
Messenger from De Goes to Ricci | 1A | 1605-7
Andrade | 2 | 1624, 1625
Cabral & Cacella | 3 | 1626-8
Cabral | 3A | 1628-9
Cacella | 3B | 1628-30
Cabral | 3C | 1631-2
Azevado | 4 | 1631-2
Grueber & D'Orville | 5 | 1661-2
Desideri | 6A | 1713
Desideri & Freyre | 6 | 1714-6
Freyre | 6B | 1716
Desideri | 6C | 1721-2
Desideri | 6D | 1725
Huc (with Gabet) | 7a | 1844-6
Huc | 7b | 1848-9

Cacella set out again for Shigatse, but when he arrived in February 1630 he was gravely sick, and only seven days later he died. The following year, Cabral too returned to Shigatse, but he was recalled to India in 1632.

The next Jesuits to reach Tibet traveled there by a far longer and even more hazardous route—they came all the way from China, an overland journey made necessary by the Dutch closure of sea routes to the East. **Johann Grueber** (1623-1680) and **Albert d'Orville** (1621-1662) trekked from Peking to Koko Nor, then southwest to Lhasa, where they stayed for some six weeks. They were the first Europeans to visit Lhasa—Tibet's capital—for 300 years. After leaving Lhasa, the Jesuits made their way through Nepal to Agra, and there D'Orville died. Grueber, however, continued his journey westward, traveling down the Indus and through Makran, southern Persia, and Mesopotamia to the Mediter-

▼ *Matteo Ricci.*

Mana Pass to the city of Tsaparang. There, although he found no Christians, the Buddhist ruler received him warmly and the following year Andrade returned to found a church. He remained in Tsaparang until 1630, when he was recalled to become Jesuit superior in Goa. Not long after he had left, his mission was overthrown by the Buddhists. In 1631, therefore, **Francisco de Azevado** (1578-1660) was sent to Leh to persuade the king of Ladakh to allow the mission to continue. The king granted the necessary permission and, with this good news,

the Jesuit returned to India. The rejoicing was, however, short-lived, for the Buddhists remained hostile to the Jesuits, and in 1635 the mission was abandoned for good.

Meanwhile, in eastern Tibet, **João Cabral** (1599-1669) and **Estevão Cacella** (1585-1630) had founded a mission at Shigatse but soon Cabral had to return to India for supplies. Cacella, meanwhile, tried to reach the Tsaparang mission, but snow forced him to abandon his attempt, and he therefore continued to India by the usual route, to rejoin Cabral at Cooch Behar. In September 1629,

ranean Sea and Rome. His account of his journey describes the route in detail, and added much to European knowledge of Asia in his day.

In 1714, **Ippolito Desideri** (1684-1733), who had the previous year arrived in India, set out for Tibet with **Emmanuel Freyre** (1679-?). In Leh, they were received kindly, and the king tried to persuade them to found a mission, but Freyre was determined to return to India. Hoping to find a safer route, Desideri and Freyre set out east for Lhasa, traveling from Gartok to the Tibetan capital over a road that no other European

113

would use for nearly 200 years. From Lhasa, Freyre returned south through Nepal, but Desideri remained in Tibet until 1721. For six months after Freyre's departure, he was the only European in Lhasa and he wrote an excellent account of Tibet.

Desideri's was the last attempt by the Jesuits to found a Tibetan mission, and other religious orders met with no more success. In the mid-1800's, however, two missionaries did manage to reach Lhasa. **Evariste Régis Huc** (1813-1860) and **Joseph Gabet** (dates unknown), while working in China, decided to preach in Tibet and they set out for that country in 1844. In Lhasa, they were welcomed, but religious teaching was forbidden and the Chinese resident decided to send the missionaries back to China. They left Lhasa, under escort, in March 1846 and reached China again in June. Their route—the main road from Lhasa to China—passed through treacherous

▼ *Leh, the capital of Ladakh.*

and was led by **George Bogle** (1746-1781). Bogle was the first Englishman to travel beyond Nepal and Bhutan, and the first European for over 100 years to reach Shigatse. There, he met the Tashi Lama, Tibet's second most powerful Buddhist leader. Bogle established good relations with the Tashi Lama, and made a detailed report on the trade of the northeast frontier of India, but the British were unable to take advantage of what he had learned because the authorities in Lhasa refused to allow other foreigners into Tibet. The ruler of Bhutan, a Himalayan country through which the route lay to Tibet, also proved intransigent. Although he would allow goods to pass through his country, he refused permission for English merchants themselves to use the route.

In 1783, Hastings sent a second mission to Tibet, led this time by **Samuel Turner** (1749?-1802). The occasion chosen for the journey was the reincarnation of the Tashi Lama—the time when, according to

Bogle	1	1774-
Turner	2	1783-
Manning	3	1811-2
Hearsey	4a	1808
Hearsey (with Moorcroft)	4b	1812
Moorcroft	5	1819-
Nain Singh (part with Main Singh)	6a	1865-
Nain Singh (with Main Singh & Kalian Singh)	6b	1867
Nain Singh (with Kishen Singh & Main Singh)	6c	1873
Nain Singh	6d	1873-
Kishen Singh (A.K.)	7a	1869
Kishen Singh	7b	1871-
Kishen Singh	7c	1873-
Kishen Singh	7d	1878-
Kintup (K.P.)	8	1879-

mountains and was no more than a track. Huc wrote a detailed—if somewhat unreliable—account of their journey across the heartland of Asia, and his marvelous report of Lhasa fascinated the world.

The Jesuits had seen Tibet as a field for their missionary activities; the British who followed them there had a different interest in the land. They regarded Tibet as a possible trading partner for the British East India Company, with its rule firmly established in India, had begun to look farther north. Later, too, knowledge of Tibet was felt to be vital to India's security, for only thus could Britain guarantee the sub-continent's northern frontier.

The first British mission to Tibet was sent there in 1774 by Warren Hastings, India's governor general,

Tibetan belief, the soul of the dead lama returns to earth in another body. When Turner was in Tibet, the reincarnated Tashi Lama was only 18 months old.

Turner's journey told the British much about Tibet, but an opportunity never arose for this information to be used. In 1788, Tibet was attacked by Gurkhas, a people from Nepal, and although they were bought off, in 1791 they returned and captured Shigatse. The Gurkhas were only driven back with the aid of a Chinese army and, in return for its help, China seized the opportunity to take control of Tibet.

Diplomatic missions might be over, but in 1811 an Englishman traveling in an unofficial capacity did manage to reach Tibet. He was **Thomas Manning** (1772-1840), and he

even entered the "forbidden city"—as Lhasa was by then known. Manning was the first Englishman to visit Lhasa and the first to see the Dalai Lama, Tibet's supreme ruler, but his visit to the Tibetan capital lasted barely four months. The Chinese officials there made it abundantly clear that he was not welcome and in April 1812 he left for India.

The first accurate geographical information about the mountain ranges of the western end of the Himalaya was obtained by **Hyder Jung Hearsey** (1782-1840), who in 1808 traveled alone in the region, and **William Moorcroft** (?-1825). Hearsey and Moorcroft disguised themselves as Indian fakirs (holy men) and traveled into western Tibet. They penetrated to the far side of the Himalaya and visited Lake Manasarowar. Seven

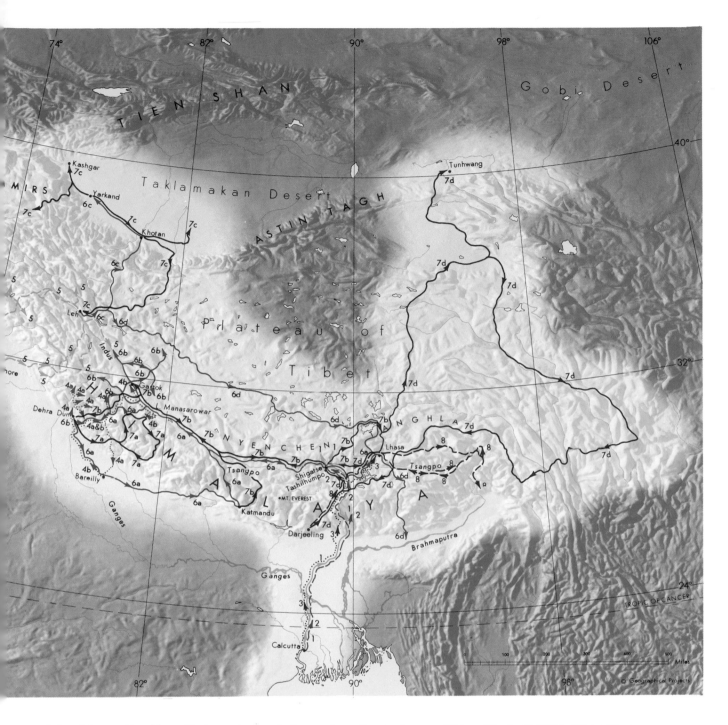

years later, Moorcroft, with an East India Company geologist, explored from Lahore to Leh, then northwest through the Hindu Kush. But somewhere in Afghanistan, in 1825, he was murdered by local tribesmen.

In 1802, Britain had launched the Great Trigonometrical Survey, an attempt to map the entire subcontinent of India and to chart the mountains guarding her northern frontier. By 1863, the work of mapping the mountains on the southern and western frontiers of Tibet had already been completed. Much of the map of Tibet, however, was still entirely blank for China, believing Britain partly responsible for the Gurkha attacks of 1788 and 1791, had closed the frontiers of Tibet to foreigners. Then a surveyor, T. C. Montgomerie, had the idea of em-

ploying Indians who, disguised as merchants or pilgrims, would make a secret survey of Tibet. With their elaborate technical training, the Indian surveyors became known as *pundit-explorers*, from the Indian word *pundit*, meaning "wise man".

Nain Singh (dates unknown), the first of the pundits, traveled more than 3000 miles in the course of his surveys, making many new discoveries and covering much previously unknown ground. He traced part of the course of the Tsangpo—the upper Brahmaputra River—and discovered a vast mountain range (the Nyenchentanghla) lying north of the river and parallel to it. His journeys were all measured in footsteps, and he traveled in the guise of a Tibetan trader, occasionally joined by another of the pundits, among whom were

Kishen Singh (?-1921), **Main Singh** (dates unknown), and **Kalian Singh** (dates unknown). Kishen Singh, whose code name in the survey was A.K., also made many journeys in his own right. He explored much previously unknown country, and he too measured how far he had traveled by his number of steps. Once, the caravan he was accompanying took to horses to escape from bandits, and for 230 miles Kishen Singh had to record distance by counting the paces of his horse.

Kintup (dates unknown), who was called K.P. in the survey code, attached himself to a Mongolian lama to make his journey. But the lama sold him into slavery and it was two years before he could escape. His journey proved that the Tsangpo and Brahmaputra rivers were one.

115

The "Great Game"—and after

The "Great Game" of maneuver and countermaneuver that Britain and Russia acted out in Persia was played too in central Asia. There, in the bleak deserts and lofty mountain ranges of the continent's heartland, explorers forged the way for the expansion of their country's power. In their wake, Russia, feeling that Asia fell naturally within her sphere of influence, gradually extended her boundary southward, while the British pushed north from India, determined to protect their vital frontier.

Nowhere was the "Great Game" played with greater feeling than in Tibet. For both nations, that country was the key to control of Asia, but their hopes of winning power there were for a long time little more than a dream. Tibet remained closed to foreigners, cut off by the hostility of the Tibetan government and its Chinese advisors, as well as by its extreme climate and hazardous mountain terrain. For many years, the only European to get near Lhasa, the Tibetan capital, was the Russian explorer **Nikolai Przhevalski** (1839-1888). In his efforts, Przhevalski revealed more of central Asia than any man before him.

In 1871, Przhevalski crossed the eastern end of the Gobi Desert to Kalgan, near Peking, then, after sorties into northeast Mongolia and the Ordos Desert, he left Peking for Koko Nor. He followed roughly the same route as Huc and Gabet, correcting many of the exaggerations in Huc's story. Przhevalski had hoped to visit Lhasa, but he had only reached a point southwest of Koko Nor, on the eastern edge of the Plateau of Tibet, when winter set in, and he was forced to turn back. He had, however, explored much previously unknown country, and collected many specimens of animals and plants.

Przhevalski made his next attempt

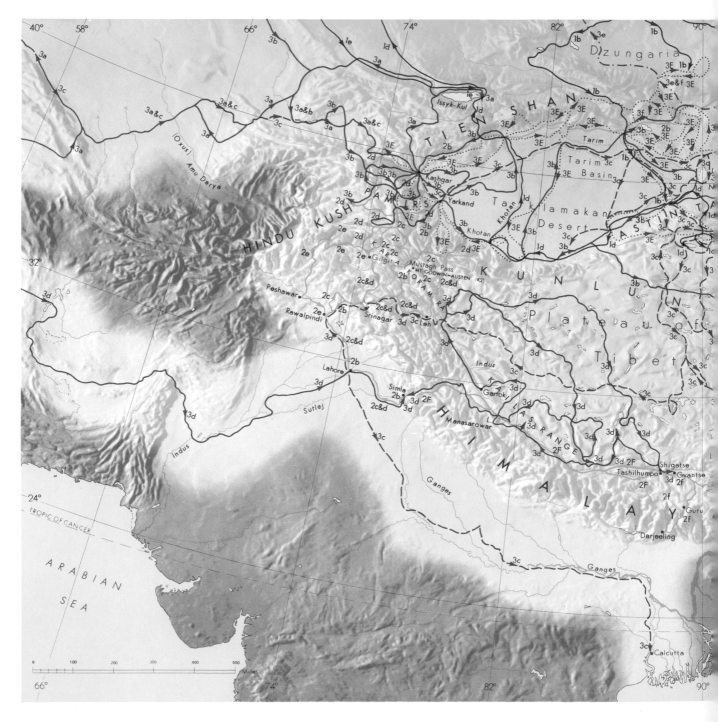

on Lhasa farther west, from Dzungaria. Unsuccessful in pushing south, he retraced his steps and skirted the mountains at the southwestern edge of Dzungaria, then crossed the Tien Shan. He located the seasonal lake Lop Nor, and discovered the Astin Tagh but, unable to find a way through the mountains, he was forced to turn back. In 1879-80, however, traveling farther east through Tsaidam and visiting Koko Nor, he managed to penetrate deep into the Plateau of Tibet but, only 170 miles from Lhasa, a party of Tibetan officials refused to allow him to go on. It was rumored in Lhasa that Przhevalski intended to

kidnap the Dalai Lama, and the Tibetans were not prepared to give him the chance. He did, however, carry out the first exploration of much of northern Tibet, of which he wrote a valuable account.

Przhevalski never got nearer to Lhasa than he had on his 1879-80 journey. In 1884, he crossed the Gobi Desert, and explored the country around the source of the Hwang Ho, then made his way to Lop Nor, intending to push south from there into Tibet. He was, however, prevented from traveling south, so turned east to Khotan, then traversed the Taklamakan Desert and Tien Shan

to Issyk-Kul. Przhevalski intended to lead another expedition in 1888, but he died before it began. Although he never reached Lhasa, he made vast areas of Asia known to Russia, opening the way for her empire to expand.

Up until this time, few British explorers had entered central Asia but, in response to the Russian threat, the British now began to move into the heartland. The most famous of their explorers was **Francis Younghusband** (1863-1942). In 1886, Younghusband, after traveling widely in Burma, accompanied a British expedition into Manchuria, north-

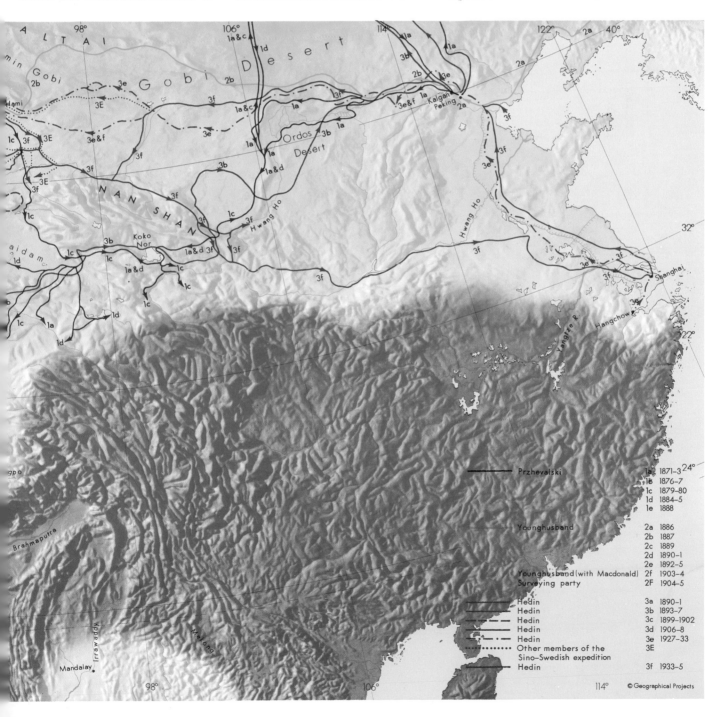

Przhevalski	1a 1871-3
	1b 1876-7
	1c 1879-80
	1d 1884-5
	1e 1888
Younghusband	2a 1886
	2b 1887
	2c 1889
	2d 1890-1
	2e 1892-5
Younghusband (with Macdonald)	2f 1903-4
Surveying party	2F 1904-5
Hedin	3a 1890-1
Hedin	3b 1893-7
Hedin	3c 1899-1902
Hedin	3d 1906-8
Hedin	3e 1927-33
Other members of the Sino-Swedish expedition	3E
Hedin	3f 1933-5

© Geographical Projects

east of Peking. The following year, he left Peking to cross central Asia to Kashmir. In July, Younghusband reached Hami, having traveled more than 1250 miles' through the Gobi Desert, then he proceeded along the edge of the Taklamakan Desert to Kashgar, whence he set out south. He crossed the Karakoram range by the Mustagh Pass, which he discovered, and continued to Lahore and Simla.

During the following years, Younghusband made a number of important expeditions into the complex of mountain ranges on India's northwest frontier. Surveying the passes leading to the Pamirs in 1891, he was arrested by a Russian force. His ambition, however, was to explore Tibet, and in 1903 he was chosen to lead a mission to Lhasa. The Dalai Lama's agent, a Russian by nationality, was trying to foster links with Russia, and to counter the Russian influence Lord Curzon, viceroy of India, decided that a show of British strength was called for. The mission Younghusband headed consisted of 3000 Indian soldiers commanded by **James Macdonald** (1862-1927), besides 10,000 Indian porters and a survey corps.

Geographically, the work of the surveyors who accompanied Younghusband was of great importance, for they explored the Tsangpo (Brahmaputra) River from Shigatse almost to its source, then went on to survey the Sutlej River from its source as far as the Indian frontier. Politically, the results of the expedition were just as impressive, though they were not achieved without bloodshed. At Guru, Younghusband's force was met by 2000 Tibetan soldiers, but won through owing to superior training and arms, while at Gyantse, Macdonald captured a Tibetan fort. Younghusband entered Lhasa on 2 August 1904, the first European to

see the city since Huc and Gabet. Hearing of the approach of the British expedition, the Dalai Lama and his Russian agent had fled, and the regent was forced to concede all Younghusband's demands. But communications were so bad between British India and Lhasa that in 1906 Britain made a treaty with China, giving the latter sovereignty over Tibet. In 1907, Russia agreed to this arrangement. The "Great Game" was at an end.

Exploration in Asia still went on, however, for vast areas remained unknown. In 1890-1, **Sven Hedin** (1865-1952), a member of the Swedish embassy in Persia, traveled to Kashgar and over the Tien Shan to Issyk-Kul. This first expedition whetted his appetite for exploration, and in 1893 he began the first of five great central Asian journeys. He explored around Kashgar, south and west into the Pamirs, and east into the Taklamakan, then from a point near Khotan, he crossed the Taklamakan from south to north. Continuing to the western shores of Lop Nor, he discovered that the lake's position had changed since Przhevalski had located it. From Lop Nor, Hedin turned west along the edge of the Taklamakan. Then he made his way east, keeping south of the Tsaidam Depression, to Koko Nor. He continued to Peking, turned north, and crossed the eastern end of the Gobi Desert to Mongolia. During his journey, he had made a discovery of great value, in particular to archeologists. In the Taklamakan Desert, he had found ancient cities buried under the sand.

In 1899, Hedin set out on another journey, traveling via Kashgar and Yarkand, then along one branch of the Tarim to explore in the region of Lop Nor. Thence, he turned south, and crossing the Astin Tagh started out across the Plateau of Tibet. He

▲ *The peoples of Tibet, cut off in their mountain country, over the centuries evolved their own way of life, religion, customs, and clothes. These three watercolors of Tibetans are by Sven Hedin who, during his journeys in central Asia, made hundreds of drawings and watercolors of people and places. They show (left to right) two youths exchanging a traditional greeting, a woman in traditional costume, and a soldier armed with an ancient musket.*

had disguised himself as a Mongol, and hoped that thus he would be able to enter Lhasa, but he was still more than 150 miles from Lhasa when a party of Tibetan warriors turned him back. Hedin then attempted to push south to India, but that route passed through forbidden country, and instead he had to travel west, across the plateau to Leh. This meant Hedin could explore an area that was unknown.

So totally unfamiliar was the region Hedin covered on his next expedition that the most up-to-date British map simply designated it "unexplored". This was the western part of the Tibetan plateau, lying between Leh and Shigatse, an area which included a new mountain range—the Kailas—on the Tibetan side of the Himalaya, and also the sources of the Indus and Brahmaputra (Tsangpo) rivers. Hedin discovered the Kailas Range, and the source of the Brahmaputra. He also confirmed the source of the Indus, which the pundits had discovered.

Nearly 20 years passed before Hedin made his next expedition in central Asia. Then, in 1927, he led a joint expedition of Swedish and Chinese scientists there. During this six-year scientific mission, an enormous amount of ground was covered by the various members of the expedition, and valuable work accomplished, by which many of the outstanding blanks on the map were filled. This venture had no sooner ended, than Hedin left Shanghai, China, on his last journey. He surveyed the eastern part of the Silk Route—the great ancient trade route between China and Europe, along which, in the time of the Roman Empire, Chinese silk reached the west. On this expedition, Hedin worked chiefly between Lop Nor and the Nan Shan.

Hedin's report of ancient cities lying under the sands of the Taklamakan Desert fascinated **Aurel Stein** (1862-1943). Stein, a British archeologist, resolved to study in the area to learn about its past. He made many expeditions into central Asia, accompanied always by trained surveyors who made maps of the regions he had traveled. His first journey to the Taklamakan, in 1900-1, was a reconnaissance of the Khotan area, which confirmed its possibilities for archeological research.

Stein's excavations on his next expedition in 1906-8 showed that central Asia was once a fertile plain. He found documents with seals depicting Hercules and Eros—which proved that the region had once been closely connected with Greece and Rome—uncovered the lost cities of Miran and Loulan, and, near Tunhwang, discovered the Caves of the Thousand Buddhas, cave-temples which were a treasure house of ancient Chinese culture. For part of his journey, he followed the route Hsuan-tsang had traveled some 1300 years earlier. Stein's explorations took him as far east as the Nan Shan. On his return journey, in the Kunlun, he was severely frostbitten and had to be carried back to India in a litter. Following this expedition, in 1912, Stein was knighted.

In 1913, Stein set out again for the Lop Nor area, where he made more important discoveries. Although his most valuable work on this expedition was done around Lop Nor, he also traveled east to the Nan Shan, and surveyed in the region of Turfan, before returning to India.

During the 1920's, Stein made two more short expeditions, the first northeast of Peshawar and the second in Quetta province on the Afghan frontier. These journeys—with those of Hedin—filled in virtually the last blanks on the map. But central Asia was not long to remain open to Europeans. With the communist takeover of China and—later—of Tibet, the heartland, which had been explored with so much difficulty, was closed to foreign travelers once more.

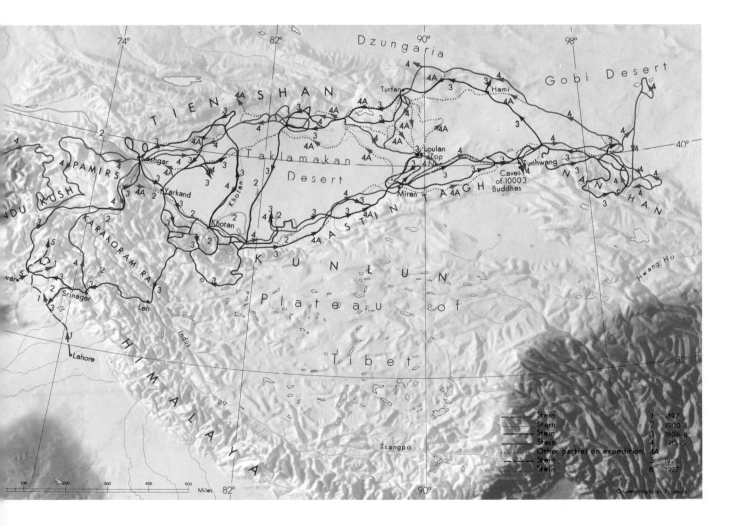

Arabia Felix

No part of Asia was to remain longer unexplored than Arabia. In that desert land, travel was rendered perilous, not only by the harsh climate and terrain, but by the danger of death at the hands of wandering tribesmen. For in Arabia, the birthplace of the religion of Islam, the people were fanatical in their hatred of those who did not share their beliefs.

In classical times, the Arabian Peninsula was known as Arabia Felix ("happy Arabia") because from there came precious incense and spices to meet European demand. But the name seemed little merited to the Europeans who tried to open up the country and, indeed, for many years only Arab traders and Moslems making the annual pilgrimage to the holy cities of Mecca and Medina attempted to travel there. It is to a Moslem pilgrim that we owe one of the first accounts of the holy places. **Sheik Muhammad ibn-'Abdullah ibn-Batuta** (1304-1377), a young lawyer from Tangier, tried to reach Mecca by crossing the Red Sea but for lack of a ship he had to travel to Damascus to join the pilgrim caravan there. After his pilgrimage, Ibn-Batuta continued his journey in Arabia, visited East Africa, Persia, and southern Russia, and made his way as far east as China. His account of his travels includes a vivid report of the pilgrimage and he can claim to be the first true explorer of Arabia.

The first Christian who is known to have made the pilgrimage to Mecca, and the first European to record it, was **Ludovico di Varthema,** who reached the city in 1503. Di Varthema avoided the ban on non-Moslems entering Mecca and Medina by pretending to be a Moslem, and joining the guard accompanying the pilgrim caravan from Damascus. He later visited inland Yemen before taking a ship for the Far East, where he continued his travels.

Not until more than 250 years after Di Varthema's journey was a serious attempt made to explore Arabia—by a scientific expedition sponsored by King Frederick V of Denmark in 1761. The expedition consisted of five scientists, each a specialist in a particular field, but only one, **Carsten Niebuhr** (1733-1815), survived to return to Europe. Detailed studies were made of Yemen, and information gathered about other parts of Arabia, all of which Niebuhr included in his *Description of Arabia,* one of the 1700s' most important geographical works.

During Niebuhr's visit, Moslem fanaticism in Arabia was at low ebb, but Wahhabism, an Islamic revival of the mid-1700's, would soon make travel there more dangerous for non-Moslems than it had ever been. When **Johann Burckhardt** (1784-1817) made the pilgrimage in 1813-5, he disguised himself as a Moslem. Burckhardt had visited Damascus, and explored in Jordan, discovering Petra, before setting out for Mecca, and he traveled to Mecca from Africa, crossing the Red Sea to Juddah. His journey provided Europe's first detailed knowledge of the Hejaz, the region which includes the holy cities, and so minute was his description that **Richard Burton** (1821-1890), Mecca's next European visitor, could add little to it geographically. Burton's greatest interest was, however, the Arab peoples, and he studied them closely, both on the pilgrimage and on his 1877 journey into Midian, east of the Gulf of Aqaba. It was Burton who made the first English translation of *The Arabian Nights.*

The first European to penetrate the interior of the Hadhramaut, the hilly plateau in southern Arabia, was a naval officer, **James Wellsted** (dates unknown). In 1834, while serving on the survey ship *Palinurus* in Arabian waters, Wellsted sighted ruins on the cliff of Hasan Gorab, near Bi'r 'Ali. In 1835, some 50 miles inland, he discovered the ruins of Nakab-al-Hayar and at both these sites he copied inscriptions in the ancient Himyaritic tongue. Nearly 60 years later, **James Theodore Bent** (1852-1897) and his wife **Mabel** (dates unknown) led a party into the Hadhramaut. The Bents completed their journey safely despite Arab hostility, and later visited the Qara Mountains, and southern Yemen.

Between his two visits to the Hadhramaut, Wellsted had traveled in Oman where, although the tribes were fanatical Wahhabis, he was hospitably received. He penetrated inland to the edge of the Rub' al Khali, the "Empty Quarter", Arabia's great southern desert, but he never tried to enter its wastes. Indeed, he wrote that there ". . . even the hardy Bedouin scarcely dares to venture. . . ."

Even in the last quarter of the 1800's, no European had penetrated far into the Arabian interior, although the heart of the peninsula was

——— Ibn-Batuta	1a	1325-32
	1b	1341-9
——— Di Varthema	2	1502-8
——— Niebuhr	3	1761-3
——— Burckhardt	4a	1812
	4b	1813-5
·········· Wellsted	5a	1834
	5b	1834-5
	5c	1835
·········· Burton	6a	1853-4
	6b	1877
——— Bent, T.& M.	7a	1893-4
	7b	1894-5
	7c	1897

© Geographical Projects

CASPIAN
SEA

Tabriz
1a

1a

1a

Euphrates

2
1b

Tigris

1b

1a

Baghdad

1a

1a

Isfahan
1b

1b

1a

Euphrates

Damascus

H a m a d

Wadi as Sirhan

Basra
3a

1a

1a

1a

2

1b

PERSIAN GULF

Al Hasa

HORMUZ

1a

A n   N a f ū d

Wadi al
Ukhaydir

Medā'in Sālih
Al 'Ula

1a & 1b

2

Khaybar

6a 4b

Medina

2

6a

1a

TROPIC OF CANCER

5b

5b

5b

5b

BAHRAIN

1a

GULF OF OMAN

2 1b

5b

Muscat

5b

5b

2

Yanbu

3

1a
& v

1b

4b

2

6a

1a

Juddah
4b

3

Mecca

1a

1a

5b

R u b '   a l   K h a l i
(E m p t y   Q u a r t e r)

AL MASIRAH

1a

1b

1a

RED SEA

1a

6a

2

1a

1a

3

Dhafar

7b MTS. Hasik
GARA

1a

2

1b

3

Y e m e n

Say'un Tarim
Shibam

H a d h r a m a u t

7a 7a

7a

Al Luhayyah

3

San'a 3

Marib

2

1a

1a

Bayt al Faqih

Yarim

2

5c Bi'r
Belha Ali

Al Mukallā
5a

5a

Ta'izz

2

2

7c

3

2

Al Mukhā

3 2

3

Aden

2

1a

GULF OF ADEN

2

I N D I A N

1a

1a

2

O C E A N

1a

1a

0   100   200   300   400   500
Miles

121

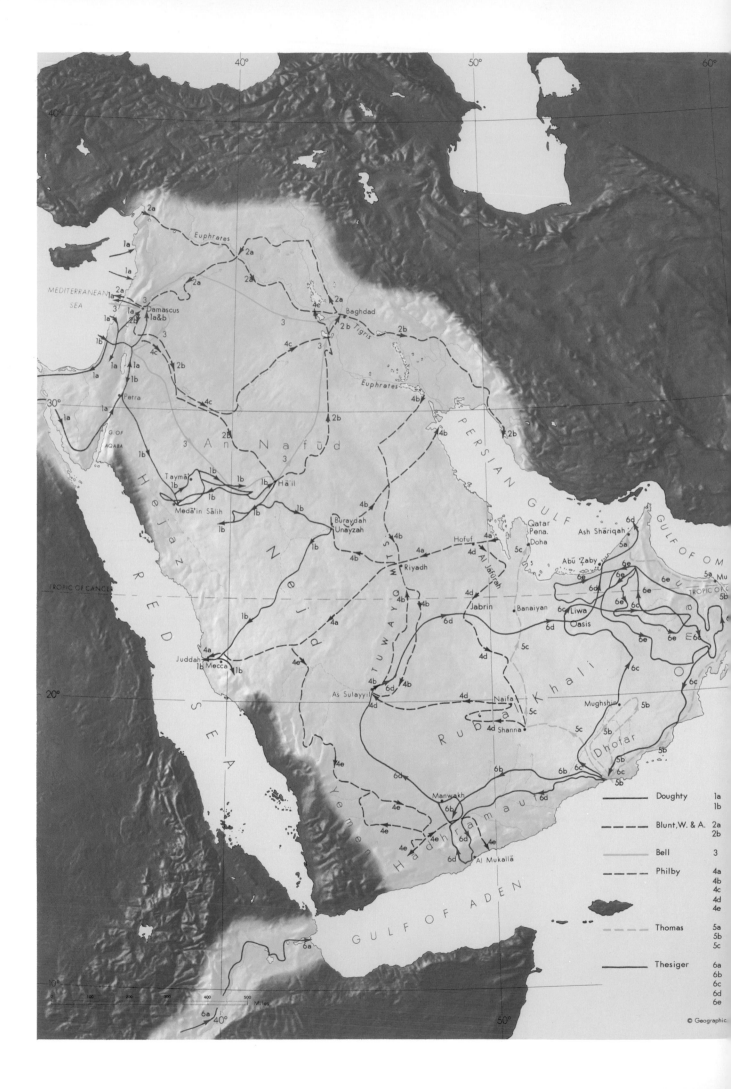

MEDITERRANEAN SEA

Euphrates

2a

1a

1a

2a

3

3

Damascus

1a&b

1a

1b

2b

1a

4c

2b

1a

4e

Baghdad

2b Tigris

2b

2a

3

4c

3

Euphrates

2b

Petra

1a

4c

2b

1b

30°

2b

G. OF
AQABA

1b

An   Nafūd

3

2b

4b

PERSIAN   GULF

2b

4b

1b

3

3

Taymā'

1b

1b

1b

Hā'il

1b

1b

4b

Medā'in Sālih

1b

Qatar
Pena.
Doha

Ash Shāriqah

6d

GULF OF OM

1b

Buraydah
Unayzah

4b

4b

Abū Ẓaby

5a

Mu

1b

4a

Hofuf

4a

5c

6e

5a

Riyadh

4d

Al Jafūrah

6e

6e

6e

5a

TROPIC OF CANCER

1b

4b

Jabrin

Banaiyan

6c

Liwa

6d

6e

6e

TROPIC OF C

4a

4b

4d

6d

Oasis

4e

As Sulayyil

4b

6d

4b

4d

Naifa

Khali

6d

6c

6e

6e

6e

20°

4d

5c

Mughshin

5b

R u b a '

5b

Dhofar

5b

4d Shanna

5c

5c

5b

6b

6b

6c

5b

4e

6c

6c

5b

4e

6d

Manwakh

6b

H a d h r a m a u t

6d

5b

Juddah
1b Mecca 1b

4a

Yemen

4e

6b

4e

4e

4e

4eh

6d

4e

6d

Al Mukallā

GULF   OF   ADEN

6a

10°

100   200   300   400   500   Miles

6a

40°

50°

© Geographic

Doughty   1a
                   1b

Blunt, W. & A.   2a
                   2b

Bell   3

Philby   4a
                   4b
                   4c
                   4d
                   4e

Thomas   5a
                   5b
                   5c

Thesiger   6a
                   6b
                   6c
                   6d
                   6e

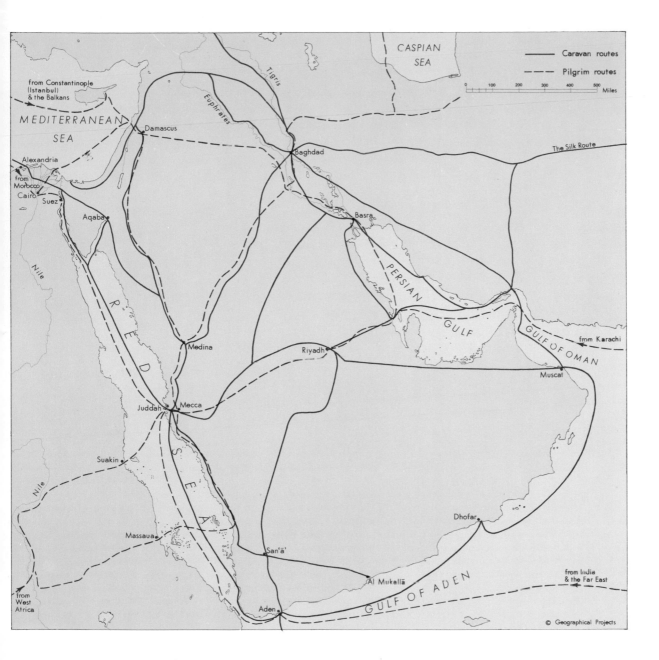

▲ *The age-old routes the merchants and pilgrims followed across Arabia.*

regularly crossed by traders, and by pilgrims following the traditional routes to Mecca. But the traders and pilgrims were Moslems, and as such safe from the religious fanaticism of the Arabs, who reserved their hostility for any infidel intruder. In 1875, however, **Charles Doughty** (1843-1926), while traveling with Bedouin tribes beyond the Jordan, heard of, and resolved to visit, the ancient monuments at Medā'in Sālih. In 1876, he joined the pilgrim caravan from Damascus, and traveled with it to Medā'in Sālih. Then, traveling as a Christian and an Englishman, but in the guise of a healer, he spent two years wandering with the Bedouins through Arabia. Doughty suffered much hardship, being expelled from Hā'il, robbed, and nearly killed, and was often in great danger. Yet he survived to write *Arabia Deserta,* a vivid picture of the country.

In 1878, two English travelers, **Wilfrid Scawen Blunt** (1840-1922) and his wife **Lady Anne Blunt** (dates unknown), journeyed down the Euphrates to Baghdad, and the following year they set out for Hā'il to see the peoples of Arabia, and to buy Arab horses for breeding. Although they traveled undisguised, and made no secret of being British, they completed their journey safely, most probably because they traveled in company with an Arab sheik. **Gertrude Bell** (1868-1926) was less lucky, for Arab hostility forced her to curtail her journey at Hā'il instead of continuing to Riyadh as she had originally intended. Nevertheless, she learned much about Arabia, and her knowledge was of more than geographical importance, for she put it at Britain's service during World War I.

Not until 1930-1 did a European cross the great Rub' al Khali, the desert that had so impressed Well-sted nearly a century before. **Bertram Thomas** (1892-1950), who had worked for some years for the Sultan of Muscat, reached the edge of the Rub' al Khali in 1928-9 while traveling in Dhofar. The following year, he crossed the desert from south to north. Another Englishman, **Harry St. John Philby** (1885-1960), who, like Thomas, worked for an Arabian ruler, made the crossing the very next year. Before his magnificent feat, Philby had already traveled widely in Arabia, crossing the peninsula from east to west in 1917 and in 1918 traveling south to As Sulayyil.

The exploration of the Rub' al Khali was completed by **Wilfred Thesiger** (born 1910) who made two crossings of the desert, in 1946-7, and 1947-8. Thesiger was the last of the great explorers of Arabia, for by then the face of the country was changing. Oil had been discovered in the desert and the peninsula's new challenge would be the exploitation of its hidden wealth.

123

9 The Dark Continent

Even as recently as the late 1700's, the interior of Africa was almost totally unknown. During the Great Age of Discovery, the continent had been regarded more as an obstacle in the sea route to India than as a land worthy in itself of exploration and, although some missionaries and traders had subsequently traveled to Africa, none had penetrated far inland. In southern Africa, most rivers—the usual routes to the interior—are navigable for only a short distance inland before their course is broken by rapids and falls. Over these falls, the rivers drop from the interior plateau down to the narrow coastal plain. Many of the African peoples, too, were hostile to intruders and, in that unfamiliar climate, Europeans were always at the mercy of some tropical disease. In the north, the wastes of the Sahara divide the Mediterranean coastlands from tropical Africa, and there explorers faced fanatical Moslem tribesmen, besides the dangers of travel in desert lands.

Rumors of course abounded about a land so little known, and Africa came to be called the "Dark Continent", so mysterious did it seem. Theories, often wildly mistaken, persisted about Africa's geography and her peoples, and many believed that the continent held hidden stores of wealth. Only with the coming of the explorers toward the end of the 1700's did the aura of mystery begin to be dispelled. Discovery centered on three main areas: the Nile and the lake region of eastern Africa; the southern and central parts of the continent; and the Niger and the Sahara desert. Gradually, the geographical problems of each region were unraveled and the true face of Africa slowly became clear.

In classical times, northern Africa was an integral part of the civilized world of the Mediterranean. One of the world's first civilizations developed in Egypt; the city of Carthage in present-day Tunisia was the hub of a powerful empire; and the Roman Empire included all Africa's Mediterranean shore. Then, in the A.D. 700's, the Arab onslaught brought the Islamic religion to north Africa. Because of the great barrier of the Sahara, however, the influence of civilization never spread far to the south, and as late as 1800 most of Africa's inhabitants still followed a primitive way of life. To these people, the arrival of Europeans inevitably brought change. Missionaries traveled to Africa to convert the heathen, and humanitarians to abolish the slave trade, through which, between about 1450 and 1880, some 10 million black Africans were sold. In the wake of the explorers and reformers, the colonizers reached Africa, and by 1900 almost all the continent was under European rule. The European empires in Africa were short-lived, for by 1970 most African countries were self-governing, but in those few years, the evolution of centuries had been achieved. Africa had stepped forward to take her place in the modern world.

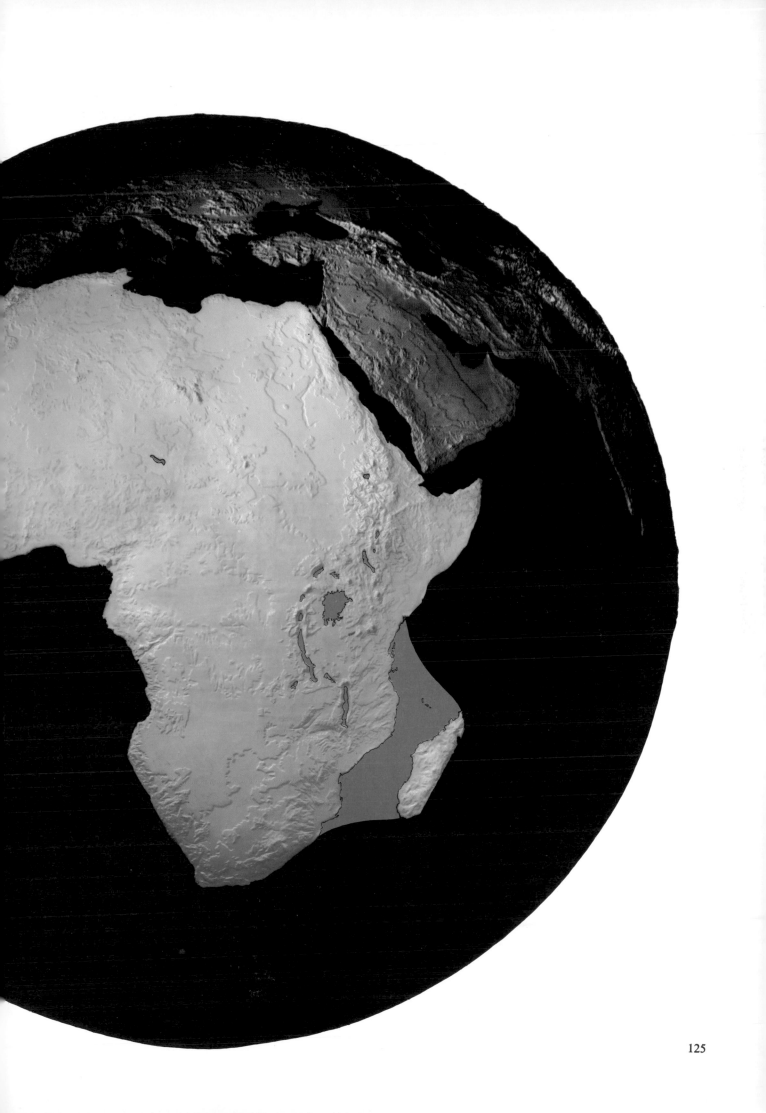

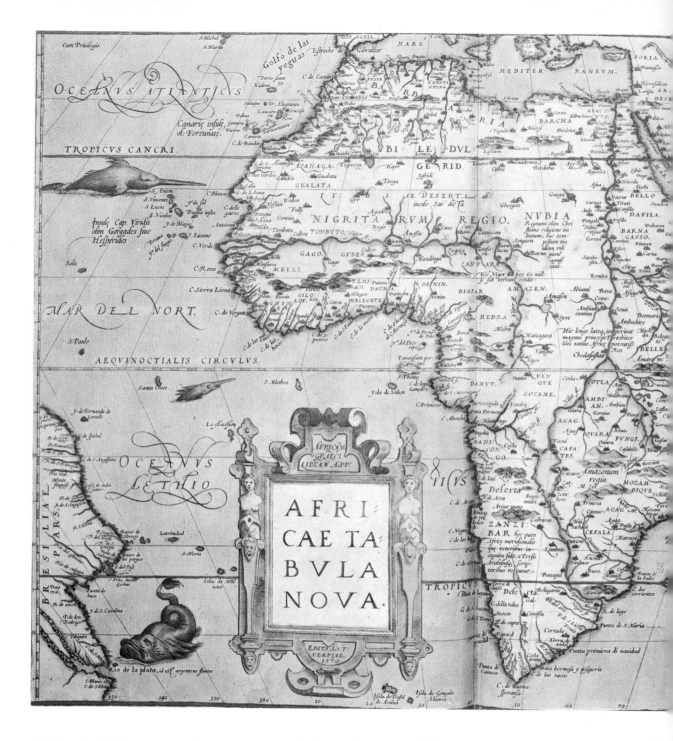

Africa in 1570 was a continent known and yet unknown, a continent of which, although its existence had long been recognized, little that was definite had been learned. Such knowledge as Europe had of Africa related to the coastlands, and not to the interior—the Portuguese who forged the sea route to India had traced the outline of the continent, and from missionaries and traders Europe had acquired some information about the lands bordering the coasts.

Knowledge of Africa might be limited, but the continent's existence was certain, and its place was therefore assured in Abraham Ortelius' atlas *Theatrum Orbis Terrarum*. This map was among the 70 in the first edition of Ortelius' work. The outline of the continent was laid down with some accuracy, and one might believe that the map maker also knew something of the interior, for he depicts mountains and rivers with conviction, and includes numerous towns. This picture is, however, rather the result of an imaginative interpretation of classical works of geography, and of contemporary rumor, than of definite geographical knowledge.

The cartographer's picture of the Nile derives most probably from the Greek geographer Ptolemy's work of before A.D. 150. Ptolemy had envisaged the river rising in two lakes deep in the interior, and fed by melting snows from what he called the Mountains of the Moon. On the map in Ortelius' atlas, too, the Nile rises in two lakes in the heart of Africa, and the rivers debouching from these lakes join north of the equator to flow north. The map maker reveals just how persistent was the Prester John legend, for near the confluence of the Nile's branches, he marks the region that he believed was ruled by that legendary king.

The great lake where the westernmost branch of the Upper Nile rises is shown as the source of two other rivers as well. To the west flows the Zaire—the river generally known as the Congo—and to the south the Zuama, which branches to enter the sea as two separate rivers. Here, Ortelius may have had definite knowledge, for the northernmost river could well be the Zambezi, and the southernmost the Limpopo River.

126

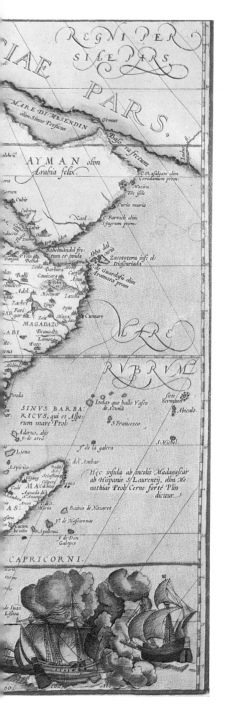

The Source of the Nile

Northward through Africa flows the mighty Nile River. Its lower reaches have long been known, for in its fertile valley the civilization of ancient Egypt was born. Until the 1600's, however, its upper course remained a mystery, and even then it was the work of centuries to map that great stream.

In its upper reaches, the Nile is really two rivers, which join at Khartoum to flow together to the sea. These two branches are known as the Blue Nile, and the White Nile, from the color of their waters. The source of the Blue Nile was first seen by a European in 1613 when **Pedro Paez** (?-1622), a missionary at the Ethiopian court, visited the Springs at Geesh. About 15 years later, another missionary, **Jerônimo Lobo** (1593-1678), traveled from Lake Tana down the river past Tisisat Falls. But it was **James Bruce** (1730-1794) who made the first scientific exploration of the Blue Nile. He visited the Springs at Geesh, and verified their position, then, via Gondar, he traveled overland to Sennar on the Blue Nile. From Sennar, Bruce followed the Blue Nile to Khartoum, then continued down the mainstream of the Nile past Berber. He crossed the Nubian Desert, rejoined the Nile at Aswan, and eventually reached Cairo, convinced that he had seen the source of the Nile. In fact, Bruce was mistaken, for the White Nile is the longer of the river's branches, and the point where the White Nile rises is considered the source of the Nile.

The Ortelius map gives a totally false impression of the course of the Niger River. It is shown rising a little north of the equator in a lake also named Niger, and flowing north, then west, to enter the sea through a great delta around Cape Verde— in the region where the Senegal and Gambia rivers enter the sea. Farther south, a region named Zanzibar is marked. In short, the Ortelius map reveals Europe's almost total ignorance of the African continent. This picture would not, however, be improved for some 200 years. Even in the 1730's, the English satirist Jonathan Swift was writing that:

". . . geographers, in Afric-maps,
With savage-pictures fill their gaps;
And o'er unhabitable downs
Place elephants for want of towns."

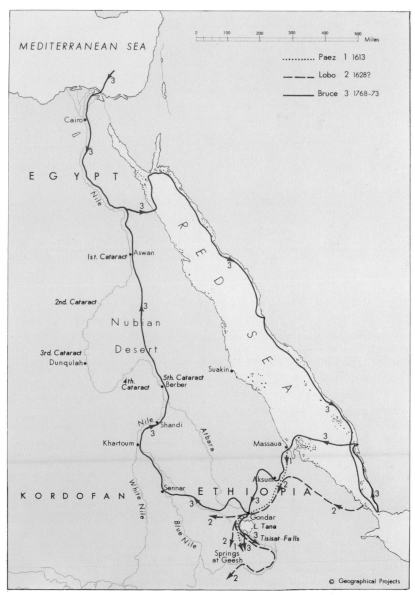

The first clues to the origins of the White Nile were discovered by missionaries journeying inland from the east coast of Africa. They were **Johannes Rebmann** (1820-1876)—who in 1848 discovered Mount Kilimanjaro, Africa's highest mountain—and **Johann Krapf** (1810-1881)—who sighted Mount Kenya in 1849. From Arab caravan leaders Krapf

▲ *John Hanning Speke.*

had heard in 1848 of an inland sea and a range of mountains. Could such a lake be the source of the Nile?

The Royal Geographical Society of London took the missionary's report so seriously that an expedition was commissioned to find his inland sea. It was led by **Richard Burton,** who in 1853-4 had made the pilgrimage to Mecca, and who was accompanied now by **John Speke** (1827-1864). The two men discovered Lake Tanganyika, and sailed up the east coast from Ujiji. But they neither found which way the lake drained nor reached its northern end.

From Arab traders, Burton and Speke heard of another lake northeast of Tanganyika, but when they reached Tabora Burton was too sick to continue the search. Speke went on

alone to discover Lake Victoria. He returned convinced that he had found the source of the White Nile. In England, the discovery of Lake Tanganyika was largely ignored in the excitement of Speke's claim. He was given command of another expedition and, with **James Grant** (1827-1892), he traveled around the west side of Lake Victoria and discovered Ripon Falls. There, a river—the White Nile—leaves Lake Victoria. But Speke did not follow the White Nile from Lake Victoria. He set out inland and, crossing the river between the Karuma Rapids and the Murchison Falls, he rejoined it downstream of Lake Albert. Thus, he still had no definite proof of his claim and Burton, who had never believed the Lake Victoria theory, was quick to question it. Before the truth could be discovered, Speke died in a shooting accident. He never knew he was right, and Burton wrong.

At Gondokoro on the White Nile, Speke and Grant had met **Samuel Baker** (1821-1893). Baker had left England to seek the source of the Nile but, hearing that Speke had "settled" the Nile question, he started in search of the Luta Ngizé, a lake of which Speke had told him.

Baker reached the lake, naming it after Prince Albert. Later, he discovered the Murchison Falls.

Baker had fitted another important piece into the Nile puzzle by his discovery of Lake Albert and its connection with the White Nile. But the picture was still incomplete, for Lake Edward and the Kagera River were unknown. Lake Kivu had not been discovered either, but Lake Kivu belongs to the Congo river system, and not to that of the Nile.

Georg August Schweinfurth (1836-1925), a German botanist, was the first European to cross the Nile-Congo watershed. He discovered the Uele River, and although he did not explore it, he wrote a valuable account of the region. Schweinfurth thought the Uele was the upper course of the Chari, but in fact it flows into the Ubangi which joins the Congo. Further explorations on the Nile-Congo watershed and around the White Nile's headwaters were made by **Emin Pasha** (1840-1892), whose real name was Eduard Schnitzer. From 1876, as an Egyptian government official, Pasha lived in the Upper Nile country, but in 1885, when the fanatical Moslem forces of the Mahdi captured Khartoum and won control of the Sudan, Emin Pasha was cut off from the outside world. Not until 1888 was he rescued by **Henry Stanley** (1841-1904). Pasha later set out with **Stuhlmann** (dates unknown) to try to cross Africa but he was murdered near the Congo.

In 1878-80, with a Royal Geographical Society expedition seeking a good route from the coast to Lake Nyasa, **Joseph Thomson** (1858-1895) traveled via Lake Nyasa to Lake Tanganyika, finally establishing that the Lukuga River was the outlet of the lake. From the Lukuga, he tried to reach the Congo, but native opposition forced him to turn back and he therefore returned via Tabora to the coast. On this expedition, Thomson discovered Lake Rukwa. His next journey led him to the Rovuma River, to investigate an unfounded report that there was coal there, and, in 1883-4, with **James Martin** (dates unknown), he opened a new route from the coast to Lake Victoria, forging a path through the country of the warrior Masai. He visited Lake Naivasha, and discovered Lake Baringo and Mount Elgon. In 1890-1, in the service of the British South Africa Company, Thomson traveled in the unmapped country between lakes Nyasa and Bangweulu. Two years earlier, **Samuel Teleki** (dates unknown) and **Ludwig von Höhnel** (dates unknown) had discovered lakes Rudolf and Stefanie. A few blanks still remained, but with their discovery the map of eastern Africa was virtually complete.

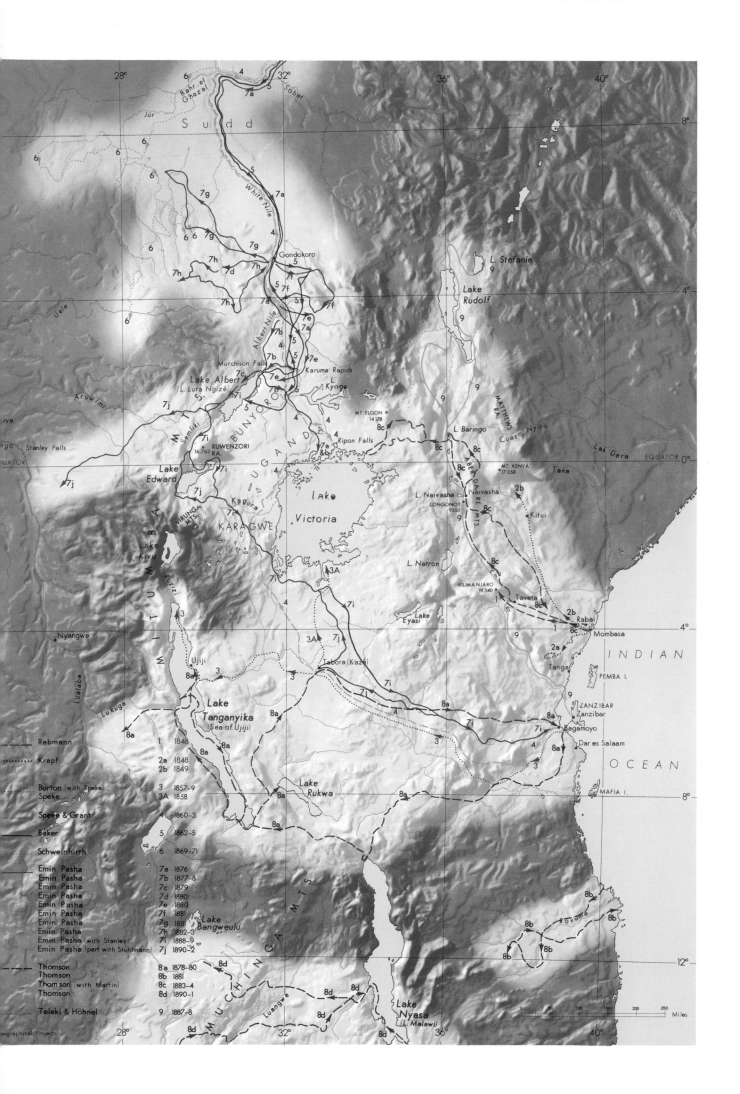

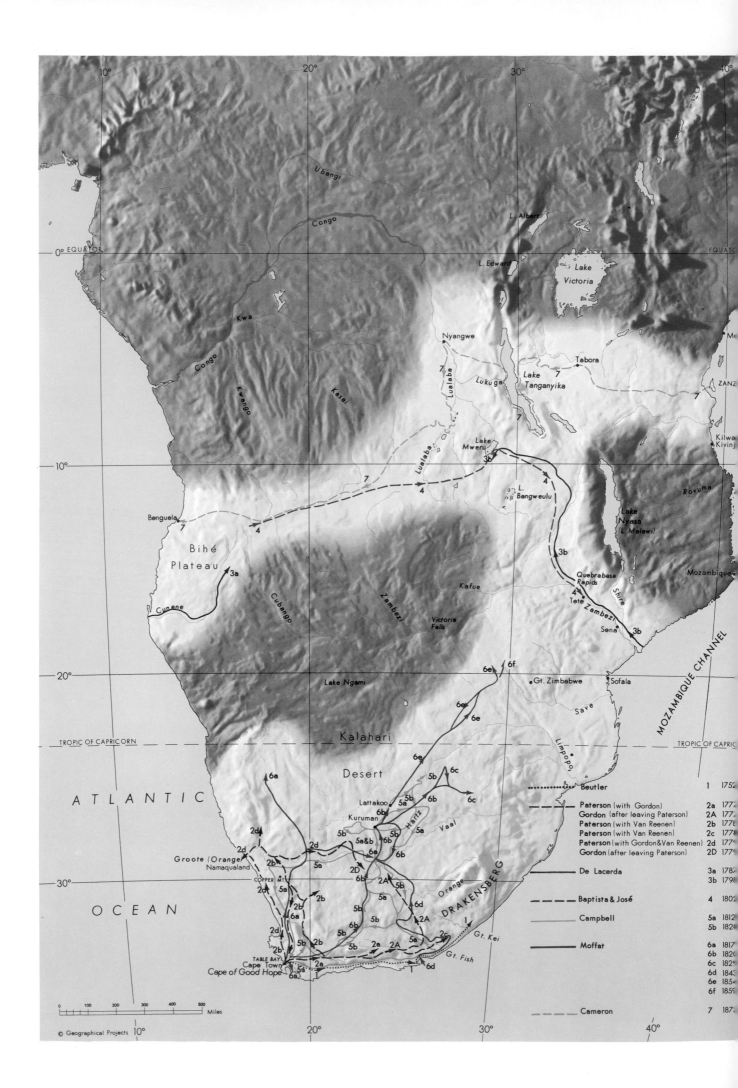

EQUATOR

Ubangi

Congo

L. Albert

L. Edward

Lake
Victoria

Kwa

Congo

Nyangwe

Kasai

7

Lualaba

Lukuga

Tabora

Lake
Tanganyika

7

ZANZ

Kwango

7

Lualaba

7

Lake
Mweru
3b

4

Benguela

7

4

L.
Bangweulu

4

Rovuma

Bihé
Plateau

3a

Kafue

Zambezi

Lake
Nyasa
(L. Malawi)

3b

Quebrabasa
Rapids

Mozambique

Cubango

Cunene

Victoria
Falls

4

Tete Zambezi
Sena 3b

Shire

MOZAMBIQUE CHANNEL

Lake Ngami

Kalahari

6e 6f

Gt. Zimbabwe

Sofala

Save

6e

6e

TROPIC OF CAPRICORN

Desert

6e

TROPIC OF CAPRIC

ATLANTIC

6a

5b 6c

Lattakoo 5a 6b 6c

Kuruman 6b

5b Hartz

Vaal

Limpopo

2d

2d

2d

Groote (Orange)
Namaqualand

2b

5a

5b 5a&b 6b

6a

6b

5a

2d

COPPER MT.

2d 5a

2b

6a

2D

6b 2A 5b

5a

Orange

6d

DRAKENSBERG

OCEAN

2b

2b

5b

5a

2A

1

2d

6a

5b

6b

5b

5a

6d

2A

Gt. Kei

2d

5b 2b

5b

2a 2A 5a

2c

Gt. Fish

TABLE BAY
Cape Town
Cape of Good Hope

5a 2a

6a

6d

.... Beutler 1 1752

—————— Paterson (with Gordon) 2a 177?
————— Gordon (after leaving Paterson) 2A 177?
————— Paterson (with Van Reenen) 2b 1778
————— Paterson (with Van Reenen) 2c 177?
————— Paterson (with Gordon&Van Reenen) 2d 177?
————— Gordon (after leaving Paterson) 2D 177?

—————— De Lacerda 3a 1787
  3b 1798

– – – – Baptista & José 4 1802

———— Campbell 5a 1812
  5b 1820

———— Moffat 6a 1817
  6b 1820
  6c 1820
  6d 1843
  6e 1854
  6f 1859

– – – – – Cameron 7 1873

0 100 200 300 400 500 Miles

© Geographical Projects 10°

20° 30° 40°

The Heart of Africa

In 1652, the Dutch founded the first settlement at the Cape of Good Hope. Intended by the Dutch East India Company as a port of call for Dutch ships en route to the Indies, the colony was at first concentrated around Table Bay. Gradually, however, the settlers made their way into the interior. In 1752, *August Beutler* (dates unknown) led a party across the Great Kei River, and was only prevented from traveling even farther afield because his men were fatigued.

The Groote (Orange) River, which flows from the Drakensberg to the Atlantic, was first crossed in 1760, and in 1777 **Robert Gordon** (dates unknown) reached the river near its junction with the Vaal. For part of his journey, Gordon was accompanied by **William Paterson** (1756-?) who, the following year, with a young Dutchman, **Van Reenen** (dates unknown), crossed the Groote near its mouth. In 1778-9, Paterson and Van Reenen traveled east beyond the Great Fish River. In 1779, with Gordon, they pushed north to the mouth of the Groote which Gordon renamed the Orange.

In 1806, Britain finally took possession of Cape Colony and British missionaries were soon traveling to South Africa to preach. Returning from a mission to Lattakoo, the Batswana capital, in 1812-4, **John Campbell** (1766-?) reached the confluence of the Hartz and Vaal rivers, and traced part of the course of the Orange. Six years later, he discovered the source of the Limpopo River. **Robert Moffat** (1795-1883), who was to spend more than 50 years among the Batswana people, in 1817-9 crossed the lower Orange and continued far to the north. Moffat moved the Batswana mission from Lattakoo to Kuruman, and explored the fringes of the Kalahari, then pushed north to the Save.

In 1841, Moffat was joined at the Kuruman mission by **David Livingstone** (1813-1873). Livingstone, in his travels, was to redraw the map of Africa, and to him discovery was as important as missionary work. Still, throughout his time in Africa, he worked to better the Africans, and above all to abolish the slave trade.

Two years after his arrival at Kuruman, Livingstone founded a new mission at Kolobeng and in 1849 he set out from there with **Cotton Oswell** (1818-1893) and **Mungo Murray** (dates unknown) for Lake Ngami in the north. The following year, Livingstone and Oswell tried to reach Linyanti and, although on their first attempt they were unsuccessful, in 1851 they managed to push north beyond Linyanti to the Zambezi. Returning they visited Linyanti.

Although, until Livingstone's journey, nothing had been known of the upper reaches of the Zambezi, the Portuguese had long been familiar with its lower course. In 1798, the river had even been explored as far as the Quebrabasa Rapids by **Francisco de Lacerda** (?-1798). Lacerda, who in 1787 had traveled on the Cunene River, was seeking a practicable route across Africa, but he died near Lake Mweru, and his party returned to the coast. Soon, however, his ambition was realized by two Portuguese traders, **Pedra Baptista** (unknown) and **Amaro José** (dates unknown), who traveled from the Bihé Plateau to the Zambezi.

After his journey to Linyanti, Livingstone returned to Cape Town, but in 1852 he set out again. His goal was to complete the exploration of the Zambezi. Reaching the river near Linyanti, he traveled to the Atlantic coast at Luanda. On his return journey, he crossed Africa from Luanda to Quelimane (formerly Kilimane), discovering the Victoria Falls.

In 1858, Livingstone left Quelimane with his brother **Charles** (1822-1875) and **John Kirk** (1832-1922). They made a number of expeditions on the Zambezi and the Shire rivers, discovering lakes Shirwa and Nyasa, then traveled up the Zambezi to Linyanti. In 1861, they tried to sail up the Rovuma River to Lake Nyasa, but the river proved unnavigable, and the route up the Shire had to be used again. Once on Lake Nyasa, much of the western shore was explored. A second attempt was later made to sail up the Rovuma, but it too was unsuccessful and in 1863 the expedition was recalled. By this time, Livingstone's reputation as an explorer was prodigious and when, after Baker's discovery of Lake Albert in 1864, the Royal Geographical Society planned an expedition to complete the mapping of the Nile's sources, it was to Livingstone they turned. He left the coast near the mouth of the Rovuma and trekked via Lake Nyasa to Lake Tanganyika, going on to discover Lake Mweru and Lake Bangweulu. Then, he turned for Ujiji to collect his letters and stores. By this time, Livingstone was suffering from the effects of years of hardship and sickness and his position was made no easier when he found his stores had been stolen.

Undeterred, Livingstone traveled west to the Lualaba River, which at first he was inclined to believe to be a source of the Nile. Later, he

Victoria Falls. ▶

guessed rightly that it belonged to the Congo. From the Lualaba, he returned to Ujiji and there, on 10 November 1871, **Henry Stanley's** expedition arrived. Stanley had been sent by the *New York Herald* to find Livingstone, who had been for long "lost" to the outside world. The two men together explored the northern end of Lake Tanganyika but, although Livingstone accompanied Stanley as far as Tabora, he would not return with him to the coast. The problem of the Nile was still unsolved, and Livingstone, believing its ultimate source must lie near Lake Bangweulu, insisted on going there. Near the source of the Luapula River, south of Lake Bangweulu, on 1 May 1873, David Livingstone died.

Just a month before Livingstone's death, **Verney Cameron (1844-1894)** led an expedition from Zanzibar to take supplies to Livingstone. At Tabora, from the explorer's servants, he learned of their master's death, but nevertheless he continued his journey to carry on Livingstone's work. Cameron made the first maps of much of the coast of Lake Tanganyika, and discovered the Lukuga River, which he correctly believed to be the lake's outlet even though he did not follow it. On reaching the Lualaba, he concluded that it was part of the Congo, but Arab hostility prevented him procuring boats to sail down the river and prove his claim. Cameron did, however, continue his journey westward to the Atlantic coast.

A contemporary newspaper picture of
▼ *Stanley's meeting with Livingstone.*

Henry Stanley, the man who had "found" Livingstone, set out in 1874 for Lake Victoria and, after circumnavigating the lake, he confirmed that its only outlet was Ripon Falls. He crossed the Kagera River to discover Lake Edward, and thoroughly explored the country between that lake and Lake Victoria. He then continued to Lake Tanganyika, and sailed around the southern end of the lake, concluding incorrectly that the lake only flowed through the Lukuga River when it was exceptionally high. The Lukuga was finally proved to be the lake's outlet by Joseph Thomson in 1878-80.

In 1876, Stanley left Ujiji, and trekked west to the Lualaba River. There, by threatening force, he succeeded in obtaining boats where Cameron had failed. In the face of horrific dangers, and suffering constant hardship, he sailed down the Lualaba past the point where it becomes the Congo. He reached Boma, at the mouth of the Congo, 999 days after he had left Zanzibar for Lake Victoria in 1874.

In 1879, Stanley was back on the Congo, sponsored by the King of the Belgians to open up access to the interior. He traveled upstream to Stanley Falls and, in 1883, discovered lakes Tumba and Leopold II. In 1888, Stanley left the Atlantic coast on his last great journey, the rescue of **Emin Pasha.** He traveled through the Congo forests to meet Pasha on the Upper Nile, and finally led his party down to the east coast. On his way, he explored the Semliki River, linking lakes Albert and Edward, and discovered the Ruwenzori Range.

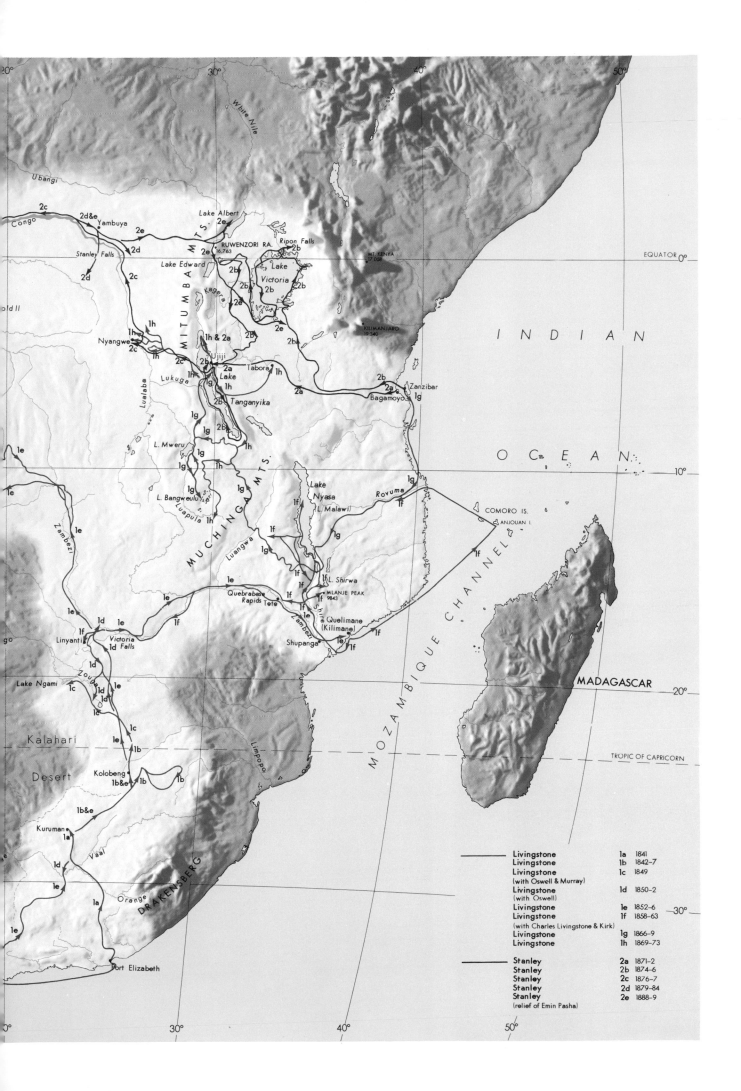

20°   30°   40°   50°

Ubangi

2c
Congo   2d&e
              Yambuya   2e   Lake Albert
                            2d   2e
        Stanley Falls   2c   RUWENZORI RA.   Ripon Falls
                    2d   16,763   2b
              2c   Lake Edward   2e   Lake   MT. KENYA
        1h   2b   Victoria   2b   17,058
  1h   2b   2b   EQUATOR 0°
Nyangwe   1h & 2a   1h   2e   Kagera   2e
        2c   1h   2e   KILIMANJARO
              1h   2c   Ujiji   2b   2e   19,340   INDIAN
                    1h   2b   2a   Tabora   1h
                    1g   Lake   2a   2b
                    1g   Tanganyika   2a   Bagamoyo   2b   Zanzibar
                        2b   2a
                    1g
              L. Mweru   1g   2b   1h
                    1g   O C E A N   10°
                    1g   1h   Lake
        L. Bangweulu   1g   Nyasa   Rovuma   1g
                    Luapula   1h   1f   L. Malawi   1f
                                            COMORO IS.
                    Luangwa   1f   ANJOUAN I.
                        1e   1f
              1e   Quebrabase   1f   L. Shirwa
                    Rapids Tete   1f   MLANJE PEAK
        1e   1d   1e   1f   9843
        1f   Victoria   Shupanga   Quelimane
  Linyanti   1d Falls   (Kilimane)
              1d   Shupanga   1f
        Lake Ngami   1d   1e   MADAGASCAR   20°
              1c   TROPIC OF CAPRICORN
                    1c
        Kalahari   1e   1b
        Desert   Kolobeng
              1b&e   1b   1b
              1b&e
  Kuruman   1a
        1d
        1e   Orange   DRAKENSBERG   30°
                    Vaal
              1a
        Port Elizabeth

              ———   Livingstone   1a   1841
                    Livingstone   1b   1842-7
                    Livingstone   1c   1849
                    (with Oswell & Murray)
                    Livingstone   1d   1850-2
                    (with Oswell)
                    Livingstone   1e   1852-6
                    Livingstone   1f   1858-63
                    (with Charles Livingstone & Kirk)
                    Livingstone   1g   1866-9
                    Livingstone   1h   1869-73

              ———   Stanley   2a   1871-2
                    Stanley   2b   1874-6
                    Stanley   2c   1876-7
                    Stanley   2d   1879-84
                    Stanley   2e   1888-9
                    (relief of Emin Pasha)

The Search for the Niger

In 1788, not long after James Bruce had, as he thought, fixed the source of the Nile, the "Association for Promoting the Discovery of the Interior Parts of Africa" was founded in London. The African Association, as it was generally called, first turned its attention to the Niger River, about which little was known. In the 1300's, **Ibn-Batuta,** the great Arab traveler, had crossed the Sahara to the Niger, and had visited the trading town of Timbuktu, but 400 years later Europeans did not even know which way the river flowed.

Although neither of the association's first explorers reached the Niger, they did acquire some information about the African interior. The next attempt on the river was made from the mouth of the Gambia by **Daniel Houghton** (1740?-1791). After crossing the Senegal River Houghton was decoyed into the desert by Moslem tribesmen, his possessions were stolen, and he was left to die. **Mungo Park** (1771-1806), who set out in 1795 for the Niger, saw the place where Houghton died.

Park himself was captured by Moslems, and, for three months, he was held prisoner at Benown. At last he escaped, and made his way southeast. At Ségou, he saw the Niger River, flowing steadily east. Park did not follow the river far on this occasion, but in 1805 he led a party to Africa to travel to its mouth. Before reaching the Niger, however, most of his men died. The survivors built a boat at Sansanding, and set sail down the river, but all were drowned at Bussa, escaping from an African attack.

Between Park's two journeys, **Friedrich Hornemann** (1772-1801) traveled from Cairo across the Sahara to Lake Chad, then on toward the Niger, but he died at Bokani, little short of his goal. Then, in 1818, the British government sent an expedition across the Sahara. After leaving Marzūq, however, **Joseph Ritchie** (?-1818) died, and **George Lyon** (1795-1832) was unable to travel much farther south.

In 1822, **Hugh Clapperton** (1788-1827), **Dixon Denham** (1786-1828), and **Walter Oudney** (1792?-1824) crossed the Sahara to Lake Chad then, while Denham explored around the lake, and along the Chari River, Clapperton and Oudney pushed west. But Oudney died at Kano, and Clapperton continued to Sokoto alone. There, he tried to find a guide to lead him to the Niger but, as he was unsuccessful, he had to turn back. In 1825, however, Clapperton returned to Africa with **Richard Lander** (1804-1834) to seek the river's mouth. From the Gulf of Guinea, they struck northeast and crossed the Niger, intending to return to the river from Sokoto and sail down it to its mouth. But Clapperton died at Sokoto, and Lander abandoned the attempt. In 1830-2, however, with his brother **John** (1807-1839), Lander traveled inland to Bussa, then sailed down the Niger to the sea.

Meanwhile Timbuktu, long the goal of Europeans, had been visited by two travelers. In 1825-6, **Alexander Laing** (1793-1826) trekked from Tripoli to the city, but was murdered soon after leaving there. Two years later, **René Caillié** (1799-1838), who had already made two journeys to west Africa, arrived in Timbuktu from the coast. From the city, he continued to Fez across the Sahara.

In 1850, a British "mixed scientific and commercial expedition" left Tripoli. Its leader was **James Richardson** (?-1851), but he died after the long Sahara crossing, before reaching Kukawa, and it was to **Heinrich Barth** (1821-1865) that the expedition's success was due. Barth had already traveled the length of the north coast of Africa, and now, with **Adolf Overweg** (1822-1852), he completed the exploration of Lake Chad. The expedition's next aim was Timbuktu, but Overweg died before the journey began. Barth continued alone, carrying out the first scientific exploration of much of central and west Africa, and opening the way for the conquest of the Sahara to begin.

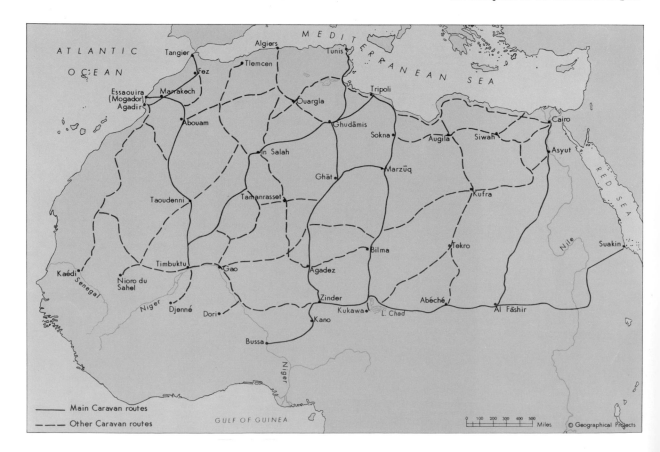

--- Main Caravan routes

-- -- Other Caravan routes

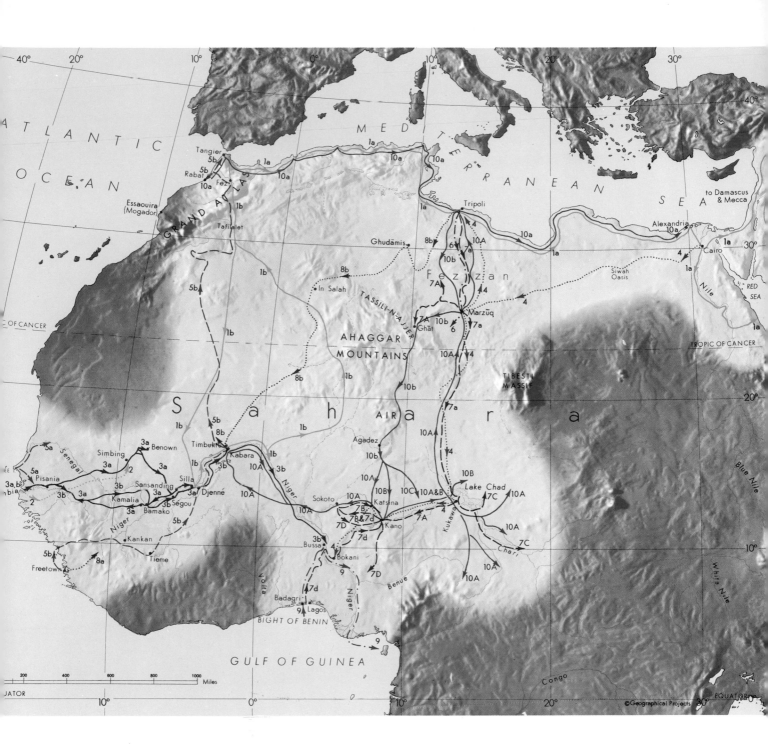

From the days of the Roman Empire, trains of pack camels wound their way across northern Africa carrying the treasures of Africa north across the Sahara desert, and goods from Europe south. These camel caravans followed traditional trails which had grown up along routes where there were known to be waterholes. There, even though the desert oases might be several hundred miles apart, travelers crossing the Sahara could be reasonably sure that they would not die of thirst. But they still had other dangers to contend with, quite apart from the heat, and the harsh desert climate. The caravan routes across the Sahara were controlled by the fierce Tuareg tribesmen, and it was on the good will of the Tuareg that the success of any journey would ultimately depend.

———————	Ibn–Batuta (part of journey)	1a	1325-32
	Ibn–Batuta	1b	1349-53
·················	Houghton	2	1790-1
———————	Park	3a	1795-7
		3b	1805-6
··············	Hornemann	4	1798-1801
— — —	Caillié	5a	1816, 1824
		5b	1827-8
———·—·—	Ritchie & Lyon	6	1818
— — — —	Clapperton (with Oudney & Denham)	7a	1822-5
	Clapperton (with Oudney)	7A	1823-4

— — — —	Clapperton (after death of Oudney)	7B	1824
	Denham	7C	1823-4
	Clapperton (with R. Lander)	7d	1825-7
	Lander, R. (after death of Clapperton)	7D	1827-8
··············	Laing	8a	1822
		8b	1825-6
—·—·—·—	Lander, R. (with J. Lander)	9	1830-2
———————	Barth	10a	1845-7
	Barth (with Richardson & Overweg)	10b	1850-5
	Barth } after explorers	10A	
	Overweg }	10B	
	Richardson } separated	10C	

135

The Conquest of the Desert

The Sahara stretches through northern Africa like a band burned across the face of the continent, a scorching, virtually waterless region, held in thrall by the nomad Tuareg tribes. Through the ages, its hostility to intruders has been legendary, and consequently, the Sahara was one of the very last regions of Africa to be explored by Europeans.

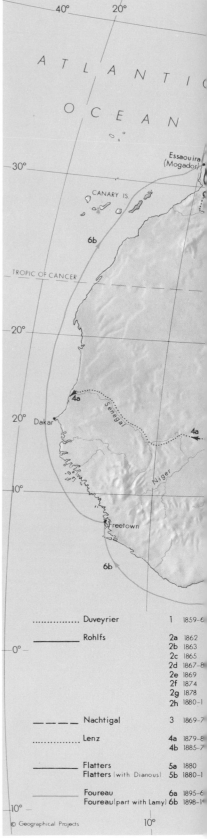

T he first explorers to venture into the desert saw the Sahara simply as a route to the Niger River, as an alternative to the route inland from the west coast. Heinrich Barth's researches, however, awakened a new interest in the desert, and after his journey it was visited by travelers concerned with the region itself. Between 1859 and 1861, a young Frenchman, **Henri Duveyrier** (1840-1892) wandered in the northern Sahara studying the Tuareg tribesmen, and, although at first he met with considerable hostility, later he was hospitably received. Illness prevented Duveyrier making another expedition in Africa, yet even so his book, *The Tuareg of the North,* remains a standard work.

Friedrich Gerhard Rohlfs (1831-1896) became interested in Africa while serving in the French Foreign Legion, and later, after his conversion to Islam, he spent nearly 20 years traveling there. Rohlfs' expeditions led him over much of the Sahara and the Libyan Desert, east to the Nile, and to the fringes of the Abyssinian Highlands. He was the first European to cross western Africa from the Mediterranean to the Gulf of Guinea.

Gustav Nachtigal (1834-1885), who, like Rohlfs, was a German, made a long and important journey in the desert between 1869 and 1874. Nachtigal's first explorations were carried out in the Tibesti Massif and later he investigated the Lake Chad

▲ *A waterhole in the Sahara desert, drawn by Heinrich Barth.*

region, before returning to the Mediterranean via Wadai, Darfur, and the Nile River. Although this was a route that had defeated many earlier explorers, Nachtigal completed his journey safely, and in so doing for the first time established a connection between the Lake Chad region and the Nile.

The achievement of **Oskar Lenz** (1848-1925) was to cross the Sahara from the Grand Atlas to Timbuktu—in effect, René Caillié's crossing of the desert in reverse. Lenz spent three weeks in Timbuktu, and learned much about the city. In 1885-7, he journeyed through central Africa, traveling up the Congo River, and to lakes Tanganyika and Nyasa.

In the year Lenz reached the mouth of the Senegal at the end of his transsaharan journey, a French military expedition under the command of **Paul-Xavier Flatters** (1832-1881) was sent to survey a route for a railroad across the desert. On this first attempt, Flatters penetrated the desert only to the Tassili-n'-Ajjer, but later the same year, with **Lieutenant Dianous** (?-1881), he set out again. This time, in the Ahaggar Mountains, the Tuareg ambushed Flatters and a small party while they were obtaining water, and every one of the Frenchmen was killed. Dianous and the main body of the force set

out to recross the desert, but food and water ran out, and they were mercilessly attacked by the Tuareg. Very few of them reached the French bases alive.

After the tragedy of the Flatters expedition, the French government temporarily abandoned the idea of forging a path across the Sahara.

·········· Duveyrier	1	1859-6
—— Rohlfs	2a	1862
	2b	1863
	2c	1865
	2d	1867-8
	2e	1869
	2f	1874
	2g	1878
	2h	1880-1
— — — Nachtigal	3	1869-7
············· Lenz	4a	1879-8
	4b	1885-7
—— Flatters	5a	1880
Flatters (with Dianous)	5b	1880-1
—— Foureau	6a	1895-6
Foureau (part with Lamy)	6b	1898-1

© Geographical Projects

136

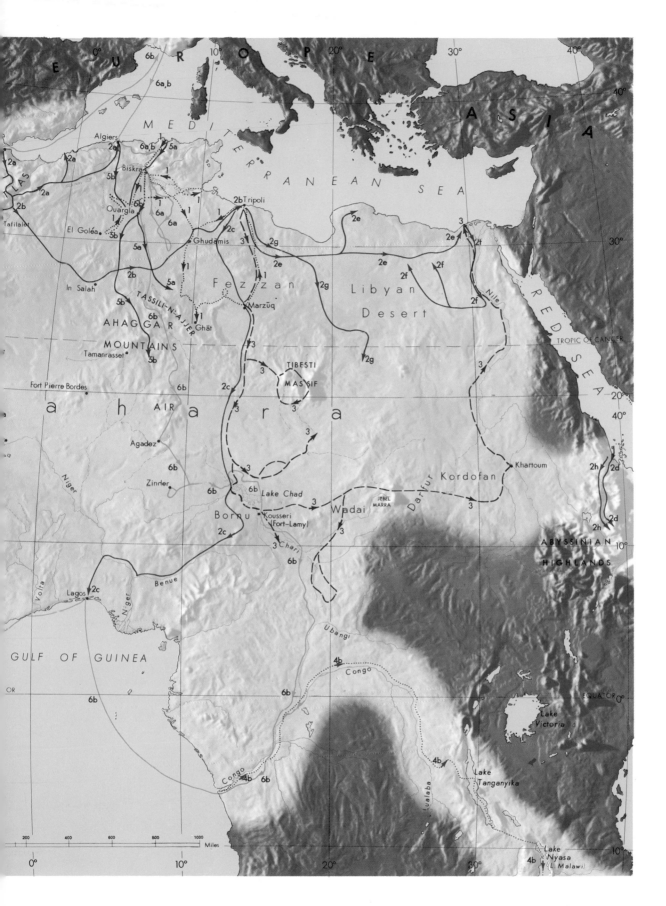

Fernand Foureau (1850-1914), however, did not. His dream was to see the establishment of a link across the desert, and he spent 15 years wandering there to prepare the way for his dream. In 1897, he went to Paris, and there he managed to obtain backing for his projected expedition to explore across the Sahara from the Mediterranean coast to the southern boundaries of the desert. The following year, his expedition set out.

Foureau's party was accompanied by a military escort commanded by **Major A. Lamy** (?-1900), an escort strong enough to deter the Tuareg from trying to attack. The desert was crossed safely, but at Kousseri, in battle with an army from Bornu, Major Lamy was killed. The mission showed, however, that a strong force could cross the desert and now the subjugation of the Tuareg became France's overriding aim. The desert would always hold dangers, but the dangers gradually became fewer as the conquest of the Sahara went on.

137

10 Terra Australis

Far away, in the unknown southern regions of the world, there lay, according to the ancients, a great continent. Such a land mass was necessary, they reasoned, to offset the weight of the continents in the Northern Hemisphere, and to balance the earth on its axis. Between A.D. 100 and 150, the Greek geographer Ptolemy placed this continent on his world map as a great land bridge joining Africa with eastern Asia. He called it Terra Australis Incognita, the unknown southern land.

European belief in Terra Australis persisted throughout the Middle Ages and in time a web of fantasy was woven around that mysterious land. Marco Polo wrote of the rich and wonderful countries he had visited in Southeast Asia, and Europe ascribed his tales to the southern continent, picturing it as beautiful and fantastically wealthy. After Vasco Núñez de Balboa's discovery of the Pacific Ocean in 1513 and Ferdinand Magellan's voyage across it $7\frac{1}{2}$ years later, it was on the Pacific that the search for the southland centered. Explorer after explorer set sail across the ocean. Some never returned. Others suffered terribly—from disease; from hunger and thirst when weeks passed without landfall; from the violent storms which all too often belie the Pacific's name. Each navigator, however, made his contribution to the map of the ocean, for it was through the search for Terra Australis that the Pacific was explored. Gradually, in succeeding voyages, its waters were charted and the bounds of the legendary continent limited until, by the end of the 1700's, Terra Australis had disappeared from the map. Gradually, too, through these voyages, the islands of the Pacific were discovered, and Australia, New Zealand, and finally Antarctica found.

With Terra Australis proved merely a legend, Europe, and in particular Britain, turned to its new discoveries, Australia and New Zealand. The exploration of these lands is a comparatively recent enterprise—only 200 years ago they were virtually unknown—and their story is largely one of settlement, and of the search for land and natural wealth. Australia especially held riches in land and minerals undreamed of by its discoverers, who described it as an unpromising country, and whose accounts contributed to its long neglect. It held dangers too, for the Aborigine inhabitants were bitterly hostile to Europeans, while in much of the continent travel was difficult, and water in short supply. In New Zealand, while the climate was milder, the terrain hindered explorers, while the colonists faced a long war with the Maori peoples for the possession of the land. In time, the Europeans ousted the Aborigines and the Maoris—the men who were the true discoverers of the lands of Australia and New Zealand. For, long years before European explorers reached those countries, the Aborigines and the Maoris had themselves arrived in Australia and New Zealand from across the sea.

Long ago, thousands of years before European ships first entered the Pacific, and before Europeans even dreamed of its existence, the exploration of that vast ocean began. From Asia first, and later, perhaps, from the Americas, as generation succeeded generation groups of men made their way across the ocean from island chain to island chain.

These first explorers were to be the first inhabitants of the Pacific islands for, in those days, from such long journeys, there was no going back. The earliest settlers came from Asia. At an early date, they began to make their way via the Malay Peninsula and the East Indian archipelago into the Pacific region known as Melanesia—"black islands". The first wave of migrants was followed by others and gradually the travelers spread throughout Melanesia and pushed south into Australia.

North of Melanesia, and east of the Philippine Islands, lies the region of Micronesia—"small islands". Cut off as it is by vast stretches of ocean, the settlement of Micronesia involved long sea voyages, and it was probably not until 3000 or 2000 B.C. that the first travelers reached the islands. Even then, colonization was a slow process. Only over generations did voyagers find their way from island group to island group.

About the settlement of Polynesia—"many islands"—the third and largest of the Pacific regions, controversy is rife. Many of the landfalls must have been accidental, made by seafarers who set out with no particular goal, and from such uncharted voyages it is almost impossible to establish a pattern of migration. Most experts agree, however, that the Polynesian settlers came originally from Asia, but they dispute when they arrived, and what route they followed.

The traditional theory is that travelers from Melanesia and Micronesia gradually spread east into Polynesia, but some believe that such journeys would have been impossible because of prevailing adverse currents and winds. They hold that far back in time the original settlers of Polynesia migrated from northeastern Asia into Alaska and that later, in two separate waves, from northwestern North America, and from western South America, these men set out across the sea.

European knowledge of these journeys is, however, a relatively recent acquisition, pieced together from legends, and from archeological remains. The first European sailors to set out across the Pacific in the 1500's knew nothing of that great ocean at all.

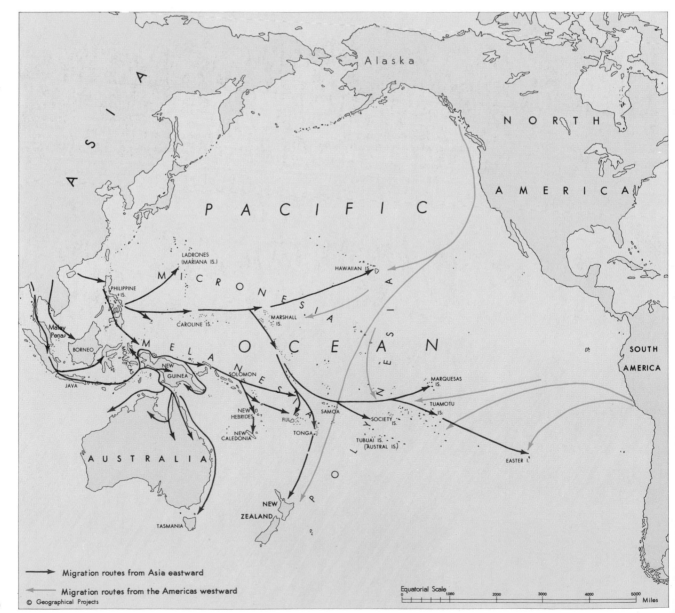

→ Migration routes from Asia eastward
→ Migration routes from the Americas westward
© Geographical Projects

Equatorial Scale

The Southern Continent

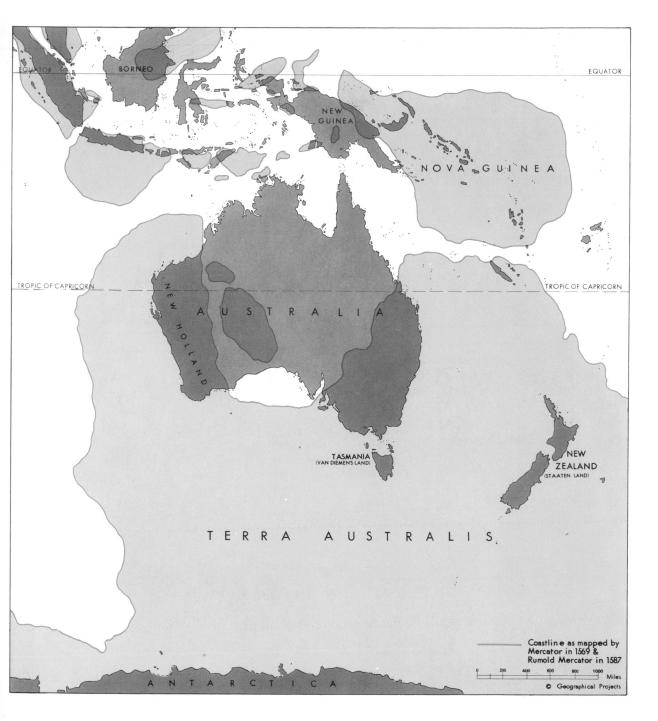

The outline of Terra Australis, the imaginary southern continent, superimposed on a map of Australasia.

In the days before European explorers had finally established the world's geography, cartographers used to speculate about the areas that were unknown. One of the most persistent of their theories related to the great continent that they believed to exist in the Southern Hemisphere, and that they knew as Terra Australis Incognita.

The theory of Terra Australis had first been put forward in classical times by Greek geographers. One of them, Pomponius Mela, believed it to be so large that he named Ceylon as its northernmost tip. But when Ptolemy drew his world map, he used the southern continent to join southern Africa with eastern Asia, thus making the Indian Ocean into a vast inland sea. During the Middle Ages, the legend of an unknown continent persisted and, with the renewed interest in the world created during the Great Age of Discovery, speculation about it was revived. To men who had no idea of the existence of Australia or Antarctica, such a huge land mass seemed logical, and Gerardus Mercator even wrote that without it nothing would prevent the earth overbalancing and "toppling to destruction amidst the stars".

Mercator depicted Terra Australis on the world map he drew in 1569 for the use of sailors. His imaginary continent extended north from the South Pole into the South Atlantic Ocean, where a broad passage separated it from Africa, and it covered part of what is actually Australia and much of the South Pacific Ocean too. According to Mercator, Tierra del Fuego was a promontory of this southern land. Unlike many of his contemporaries, however, Mercator separated Terra Australis from Nova (New) Guinea, even though no one yet knew of the existence of the Torres Strait.

141

From 1569, when his world map was published, until his death in 1595, Mercator was occupied with two great projects. The first of these was an edition of the work of Ptolemy, which appeared in 1578 and again in 1584. The second was his atlas, the first part of which was published in 1585. It was for the atlas that in 1587 Mercator's son Rumold (1545?-1599) drew a world map.

Rumold divided the world into two hemispheres, the Eastern Hemisphere —the Old World, Europe, Africa, and Asia—and the Western Hemisphere —the New World, or the Americas.

Rumold Mercator's map was in effect a redrawing of his father's 1569 map and, following his father, he filled much of the Southern Hemisphere with a huge continent, Terra Australis, covering much of the

southern Pacific Ocean, and part of Australia too. In fact, at first glance, Rumold's map gives the impression that he actually knew of Australia, for the northern peninsula of his land mass pushes through the western part of the continent, and the west coast of this peninsula is roughly parallel to Australia's west coast. In 1587, however, Australia had not yet been discovered, and

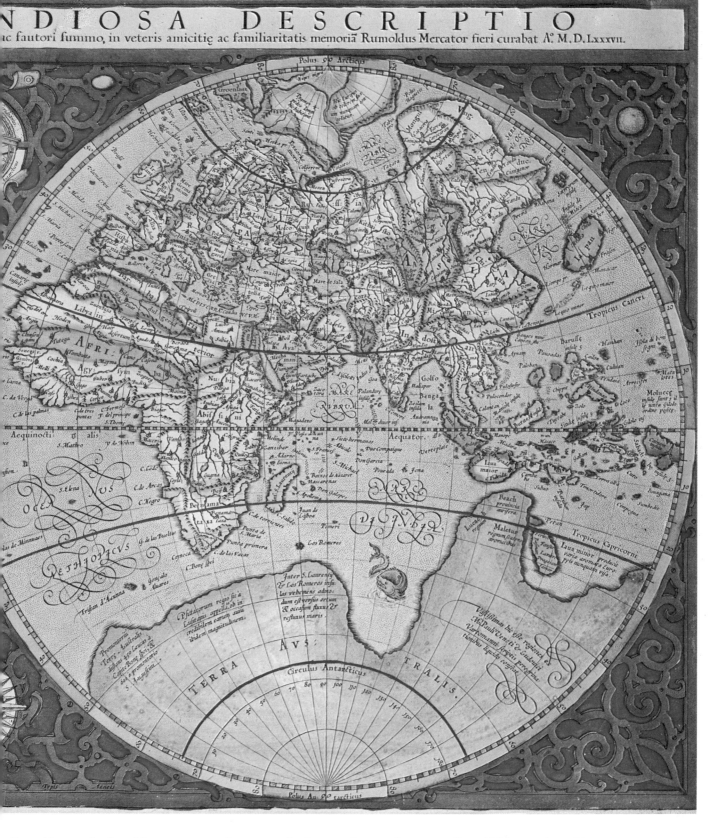

NDIOSA DESCRIPTIO

ac fautori summo, in veteris amicitię ac familiaritatis memoriā Rumoldus Mercator fieri curabat A° M.D.Lxxxvii.

▲ *Rumold Mercator's world map.*

Rumold was basing his map on Marco Polo's book. On the peninsula, he names the kingdom of Lucach, thus identifying it with the country that Polo had written of as Locach, describing it as lying to the south of China, and as a rich and splendid land. Although Polo was probably referring to Siam, or to the Malay Peninsula, both of which he had visited, Europeans thought that

he was referring to the southern continent. Soon, everything that Marco Polo had written of Locach was ascribed to the southern land.

By the time Rumold Mercator drew his map, most Europeans already thought of these tales as referring to a fact, and not to a theory, and explorers set sail in search of a continent whose existence they were convinced of, rather than to see

whether one was there. Their search revealed the Pacific Ocean, and led to the discovery of its islands, and of Australia and New Zealand, but of the legendary southern continent, not a trace was found. Gradually, the Europeans pushed the possible bounds of Terra Australis toward the South Pole until the myth dissolved.

143

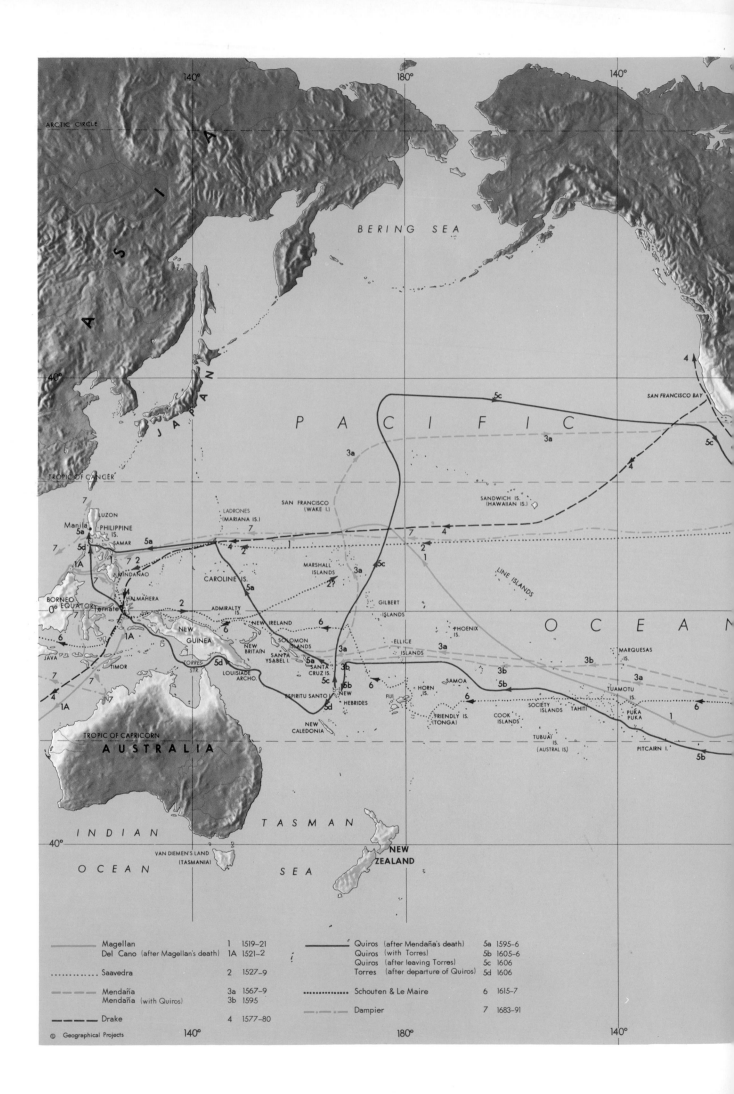

ARCTIC CIRCLE

A S I A

BERING SEA

140°   180°   140°

40°

PACIFIC

JAPAN

SAN FRANCISCO BAY

5c

3a

3a

4

5c

TROPIC OF CANCER

LUZON

Manila
PHILIPPINE
IS.
SAMAR

LADRONES
(MARIANA IS.)

SAN FRANCISCO
(WAKE I.)

SANDWICH IS.
(HAWAIIAN IS.)

4

5c

7

5a

5d

7

1A

7 2

1

5a

4 2

1

4

2

1

7

O   C   E   A   N

MINDANAO

CAROLINE IS.

MARSHALL
ISLANDS

3a

5c

2?

5a

LINE ISLANDS

BORNEO
EQUATOR
0°

HALMAHERA
Ternate

2

ADMIRALTY
IS.

GILBERT
ISLANDS

7

7

1A

NEW
GUINEA

NEW IRELAND

6

6

PHOENIX
IS.

6

JAVA

NEW
BRITAIN

SOLOMON
ISLANDS

ELLICE
ISLANDS

3a

MARQUESAS
IS.

3b

TIMOR

TORRES
STR.

5d

SANTA
YSABEL I.

SANTA
CRUZ IS.

5a

6

3a

5b

3b

3a

7

7

LOUISIADE
ARCHO.

5b

5c

6b

6

HORN
IS.

SAMOA

5b

TUAMOTU
IS.

4

1A

ESPIRITU SANTO

5d

NEW
HEBRIDES

FIJI

6

SOCIETY
ISLANDS

TAHITI

PUKA
PUKA

6

NEW
CALEDONIA

FRIENDLY IS.
(TONGA)

COOK
ISLANDS

1

TROPIC OF CAPRICORN

AUSTRALIA

TUBUAI
IS.
(AUSTRAL IS.)

PITCAIRN I.

5b

INDIAN

TASMAN

40°

OCEAN

VAN DIEMEN'S LAND
(TASMANIA)

SEA

NEW
ZEALAND

	Magellan	1	1519–21		Quiros (after Mendaña's death)	5a	1595–6
	Del Cano (after Magellan's death)	1A	1521–2		Quiros (with Torres)	5b	1605–6
					Quiros (after leaving Torres)	5c	1606
	Saavedra	2	1527–9		Torres (after departure of Quiros)	5d	1606
	Mendaña	3a	1567–9				
	Mendaña (with Quiros)	3b	1595		Schouten & Le Maire	6	1615–7
	Drake	4	1577–80		Dampier	7	1683–91

© Geographical Projects

140°   180°   140°

Across the Pacific

In 1522, **Ferdinand Magellan's** flagship *Victoria*, commanded by **Sebastián del Cano,** reached Spain after its round-the-world voyage. It had opened a new route to the Indies across the Pacific Ocean, and in 1525 Spain sent a seven-ship expedition to the Indies by that route. But one ship only reached the Moluccas and, from Mexico, **Álvaro de Saavedra** (?-1529) was sent by Cortes to its aid. He found its survivors, then turned east along the coast of New Guinea. But adverse winds prevented him returning across the Pacific, and he died on his second attempt to make the voyage back. Not until 1565 did the Spanish make the west-east crossing.

Soon, the dream of a southern continent outweighed the lure of the Indies. To find and settle the southland, and convert the heathen, **Álvaro de Mendaña** (1541-1595) left Peru in 1567. The continent proved elusive, but Mendaña discovered the Solomon Islands. Nearly 30 years later, he made a voyage to colonize the Solomons, but he could not find them. He did, however, discover the Marquesas and the Santa Cruz Islands, where he died. The voyage was continued to the Philippines by his pilot, **Pedro de Quiros** (1565-1615).

Even before Mendaña's second voyage, **Francis Drake** had sailed to find the southern continent for England—and to win booty too. Emerging from the Strait of Magellan, he was blown south of Tierra del Fuego, and concluded that it was not part of Terra Australis. Drake therefore set his course northward, plundering Spanish shipping, and the towns of Valparaíso and Callao. So rich were his rewards that future English expeditions concentrated on plunder, not on discovery. Drake sailed north past San Francisco Bay unsuccessfully seeking the Northwest Passage, then made his way across the Pacific for home.

After Mendaña's death, Quiros became obsessed with Terra Australis, and in 1605, with three ships, he sailed from Peru to find it. But, lacking the strength of will necessary in a leader, Quiros had little success. At Espiritu Santo, in the New Hebrides, his ships were separated, and he sailed back across the Pacific. However, **Luis Vaez de Torres** (?-1613?), the captain of one of the other ships, continued along southern New Guinea, and discovered Torres Strait. He proved New Guinea to be an island, not part of Terra Australis, but, for 200 years, his discovery was generally unknown.

In 1616, the Dutchmen **Willem Schouten** (1567?-1625) and **Jakob le Maire** (1585-1616) discovered Le Maire Strait, southeast of the Strait of Magellan, and first rounded, and named, Cape Horn. Crossing the Pacific, they discovered islands in the Tuamotu and Tonga groups, and the Horn Islands, but in the East Indies they were arrested for infringing the Dutch East India Company's monopoly, and both their ship and goods were confiscated. Some 70 years later, the English buccaneer **William Dampier** (1652-1715) sailed on a voyage of piracy in the Pacific. But it is to the story of Australia that his expedition really belongs.

▼ *Sketch of a ship like Mendaña's.*

The Truth and the Legend

The first mariners to cross the Pacific found no trace of Terra Australis, but their voyages did help to limit its possible bounds. The first steps in piecing together the truth from the legend were made from the Indies, not the Pacific. There, by the early 1600's, the Dutch had firmly established their power.

In 1605, **Willem Jansz** (1570-?) was sent to investigate southern New Guinea. He crossed Torres Strait, and sailed some way down Cape York Peninsula, believing it to be part of New Guinea. Then, in 1616, **Dirk Hartog** (dates unknown), following a new route east from the Cape of Good Hope, made the first of a number of

Dutch landfalls in western Australia. By 1630, the Dutch knew this coast of Australia, which they called New Holland, from the Northwest Cape to Cape Leeuwin.

In 1642, Anthony van Diemen, governor general of the Dutch East Indies, sent **Abel Tasman** (1603-1659) to explore the southern Indian Ocean, and to investigate the relationship between New Guinea and lands farther south. Tasman sailed from Batavia to Mauritius, then struck east to discover Tasmania, which he named Van Diemen's Land. Continuing east, he discovered New Zealand, which he was sure was part of the southern continent. He called it Staaten Land.

Then, via Tonga, Fiji, and northern New Guinea, Tasman made his way home. He had sailed over much of what was thought to be Terra Australis, thus pushing its northern boundary still farther south, but he had not completed his mission. In 1644, therefore, Tasman was sent out again. On this voyage, he circumnavigated the Gulf of Carpentaria, proving it a bay, not the mouth of a strait. He had missed Torres Strait, however, and still believed that the Cape York Peninsula and New Guinea were one. The last questions about the Australian coastline were not resolved until, in 1801-3, **Matthew Flinders** (1774-1814) charted most of the coast.

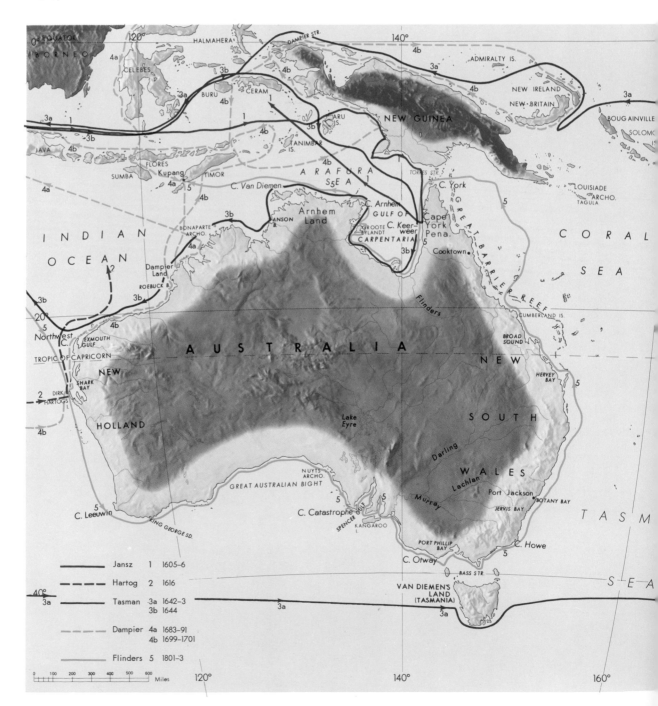

Jansz	1	1605-6
Hartog	2	1616
Tasman	3a	1642-3
	3b	1644
Dampier	4a	1683-91
	4b	1699-1701
Flinders	5	1801-3

During his buccaneering voyage, **William Dampier** spent some months on the northwest coast of New Holland, forming a poor opinion of the country. However, the journals which he published in 1697 aroused much interest and he was given command of an expedition to that land. His intention was to sail around Cape Horn into the Pacific, and to explore the unknown east coast of New Holland, continuing to New Guinea, but he was forced to abandon this plan. By using the Cape of Good Hope route, he missed his opportunity to make great new geographical discoveries, but he did prove that New Britain was divided from New Guinea by a strait.

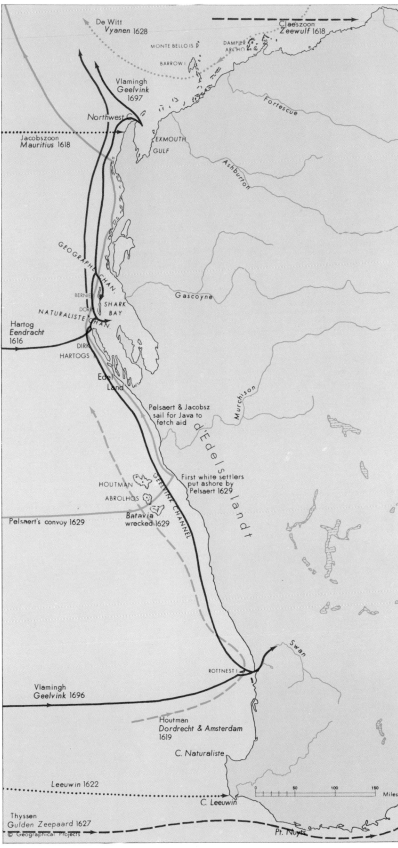

▲ *The map of the west coast of New Holland was pieced together from a number of Dutch landfalls, made following Dirk Hartog's in 1616. The first knowledge of the south coast was* obtained *in 1627 by the* Gulden Zeepaard, *commanded by François Thyssen, which sailed past Point Nuyts (named after a passenger) to the Great Australian Bight.*

147

Completing the Puzzle

By 1700, the Pacific Ocean had been crossed, not once, but many times. Australia, New Zealand, and numerous islands had been discovered. In the century that followed, the work of navigators would be to discover the final pieces of the Pacific puzzle and forge a picture of the ocean. Gradually, the remaining mysteries of the Pacific would be solved.

By 1700, too, the great days of the Dutch in the Pacific were over, although **Jacob Roggeveen** (1659-1729) did make a voyage there in 1721-3. Roggeveen sailed across the Pacific in search of the southern continent, but because he was not employed by the Dutch East India Company, after his voyage he, like Le Maire, was arrested for infringing that company's monopoly. He was, however, eventually compensated for his confiscated ships.

Roggeveen discovered Easter Island, but he found no trace of the southern continent. He remained convinced, however, that such a land mass did exist. In England, too, many believed in Terra Australis, and **John Byron** (1723-1786) set sail in 1764, commissioned to discover unknown lands in the South Atlantic. He, **Philip Carteret** (?-1796), and **Charles Clerke** (1741-1779) found no such lands, but they visited the Falkland Islands, and did discover new islands in the Pacific. Byron was also ordered to seek a strait to the Atlantic on the northwest coast of America, but he seems to have ignored this instruction, perhaps because there was sickness among his men.

The very year that Byron returned to England, one of his ships, the *Dolphin*, sailed again for the Pacific, this time under the command of **Samuel Wallis** (1728-1795). The *Dolphin*, with the *Swallow*, under the command of Philip Carteret, who had sailed with Byron, was to search for the southern continent. After passing through the Strait of Magellan, however, the ships became separated, and continued their voyages alone.

Bad weather prevented Wallis from sailing far in high southern latitudes, and he therefore made his way northwest. During his voyage across the Pacific, he discovered Tahiti—one of the most idyllic South Sea isles. Carteret, meanwhile, searched for islands reported to exist near the Juan Fernández Islands, but he could find no trace of them. He therefore sailed across the Pacific, in constant difficulty because his men were sick, and his ship so rotten that it should never have been allowed to sail. Carteret discovered Pitcairn Island and the Admiralty Islands, and rediscovered Mendaña's Santa Cruz Islands. He also sailed through the Solomons, but failed to identify them with Mendaña's discovery. Struggling home through the Atlantic, the *Swallow* was passed by another vessel north of Ascension Island. It was *La Boudeuse*, commanded by **Louis Antoine de Bougainville** (1729-1811), returning from a voyage around the world.

Bougainville left France in 1766 to hand the Falkland Islands over to the Spanish, and to seek the southern continent. His first task accomplished, he made for the Pacific to start his search. Unable to find any trace of the legendary land mass, Bougainville continued to Tahiti,

▼ *La Pérouse's men on Easter Island.*

	Roggeveen	1	172
	Byron (with Carteret & Clerke)	2	176
	Wallis & Carteret	3	176
	Wallis	3A	176
	Carteret	3B	176

© Geographical Projects

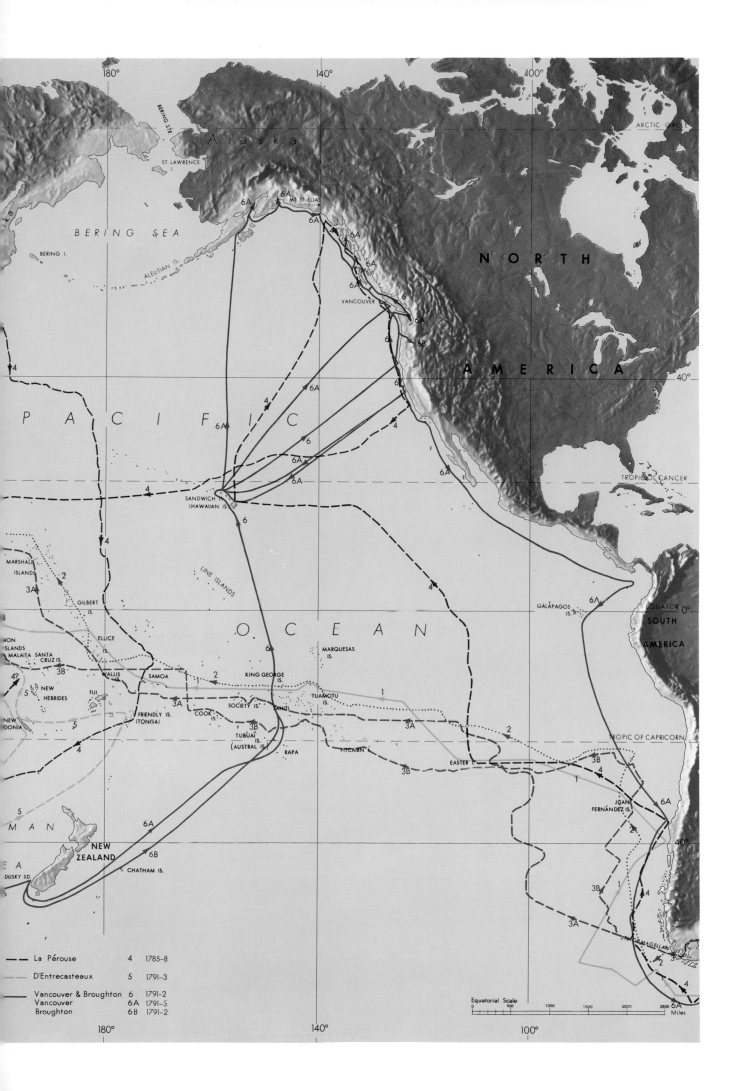

ARCTIC CIRCLE

NORTH

BERING SEA

Alaska

BERING I.

ST. LAWRENCE I.

ALEUTIAN IS.

MT. ST ELIAS

6A

6A

6A

6A

VANCOUVER I.

6

6A

6B

6L

6L

AMERICA

40°

PACIFIC

4

6A

6A

6

6A

6A

6A

4

6A

SANDWICH IS.
(HAWAIIAN IS.)

6

TROPIC OF CANCER

MARSHALL
ISLANDS

2

3A

GILBERT
IS.

LINE ISLANDS

OCEAN

GALÁPAGOS
IS.

6A

EQUATOR 0°

SOUTH

ELLICE
IS.

MARQUESAS
IS.

6

AMERICA

MON
ISLANDS
MALAITA SANTA
CRUZ IS.

3B

WALLIS

SAMOA

1

2

KING GEORGE
IS.

TUAMOTU
IS.

1

4?

5

NEW
HEBRIDES

FIJI

3A

SOCIETY IS.

TAHITI

COOK
IS.

TUBUAI
IS.
(AUSTRAL IS.)

RAPA

3A

2

3B

NEW
DONIA

5

FRIENDLY IS.
(TONGA)

3B

PITCAIRN I.

EASTER I.

3B

3B

4

TROPIC OF CAPRICORN

5

4

JUAN
FERNÁNDEZ IS.

6A

2

5

6A

NEW
ZEALAND

6B

40°

MAN

CHATHAM IS.

3B

1

4

EA

DUSKY SD.

3A

STR. OF MAGELLAN

2

4

6A

Equatorial Scale

0   500   1000   1500   2000   2500

Miles

180°   140°   100°

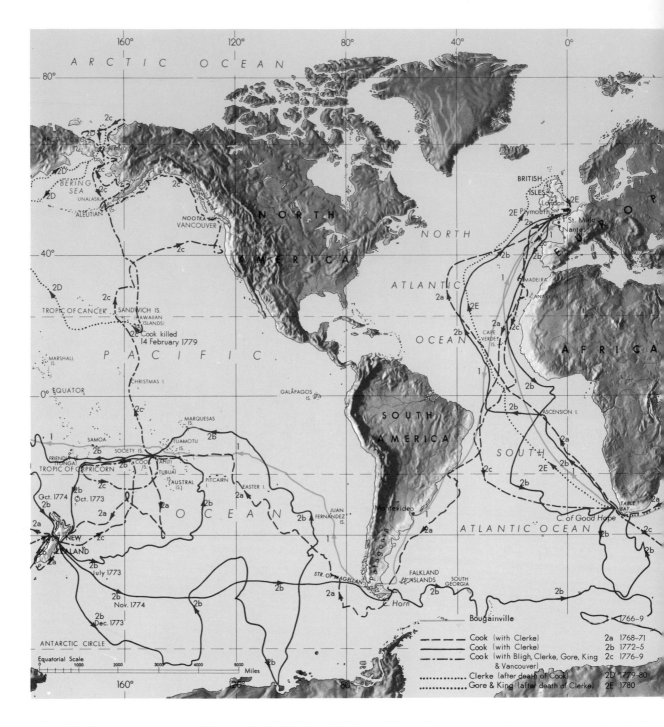

Map legend:

Bougainville 1766–9
Cook (with Clerke) 2a 1768–71
Cook (with Clerke) 2b 1772–5
Cook (with Bligh, Clerke, Gore, King & Vancouver) 2c 1776–9
Clerke (after death of Cook) 2D 1779–80
Gore & King (after death of Clerke) 2E 1780

where, like Europeans on many of the Pacific islands, he suffered from the thieving of the islanders. From Tahiti, he went on to Samoa, then sailed west as far as the Great Barrier Reef. Turning north, he discovered the Louisiade Archipelago, and passed through the Solomon Islands but, like Carteret, he failed to recognize them as such.

Bougainville did not find Terra Australis, but belief in it persisted, for no ship had yet sailed over much of the South Pacific. Even before Bougainville returned to Europe, however, **James Cook** (1728-1779) had left England on the first of three Pacific voyages. In those voyages, the legend of Terra Australis was finally disproved.

The ostensible motive for Cook's first voyage was the observation, for the British Royal Society, of a transit of the planet Venus across the sun. This was due to take place on 3 June 1769, and could be best observed in the central Pacific. Secret orders, however, instructed Cook to continue his voyage in search of the southern continent and, the transit duly recorded at Tahiti, that is what he did.

Cook sailed his ship, *Endeavour*, from Tahiti to New Zealand, and circumnavigating that country, he proved it to be two islands, not part of a southern land. He then continued to the east coast of New Holland, discovering Botany Bay, which he named because so many botanical specimens were found there. Sailing north, Cook discovered the inlet where Port Jackson (present-day Sydney) was later founded and, continuing up the east coast, and around the Cape York Peninsula, he rediscovered Torres Strait. Cook claimed all eastern New Holland for Britain, naming it New South Wales.

Cook's detailed and careful observations, with his charts of Tahiti, neighboring islands, New Zealand, and eastern Australia, gave Europe for the first time a truly accurate picture of those lands. As important as his scientific and geographical investigations, however, was the fact that he was the first commander to prevent scurvy on his ships. On 13 July 1771, Cook returned to Britain but, a year later, he set out again for the Pacific. This time, he sailed east, and pushed much farther south, crossing the Antarctic Circle on three occasions. Thus, he destroyed the possibility that Terra Australis might exist. Cook, however,

150

voyage was continued by Clerke, who charted the Asian coast of the Bering Sea. It was completed, after Clerke's death, by Gore and King.

Little remained to be done in the Pacific after Captain Cook's voyages —thereafter explorers had only to fill in the details on the map. **Jean de la Pérouse** (1741-1788) sailed to discover the prospects for a whale fishery and for the fur trade in the Pacific, and to try to find the Solomon Islands. He called at Easter Island and the Sandwich Islands, then made a coasting voyage down North America, later crossing the Pacific to sail up the Asian coast. From Kamchatka, La Pérouse sailed for Port Jackson. Thence, he set off for the Solomons, and was never seen again.

La Pérouse's disappearance occasioned the dispatch in 1791 of a search party under **Bruni d'Entrecasteaux** (1737-1793) which, although it found no sign of La Pérouse, did finally identify the Solomon Islands, and

▼ *Captain Cook.*

suspected the existence of Antarctica, believing that land lay behind the ice that turned him back. On this voyage, too, Cook rediscovered the Marquesas, which had not been sighted since Mendaña's second voyage. He also explored the New Hebrides and New Caledonia before, on 11 November 1774, finally leaving New Zealand for Cape Horn. Crossing the South Atlantic on his homeward voyage, Cook discovered the island of South Georgia.

In recognition of Cook's achievements, in 1776 he was elected a Fellow of the Royal Society, and awarded its Copley Medal for his conquest of scurvy. In July, five months after his election, he sailed again for the Pacific. His ships were the *Resolution*—with which he had sailed on his second voyage—and the *Dis-*

covery. The master of the *Resolution* was **William Bligh** (1754-1817); the captain of the *Discovery* was **Charles Clerke**, who had sailed with Cook on both of his previous voyages, and Cook's lieutenants were **John Gore** (dates unknown) and **James King** (dates unknown). **George Vancouver** (1757-1798) sailed with Captain Cook as midshipman.

Cook's object on this voyage was to explore the virtually unknown North Pacific, and to find a passage from western North America to the Atlantic. After discovering Christmas Island and the Sandwich Islands (the Hawaiian Islands) on his voyage northward, he coasted North America and passed through Bering Strait. But, returning south, Cook was killed in Hawaii during a quarrel with natives over a stolen boat. The

explored them and the Louisiade Archipelago. Then, in April 1791, George Vancouver sailed with **William Broughton** (dates unknown) for northwestern North America. Before reaching their goal, they charted 300 miles of the south coast of Australia, and discovered the Chatham Islands. By his American surveys, Vancouver proved that no easily navigable Northwest Passage opened along that coast.

In less than 100 years, the Terra Australis theory had been totally demolished. But in its place, a great ocean and many new lands had been found. The exploration of Antarctica—the true southern continent— would be the work of the future. With the exploration of the Pacific completed, it was to Australia and New Zealand that Europe turned.

151

The Birth of a Colony

In January 1788, 12 British ships sailed into Botany Bay. Their mission was not primarily to explore, but to settle. The British government, prevented by the United States newly won independence from shipping convicts to America, had become interested in Australian colonization. The fleet's mission was to found a penal colony at Botany Bay.

Botany Bay, however, proved unsuitable for a settlement, and the British founded their colony at Port Jackson, farther north. The new colony was cut off from the Australian interior by the Blue Mountains, and the first exploration was made along the coast. In 1795, **George Bass** (1771-1812?) and **Matthew Flinders** sailed some way up the Georges River from Botany Bay, then, in 1797, Bass set out to discover whether Van Diemen's Land and Australia were joined. Sailing as far as Western Port, he discovered Bass Strait. The insularity of Van Diemen's Land was proved finally when Flinders and Bass sailed around it in 1798-9.

On his return to Britain in 1800, Flinders was given command of the *Investigator* to make a voyage to Australia. He sailed along the unknown south coast, discovering Spencer Gulf and Gulf St. Vincent, before reaching Encounter Bay. There, he met the French ship, *Le Géographe*, commanded by **Nicolas Baudin** (1750?-1803). Baudin had already charted the rest of the south Australian coast.

From Encounter Bay, Flinders continued to Port Jackson, then north to circumnavigate the Gulf of Carpentaria. He had hoped to complete charting the north coast of Australia, and to map the west coast, but his ship was so rotten that he felt it would

be dangerous to continue. But even so, his voyage was a magnificent achievement: he had sailed around—and carefully mapped—more than three-quarters of the Australian coast. On his voyage back to Britain, Flinders' ship put into Mauritius for repairs, and there Flinders was imprisoned for 6½ years by the French, with whom Britain was at war. When he reached home, he found that Baudin, who had accomplished far less, had claimed Flinders' discoveries as his.

Not until 1813 was the first crossing of the Blue Mountains made by **Gregory Blaxland** (1778-1853), but then others were quick to follow him. The Lachlan and Macquarie rivers were discovered; in 1818, **Hamilton Hume** (1797-1873) discovered Lake Bathurst, and, soon afterward, Lake George, some 10 miles away, was reached. With the discovery of the Murrumbidgee sometime before 1823, the colony's most urgent problem was the charting of the river system of the interior. When, in

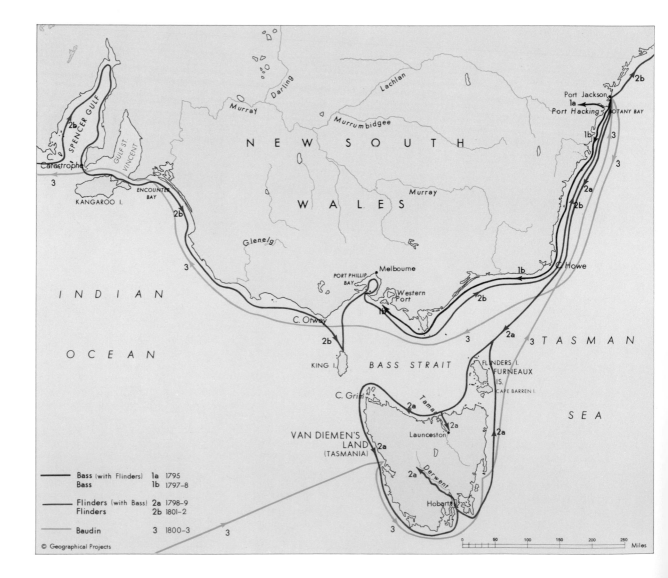

Bass (with Flinders)   1a   1795
Bass   1b   1797-8

Flinders (with Bass)   2a   1798-9
Flinders   2b   1801-2

Baudin   3   1800-3

© Geographical Projects

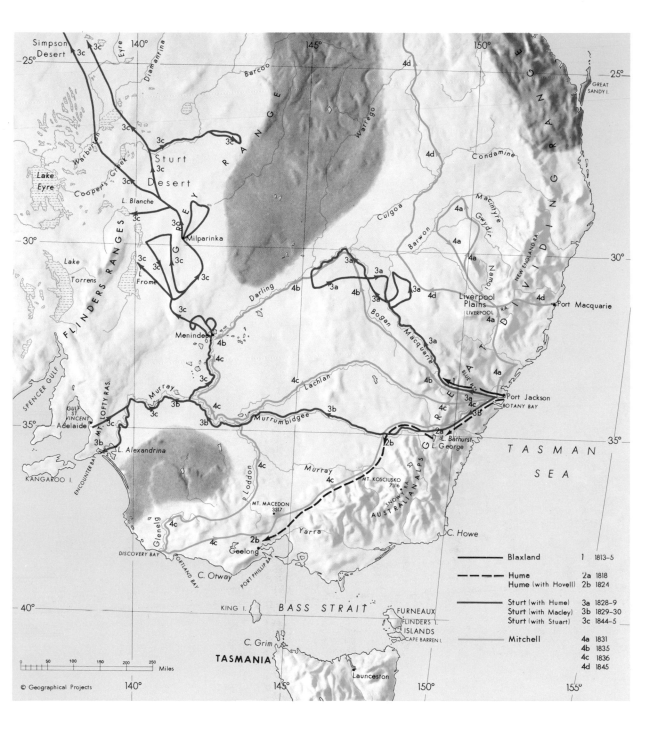

Simpson Desert
3c
Eyre
140°
Barcoo
145°
4d
150°
GREAT SANDY I.
25°
-25°
Diamantina
Warrego
3c
3c
Warburton
3c
Sturt
3c
Desert
Coopers Creek
3c
Condamine
Lake Eyre
3c
3c
L. Blanche
G
R
E
Y
R
A
N
G
E
Culgoa
Barwon
Macintyre
Gwydir
NEW ENGLAND RA.
-30°
30°
3c
Milparinka
3c
3c
3c
3c
FLINDERS RANGES
Lake Torrens
3c
3c
L. Frome
3c
3c
Darling
4b
3a
3a
4b
3a
3a
3a
3a
Namoi
Bogan
Macquarie
Liverpool Plains
LIVERPOOL
4a
4d
Port Macquarie
4d
DIVIDING
Menindee
4b
4c
3c
4c
Murray
3b
3c
4c
Lachlan
4c
3a
4b
4a
4a
GULF ST VINCENT
Adelaide
3c
Murrumbidgee
3b
3b
3b
3b
Port Jackson
BOTANY BAY
3b
3a
4c
4c
3b
BLUE MTS
GREAT
-35°
35°
SPENCER GULF
MT LOFTY RAS.
3b
L. Alexandrina
4c
Murray
Loddon
4c
MT MACEDON 3317
2b
2a
L. Bathurst
L. George
MT KOSCIUSKO 7316
AUSTRALIAN ALPS
SNOWY MTS.
TASMAN
SEA
KANGAROO I.
ENCOUNTER BAY
Glenelg
4c
4c
4c
Yarra
C. Howe
DISCOVERY BAY
4c
2b
Geelong
PORTLAND BAY
C. Otway
PORT PHILLIP BAY

Blaxland   1   1813-5
Hume   2a   1818
Hume (with Hovell) 2b 1824
Sturt (with Hume) 3a 1828-9
Sturt (with Macley) 3b 1829-30
Sturt (with Stuart) 3c 1844-5
Mitchell   4a   1831
                4b   1835
                4c   1836
                4d   1845

-40°
KING I.
BASS STRAIT
FURNEAUX
FLINDERS I.
ISLANDS
CAPE BARREN I.
C. Grim
TASMANIA
Launceston
© Geographical Projects
140°
145°
150°
155°
0 50 100 150 200 250 Miles

1824, Hume traveled with **William Hovell** (1786-1875) from Lake George to Port Phillip Bay, he came back convinced that all the rivers emptied themselves into a huge interior lake.

In 1828, Hume accompanied **Charles Sturt** (1795-1869) on an expedition to find new pastureland. They discovered the Bogan River and followed it to the Darling, then traced part of the Darling's course. The following year, with **George Macley** (1809-1891), Sturt sailed down the Murrumbidgee and on down the Murray. The Murray flows into a lagoon, Lake Alexandrina, whose outlet is to the Indian Ocean, and by this discovery Hume's theory was disproved. With **John Stuart** (1815-1866), in 1844-5, Sturt attempted unsuccessfully to reach the center of Australia. He did, however, complete

◀ *Sturt in the Australian deserts.*

the exploration of the Darling River, and he discovered Sturt Desert and Cooper's Creek.

In 1831, **Thomas Mitchell** (1792-1855) crossed the Liverpool Plains to the Namoi River, then continued north over the Gwydir to the Barwon (Macintyre). Four years later, he traveled down the Darling. The year 1836 found him on the Lachlan, Murrumbidgee, and Murray rivers, and he established their relationship, and that of the Murray to the Darling. Returning up the Murray, past its junction with the Murrumbidgee, Mitchell crossed from the Loddon to the Glenelg. In 1845, Mitchell set out north over the headstreams of the Darling and, on his return, discovered the upper course of the Barcoo River.

153

Into the Interior

While explorers were pushing outward from the British colony in southeastern Australia, the first steps were being taken toward opening up other parts of the country. Perth was founded on the west coast in 1829, and from Perth, in 1837, **George Grey** (1812-1898) sailed north to Brunswick Bay. He had intended to make the return journey overland, but his expedition had to be abandoned. Two years later, Grey set out again. This time, he landed at Shark Bay, and discovered the Gascoyne River, but lack of food forced him to turn back to Perth. During the return voyage, his ships were wrecked, and he completed the journey overland.

In South Australia, meanwhile, in 1839 **Edward Eyre** (1815-1901) sighted Lake Torrens from Mount Eyre, and that same year he explored the coast of Australia from Port Lincoln to Streaky Bay. In 1840, Eyre tried to travel north but he was unable to penetrate the salt lakes, which he believed formed a continuous horseshoe around the head of Spencer Gulf. This theory was not disproved until 1858 when **Peter Warburton** (1813-1889), on his second expedition in South Australia, traveled over the bridge of land separating Lake Torrens from Lake Eyre. That same year, **John Stuart,** Sturt's traveling companion, explored between Lake Torrens, Stuarts Range, and Streaky Bay, and in 1859, west of Lake Eyre, he discovered the Neales River. Seven years later, east of Lake Eyre, Peter Warburton discovered the river that is named after him.

Eyre followed his South Australian journeys with a greater feat of endurance—a trek from Fowlers Bay to Albany over almost waterless land. From Moreton Bay on the east coast, in 1844-5, **Ludwig Leichhardt** (1813-1848) traveled to Port Essington harbor in the north. He discovered much good pastureland, and many rivers and mountains, but he was neither a good organizer nor leader, and when, in 1846-7, he tried to walk around three sides of Australia, his expedition came to grief. Undeterred, in 1848 he set out to cross Australia. He was never seen again.

No luckier than Leichhardt, although a better leader and administrator, was **Edmund Kennedy** (1818-1848). In 1847, Kennedy was sent to discover which way the Barcoo flowed, and this he accomplished. In 1848 he was sent out again to explore Queensland. But, in the north of Cape York Peninsula, he was murdered by Aborigines when seeking help for his starving men, all but two of whom were later found dead.

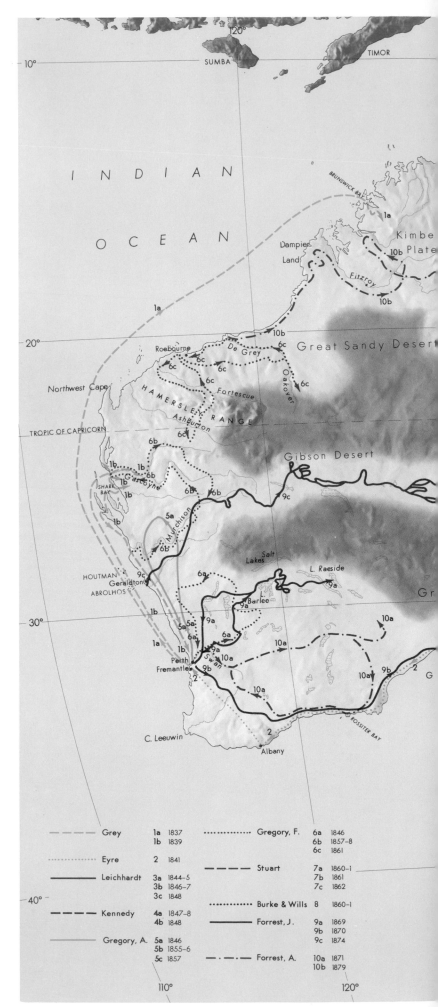

	Grey	1a	1837		Gregory, F.	6a	1846
		1b	1839			6b	1857-8
						6c	1861
	Eyre	2	1841				
					Stuart	7a	1860-1
	Leichhardt	3a	1844-5			7b	1861
		3b	1846-7			7c	1862
		3c	1848				
					Burke & Wills	8	1860-1
	Kennedy	4a	1847-8				
		4b	1848		Forrest, J.	9a	1869
						9b	1870
	Gregory, A.	5a	1846			9c	1874
		5b	1855-6				
		5c	1857		Forrest, A.	10a	1871
						10b	1879

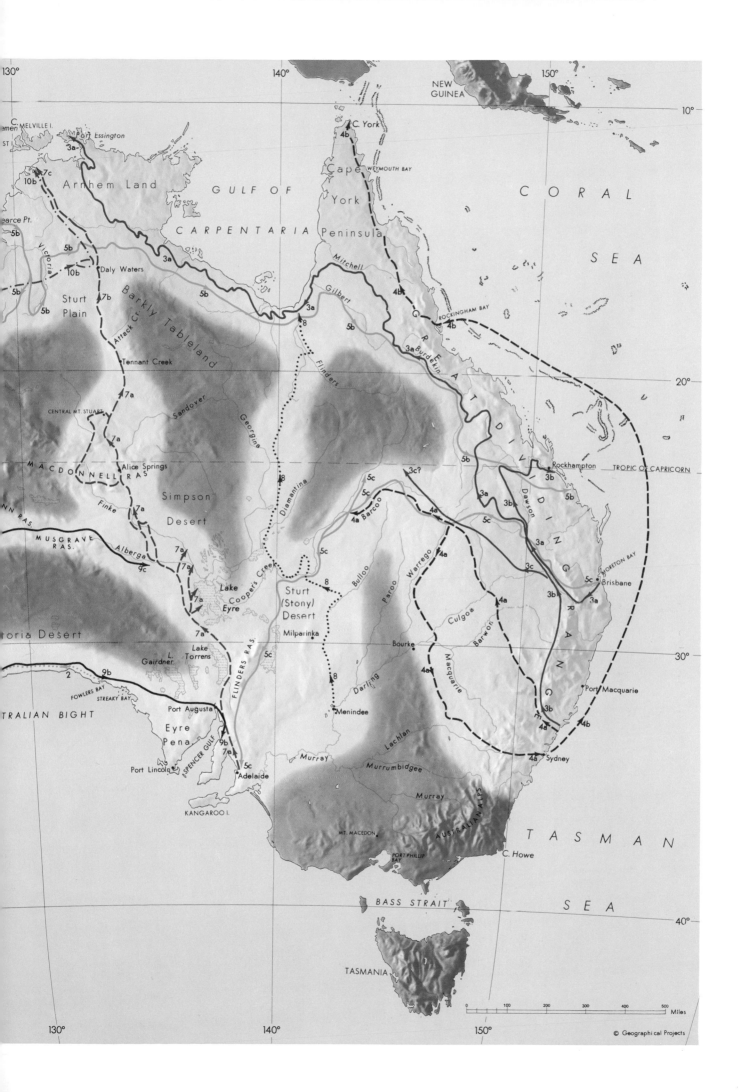

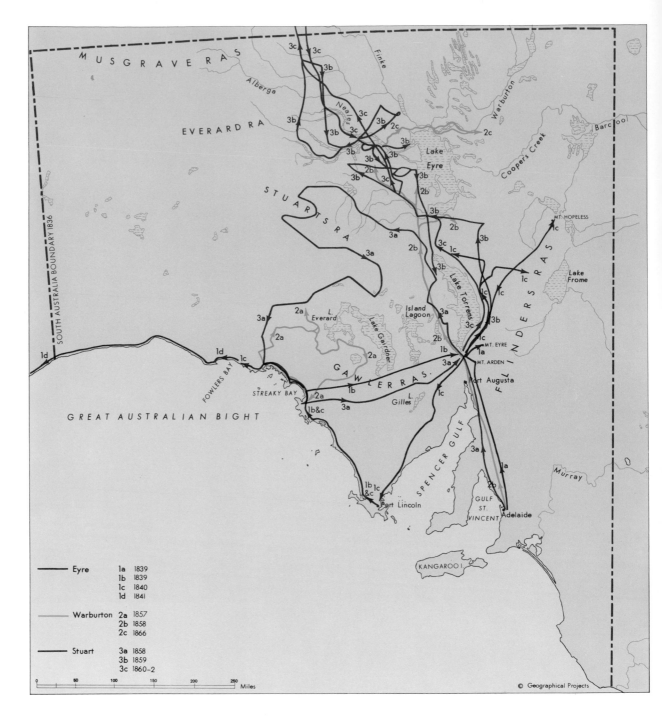

—— Eyre	1a	1839
	1b	1839
	1c	1840
	1d	1841
—— Warburton	2a	1857
	2b	1858
	2c	1866
—— Stuart	3a	1858
	3b	1859
	3c	1860–2

Two brothers, **Augustus** and **Frank Gregory** (1819-1905 and 1821-1888), did much to open up unknown Australia. Augustus Gregory made his first journey in 1846 from Perth to north of the Murchison River, then in 1855-6, in northern Australia, he discovered, and traced, Sturt Creek. From Sturt Creek, he traveled to the Victoria River, then along the south side of the Gulf of Carpentaria. He followed the Burdekin south, and eventually emerged on the east coast. In 1857, Gregory traveled from Brisbane to Adelaide, exploring the upper Barcoo River. Frank Gregory's expeditions were made in west and northwest Australia, and he discovered several fertile regions suitable for settlement.

In 1860, the government of South Australia offered a prize of £2000

▲ *Ernest Giles.*

(some $4800) to the first man to cross Australia from south to north. In the event, however, **Robert Burke** (1820-1861) and **William Wills** (1834-1861), who were the first to complete the crossing, did not live to collect their reward. Burke and Wills left Menindee in October 1860 and in November, from Cooper's Creek— the lower Barcoo River— they made a dash for the north coast with two companions. In February 1861, they were nearly at the mouth of the Flinders River, but did not continue to the sea because their supplies were running short. On the return journey, one of their companions died, and when the survivors reached Cooper's Creek, they found that the supply party they had expected to meet them had left. Before help arrived, Burke and Wills too were dead.

John Stuart also hoped to be first to cross Australia, but he was unable to achieve his ambition on his first two attempts. He chose a route which lay to the west of that followed by Burke and Wills and in April 1861 he reached the center of Australia, naming a high mountain Central Mount Sturt, after Charles Sturt. The name was later changed to Stuart, after its discoverer. Stuart nearly reached Attack Creek on this occasion, and later that year pushed north past the creek. At last, on 24 July 1862, he managed to reach the sea. Within 10 years, along his route, the Central Overland Telegraph Line was laid.

By the time the Overland Telegraph Line was opened, most of eastern Australia was known, and explorers were concentrating on the virgin country in the west. In 1872, **Ernest Giles** (1835-1897) traveled up the Finke River into the Macdonnell Ranges, but lack of water forced him to return to the Telegraph Line. The following year, with **Alfred Gibson** (?-1873),

Giles traveled into the fringes of the Gibson Desert, which he named after his companion, who disappeared there. That same year, too, **William Gosse** (1842-1881) attempted to cross western Australia, and he discovered Ayers Rock before being forced to give up. Peter Warburton, however, did manage to make a crossing that year.

The first west-east crossing of western Australia was made in 1874 by **John Forrest** (1847-1918)—later Lord Forrest, and the first premier of Western Australia. In 1869, Forrest had traveled from Perth to Lake Raeside, passing over rich goldfields without knowing it, and in 1870 he had traced in reverse Eyre's route along the Great Australian Bight. Forrest's brother **Alexander** (1849-1901) also made two journeys of exploration—the first from the Swan River to the Great Victoria Desert, and the second from the De Grey River to the coast west of Arnhem Land. On this second journey, he dis-

covered a new area of pastureland.

In 1875-6, Ernest Giles achieved his cherished dream of an inland east-west crossing of western Australia. On his return journey, he traveled through the Gibson Desert, searching unsuccessfully for traces of his missing friend. Twenty years later, two crossings of the deserts were made in a south to north direction. **Lawrence Wells** (1860-1938) led a party from Lake Barlee to the Fitzroy River, while **David Carnegie** (1871-1900) made his journey farther east and reached Sturt Creek.

Little more than a hundred years had passed since the first settlers reached Australia, yet in that short time the continent had been explored. Work still remained for pioneers in the search for pastureland and for minerals, but, by the turn of the century, few areas were entirely unknown. Parallel with exploration, too, settlement had gone forward, and now Australians could take advantage of the vast resources of their land.

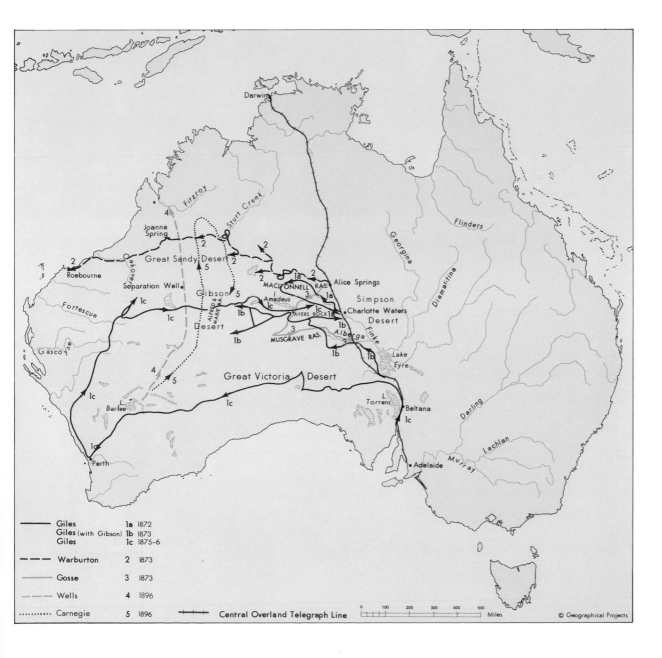

		Giles	1a	1872
Giles (with Gibson)	1b	1873
Giles	1c	1875-6
– – –	Warburton	2	1873
––––	Gosse	3	1873
– – –	Wells	4	1896
··········	Carnegie	5	1896

Central Overland Telegraph Line

0 100 200 300 400 500 Miles

© Geographical Projects

New Zealand

The navigator *Abel Tasman* returned to Batavia in 1643 convinced that he had discovered the southern continent. East of Van Diemen's Land, he had come upon a formerly unknown land mass, and he had sailed north for hundreds of miles along its coast. Surely such a discovery could only be a peninsula of an as yet otherwise unknown southern land.

More than a hundred years passed before the truth was learned about Staaten Land, Tasman's discovery, for it was not until **James Cook's** first voyage that its coast was explored. Cook discovered that Tasman's "land mass" was in reality two islands, and he learned much about the country, and was impressed by the prospects for European settlement. On his later voyages, Cook returned to that country to revictual.

As Cook had found, New Zealand —as Staaten Land became known— was an excellent watering place, and soon sealing and whaling ships were regularly visiting Dusky Sound and the Bay of Islands. Traders arrived from Australia, for the country was rich in flax and timber, and in their wake came the missionaries to convert the Maori to Christianity. The first mission station was founded in 1814 at the Bay of Islands by **Samuel Marsden** (1765-1838), chaplain to the colony of New South Wales. Marsden

was not really interested in geographical discovery, but he made three important journeys during his seven visits to New Zealand before 1837.

In 1831, Henry Williams, another missionary, visited a Maori village at Lake Rotorua, and his brother **William Williams** (dates unknown) walked right across North Island in 1839. Two years later, **William Colenso** (1811-1899) traveled from Poverty Bay to the Bay of Islands, and in 1843-4 he circled Hawke Bay, and visited Lake Waikaremoana. In 1847, Colenso visited Lake Taupo in the center of North Island, and penetrated the Ruahine Range.

Sponsored by the New Zealand Company, the first settlers arrived in 1839 on board the *Tory*, and they established their colony at what is now Wellington. That same year, Ernst Dieffenbach climbed Mount Egmont, and in 1840 New Zealand Company surveyors began exploring North Island. Through their work,

and the expansion of settlement, North Island was made known.

In South Island, however, progress was slower—there, travel is more difficult, for the Southern Alps form a barrier down the island and, even below the peaks and glaciers, the undergrowth is dense and the rivers swift. In 1843, **Thomas Brunner** (1821-1874) traveled inland from Tasman Bay, and two years later, with **Charles Heaphy** (1820-1881), **William Fox** (1812-1893), and **Ekuhu** (dates unknown), a Maori guide, he visited lakes Rotoiti and Rotoroa. The following year, he, Heaphy, and Ekuhu traveled south to the Taramakau River. At the end of 1846, Brunner set out on what has become known as "The Great Journey". It led him along the courses of the Buller and Grey rivers, and south to Tititira Head.

Once exploration had begun in South Island, settlement soon followed. The gold rush to the province of Otago, in southeastern South Island, in 1861, opened up that region, and in that same year the first recorded exploration of a New Zealand glacier —the Forbes—took place. In that year, too, surveys began in South Island and, as they progressed, they removed the blanks from the map.

▼ *New Zealand forests.*

11 The Ends of the Earth

The extreme north and the extreme south of the earth are covered by an ocean, and by a continent. There, the ice lies deep winter and summer alike, and the cold is always intense. There, the northernmost and southernmost points of our planet are situated—the ends of the earth's axis, the North and South Poles. There, for centuries, brave men have battled to explore the ends of the earth.

Explorers traveling north and south have found themselves in a cold, unfamiliar world, a world which in winter is bleak and dark. Plant and animal life are limited, particularly in the Antarctic where they are almost nonexistent. The climate is so harsh, and the dangers so numerous, that

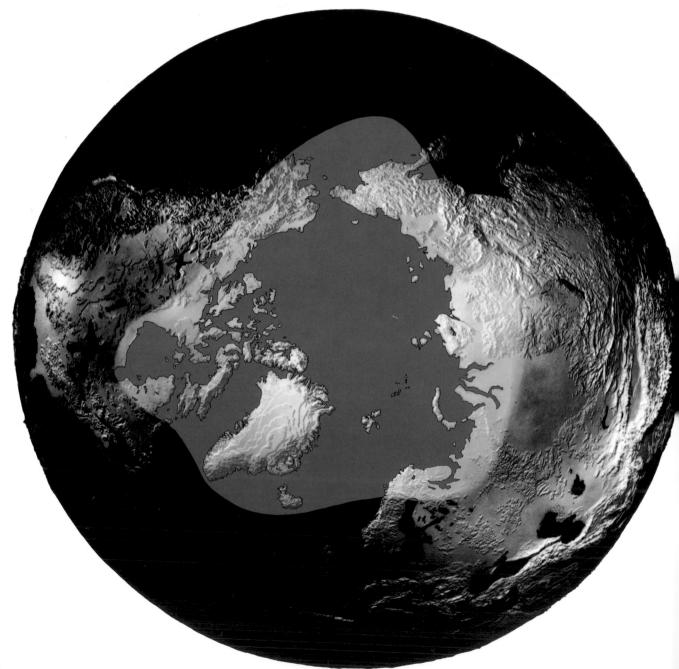

for some of its explorers, the frozen world has meant death.

After the cold, the ice is the most notable characteristic of the polar regions. The Arctic Ocean is covered by an ice pack many feet thick. In summer, with warmer weather, the outer floes break off, and great chasms appear in the main pack, so that a traveler who took to the pack by sledge in summer would be in as much danger as one entering it by ship in winter. The continent of Antarctica, with the exception of a few mountains, is entirely ice covered. From its shores, a number of vast shelves of never-melting sea ice jut out into the polar waters. Pack ice surrounds the continent, and sometimes this ice does not melt from one year to the next. Icebergs, too, break off the Antarctic icecap and drift north.

The exploring season is short in the Arctic and the Antarctic, not only because of the climate, but also owing to the phenomenon of "eternal night". At the Arctic and Antarctic circles, on one day in midwinter, the sun never rises, and the nearer one travels to the poles, the longer the period of darkness becomes. At the North and South Poles, the eternal night lasts for six months. During the polar winters, explorers' ships became icebound, and in the Arctic travelers would winter in the ice, continuing their expeditions in the spring. If supplies ran short during a land journey, particularly in the Antarctic, there was little hope of survival, for the land could not support life.

In parts of the Arctic and Antarctic, too, direction finding is difficult. Compass needles do not point to the true North and South Poles, but to the North and South Magnetic Poles, which are over 1000 miles away. In these areas, compasses are unreliable. Both the search to locate the magnetic poles, and the race to be first at the North and South Poles would in time occupy explorers. But at first it was the search for a Northwest or Northeast Passage that led explorers north.

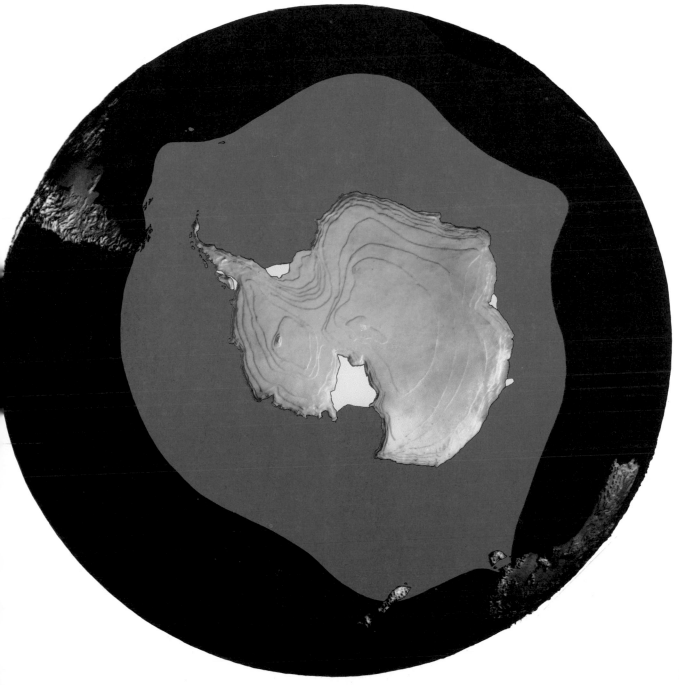

In the 1500's, although little definite was known about the polar regions, cartographers still contrived to include them on their maps. When, in 1595, four months after Gerardus Mercator's death, his son Rumold issued the third part of Mercator's atlas, a chart of the Arctic was among the 18 maps. Rumold took his picture of the Arctic from an inset in his father's world map of 1569. This had, in turn, been based on even older records, among them an account by one Jacob Croyen, and a work called *Inventio Fortunatae,* whose author may have visited Greenland and America. Both are lost, but their contents survive in the Mercators' maps.

At the center of Rumold Mercator's map lies the North Pole—the Arctic Pole as he called it—which he depicted as a "black and very high rock". The pole rises from a sea, and the sea is enclosed by islands divided by four great channels. Through these, its waters issue into an outer "icy sea". Thus, from Rumold's map, it appears that it would not only be possible to sail from Europe to Asia via a Northeast or a Northwest Passage but also directly over the North Pole.

The icy sea from Greenland east to the Ob (Oby) River contains many islands. Greenland is mapped in some detail, as is Iceland, and Novaya Zemlya is shown in outline, while Rumold also depicts other, mysterious lands. One, southwest of Iceland, is called Frisland. This was the name Martin Frobisher had given to Greenland and, after Greenland had been identified, Frisland was depicted on maps as a separate land. The other, north of Lapland and west of Novaya Zemlya, is called "S. Hugo Willoughbe's Land". Willoughby was one of the first Europeans to penetrate the Arctic, and he is believed to have reached Novaya Zemlya before he was wrecked and drowned. Here, however, his landfall is shown as a separate island, near what is actually Spitzbergen.

Although Asia had not yet been proved to be separated from America, Rumold divides them by a strait called Anian. North of the Strait of Anian, he marks two magnetic poles, one almost in the channel issuing from the polar sea. Nothing was then known of northern North America, and there Rumold's map is sketchy. Strangely, however, he names the northern point of the continent "California", although present-day California is far to the south.

162

Europe continued in ignorance of the exact nature of Antarctica long after European sailors had begun opening up the Arctic in the north. The persistence of the theory of Terra Australis long prohibited geographers from looking objectively at the Antarctic regions, and such discoveries as were made were usually believed to be part of the southern land. Even in 1739, when the French geographer Philippe Buache (1700-1773) drew his map of the earth from the South Pole to the Tropic of Capricorn, the focal point of his map was still a huge continent surrounding the pole.

Buache was a member of the Royal French Academy of Sciences, and son-in-law of Guillaume Delisle, at that time cartographer to the king of France. His principal interest in geography was to find a system governing the earth's structure. In 1754 he published an *Atlas Physique*. In it, he included a revision of his 1739 map of Antarctica, still dated 1739, but annotated as revised in 1754. Buache deduced from the geography of the Arctic that the South Pole, like the North Pole, lay in a frozen sea. This sea was surrounded by a huge continent, cut by two

vast channels. He believed that, through those channels, the ices of the polar sea flowed north to emerge as icebergs in the ocean.

Buache's continent, based as it is on the Terra Australis legend, is far larger than Antarctica. Most of that continent is contained within the Antarctic Circle, and no point reaches north of latitude 60° south. Buache's continent, however, in several places stretches north to 50° south, and once nearly to 30° south. There, it includes New Zealand, of which part of the coast was known.

On his map, Buache shows the "new discoveries" made south of the Cape of Good Hope in the very year it was first published, by a French expedition under the command of Lozier Bouvet. On Bouvet's map and memoirs, Buache based that section of his own map. An account of Bouvet's voyage is printed in the left-hand margin, and a more detailed chart of one of his discoveries at the bottom of the right-hand side. Bouvet had named his landfall Cap de la Circoncision, and Buache therefore assumed that it was part of the southern continent, and showed it as a cape. Antarctica does not, however,

stretch so far north, and Bouvet had in fact discovered the island that is now named after him. Buache's map includes too the routes followed by Bouvet's ships, as well as those of earlier voyages to the southern seas. The expeditions of Magellan, Quiros, and of Le Maire and Schouten are marked, as are those of Tasman and Dampier. The portion of the coastline of Australia (New Holland) then known is depicted, together with the southern part of Van Diemen's Land.

Buache notes on his map his theories, and information which might be helpful in drawing geographical conclusions. The ocean around the South Pole is marked as "conjectured", while on the continental coast east of New Zealand a note reads that in that region there must be a mountain range, where the rivers rise that provide the ice in the interior sea. On Bouvet's route north of Cap de la Circoncision there is a record of soundings taken between 3 December 1738 and 5 February 1739 in which no bottom was found at 180 fathoms (1080 feet). Detailed as Buache's map is, however, less than 40 years after its first publication it was rendered obsolete by Cook's discoveries.

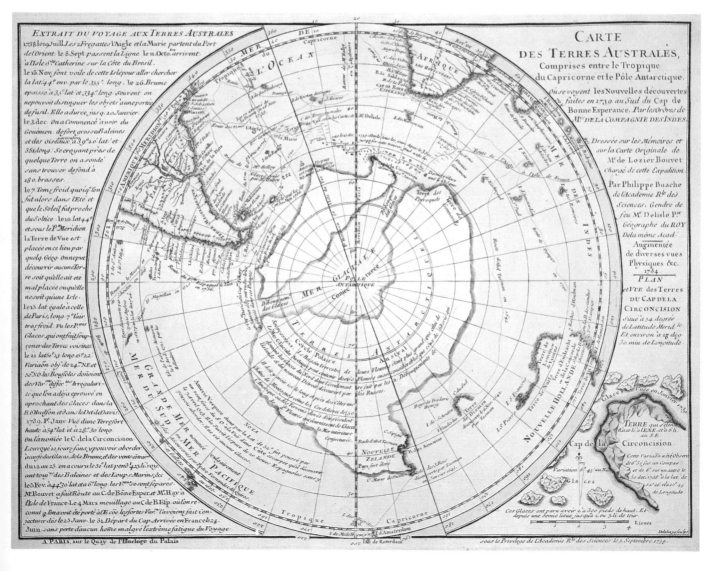

The Frozen North

The earth was round. Ferdinand Magellan had proved it by his circumnavigation, and to the nations of Europe, seeking a new route to the Indies, his discovery pointed the way to other, untried paths. If Magellan could sail southwest around the Americas, why should there not also be a passage to the northward? The search for such a passage continued long after the race to the East was over, and by the seamen who sailed north, the Arctic regions were first explored.

When Willem Barents' ship became icebound off Novaya Zemlya in 1596, he and his men were forced to winter in the Arctic. The Dutchmen built a hut to live in, and the wood they needed for building and for fuel had to be ◀ dragged for eight miles.

Seeking a Northeast Passage, Sir Hugh Willoughby probably reached Novaya Zemlya and, sailing west, Martin Frobisher discovered Baffin Island and reached Hudson Strait. Then, in three voyages west, **John Davis** (1550?-1605) opened up the Greenland coast north to Sanderson's Hope, and coasted America from Baffin Island to Newfoundland. He returned convinced that the Northwest Passage did exist.

In 1594, the Dutch commissioned an expedition to sail to China via Novaya Zemlya, and **Willem Barents** (1550?-1597) reached northern Novaya Zemlya before ice forced him back. The other members of the expedition, with **Jan van Linschoten** (1563-1611)—whose *Itinerario* spurred the Dutch to sail to the Indies—attempted a more southerly route. When they reached the open waters of the Kara Sea, they thought the way to the East was clear. The following year, therefore, it was by Linschoten's route that Barents and Linschoten sailed. The ice was bad, and they only reached Vaigach Island, but in 1596 Barents sailed north again. He discovered Spitzbergen and Bear Island, and rounded the northern tip of Novaya Zemlya, but his ship became icebound, and he and his men were forced to winter there. Almost all survived that unprepared Arctic

wintering, but Barents died on the return journey. His companions, however, did eventually reach home.

Henry Hudson made his first voyages in search of a northeasterly route to China. In 1607, he reached Spitzbergen and, on his homeward voyage, discovered Jan Mayen, and the following year he visited Novaya Zemlya. In 1609, Hudson sailed west to North America, and in 1611, seeking the North*west* Passage, he met his death in Hudson Bay.

When **Vitus Bering** sailed in 1728 from Kamchatka, he sought not a northern passage, but to discover whether a strait really divided Russia from America. With **Alexei Chirikov** and **Martin Spanberg,** he sailed through Bering Strait, then, 12 years later, he and Chirikov set out to sail to the northwest coast of America. Their ships became separated, but both reached America. Returning, Bering was shipwrecked on Bering Island, where he died.

In 1817, improved climatic conditions rendered the polar seas relatively ice free and, after an interval of more than 200 years, British interest in the Northwest Passage was renewed. In 1818, a twofold expedition was commissioned. **John Ross** (1777-1856) and **William Parry** (1790-1855) were to seek the Northwest Passage, while **David Buchan** (dates unknown) and

John Franklin (1786-1847) sailed to the North Pole. Ross and Parry, with Ross's nephew **James Clark Ross** (1800-1862), sailed into Baffin Bay, and reached the entrance to Lancaster Sound, but Ross would go no farther west, for he believed the sound was merely a bay. Buchan and Franklin were beset by ice north of Spitzbergen and were forced to turn back.

To succeed where Ross had "failed", Parry sailed in 1819 on the first of three expeditions in search of the Northwest Passage. By his voyages, the map of the Canadian Arctic was transformed. In 1819, he won a £5000 prize for passing the 110° meridian west of Greenwich and, during his voyages, he discovered many islands and waterways. He was the first Arctic explorer to extend sea voyages by land exploration, and he made remarkable efforts to keep his men healthy and amused during the Arctic winters. In 1827, Parry tried unsuccessfully to reach the North Pole and he traveled farther north than any man before.

In 1829, John Ross made another expedition to the Canadian Arctic, with James Clark Ross as second-in-command. Four winters were spent in the Arctic, and important explorations were carried out by J. C. Ross on Boothia Peninsula and King William Island. Ross fixed the position of the North Magnetic Pole.

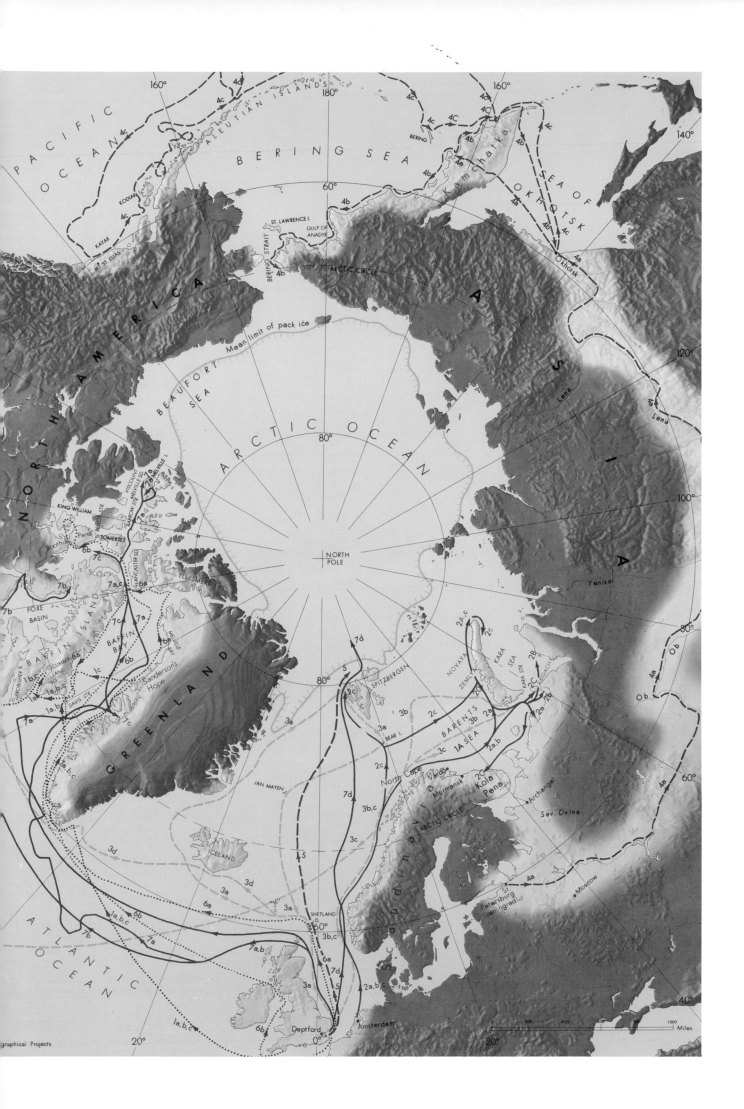

graphical Projects

The Search for Franklin

During the winter of 1846-7, Britain became anxious about an expedition commanded by **Sir John Franklin** that had sailed to find the Northwest Passage in May 1845. The expedition had not been heard of since July, the year it sailed.

To Britain, Franklin was one of the most renowned of Arctic explorers. After his voyage with Buchan, he had traveled overland with **George Back** (1796-1878) and **John Richardson** (1787-1865) from Hudson Bay to the Arctic coast of Canada, which he had mapped first from the mouth of the Coppermine to Bathurst Inlet, and later from the Mackenzie to Cape Beechey. Franklin was knighted for his achievements, and when an attempt on the Northwest Passage was mooted in 1845, he became leader.

Finding Barrow Strait blocked by ice, Franklin sailed north between Devon and Cornwallis islands. He returned to winter on Beechey Island, and in spring he pushed south. North of King William Island, his ships were beset by ice. They were never freed.

Sledging parties from Franklin's ships explored King William Island, and in a cairn at the north they left a message recording the progress of the expedition. At that time, all was well, but in June 1847 Franklin died. After another winter in the ice, **F. R. M. Crozier** (?-1848), now in command, decided to abandon ship. In April 1848, 105 men set out for Back River. Not one reached his goal.

In 1847, the first search party was sent to look for Franklin. John Richardson and **John Rae** (1839-1893) were to examine the coast east from the Mackenzie, and the strait between Victoria Island and the mainland, but ice prevented them traveling beyond the mouth of the Coppermine. Meanwhile, **Sir James Clark Ross,** with **Robert McClure** (1807-1873) and **Leopold McClintock** (1819-1907), had tried to follow Franklin's proposed route. The ice was so bad that the ships only reached Somerset Island, but sledging trips were made farther south.

In 1850, with **Richard Collinson** (1811-1883), McClure sailed via Bering Strait for the Arctic, but their ships became separated, and each searched alone. McClure sledged to the head of Prince of Wales Strait and, seeing open water ahead, realized that a Northwest Passage was found. Off Banks Island, however, his ship became icebound in 1851, and he and his crew were only rescued by Sir Edward Belcher's expedition in 1853. Collinson entered Prince of Wales Strait 10 days after McClure had left it, then rounded the southwest corner of Banks Island before returning to

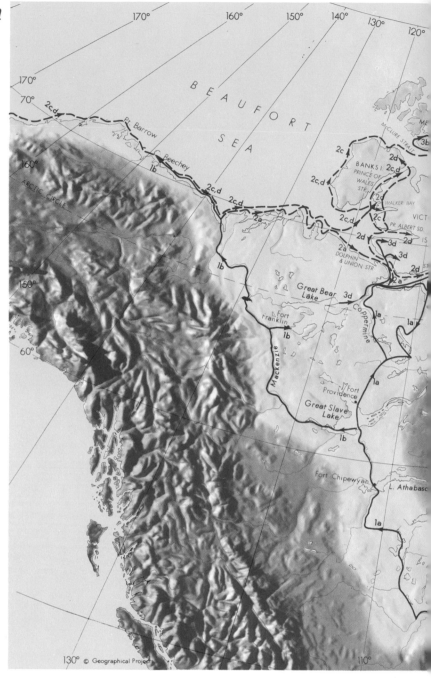

winter in Walker Bay. Next year, Collinson continued to Dease Strait, and sledges reached Gateshead Island from his ship.

In 1850, from Britain, **Horatio Austin** (1801-1865), **Erasmus Ommanney** (dates unknown), and **William Penny** (dates unknown) sailed for the Arctic with **Sir John Ross** and McClintock while from America **E. J. de Haven** (dates unknown) and **Elisha Kane** (1820-1857) joined the search. At Beechey Island, relics were found of Franklin, but sledging trips from the British ships revealed no further trace.

It was John Rae who first discovered the fate of Franklin. In 1851, he traveled from Great Bear Lake to Prince Albert Sound, then continued to Gateshead Island. Two years later, he set out from Repulse Bay for Bellot Strait. Rae met an Eskimo, who told him of the deaths of a party of white

The Death of Franklin, by Thomas Smith, mistakenly depicts Franklin as the last of his company alive. ▶

men, and from the Eskimos he bought items belonging to Franklin's men.

In 1854, the British government officially abandoned the search for Franklin. Not so Lady Franklin, who had already fitted out four expeditions to find her husband and who, in 1857, dispatched the *Fox* to the Arctic under Leopold McClintock. His expedition finally revealed the truth. The message left by Franklin's sledging party was found, with a note added that Franklin was dead, and the ships abandoned. Records of the expedition, and some skeletons, were discovered too. Twelve years after Franklin's death, the mystery had been solved. In those 12 years, the Canadian Arctic had been explored.

———— Franklin	1a 1819–22
(with Back & Richardson)	
Franklin	1b 1825–7
(with Back & Richardson)	
Franklin (with Crozier)	1c 1845–7
Winter Sledging parties	1D 1847
Crozier (with remaining	1E 1848
members of expedition on foot)	
● Position of ships in successive winters	
— — — 1st. Search expeditions:	
Richardson (with Rae)	2a 1847–9
Ross, James C.	2b 1848–9
(with McClure & McClintock)	
McClure	2c 1850–5
Collinson	2d 1850–4
———— 2nd. Search expeditions:	
British ships (with Austin,	3a 1850–1
McClintock, John Ross,	
Ommanney & Penny)	
Sledging parties from	3b 1851
British ships	
American ships	3c 1850–1
(with De Haven & Kane)	
Rae	3d 1851
—·—·— 3rd. Search expeditions:	
Rae	4 1853–4
············ Final Search expeditions:	
McClintock	5a 1857–9
McClintock & sledging	5b 1858–9
parties	

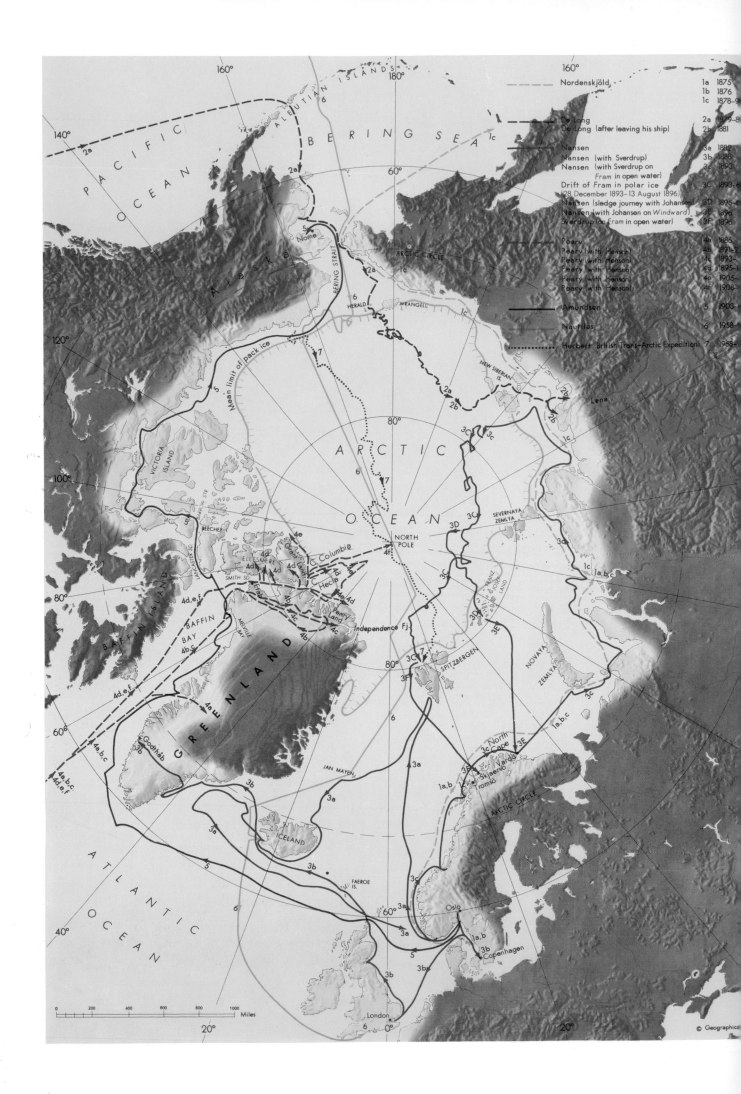

Toward the Pole

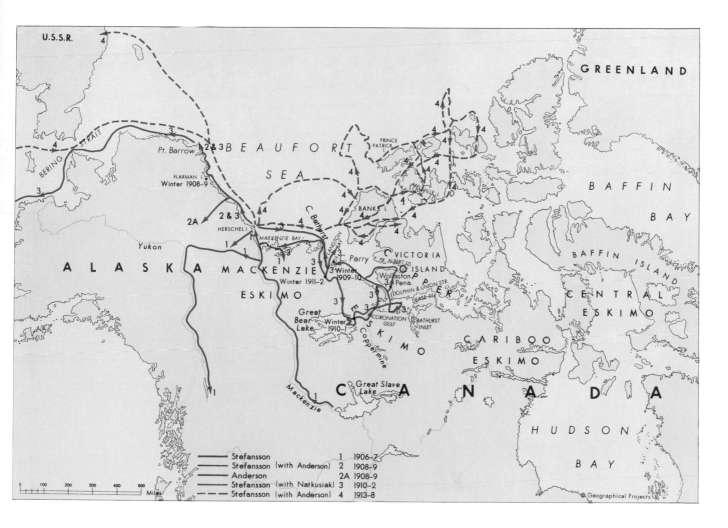

Stefansson   1   1906-7
Stefansson (with Anderson)   2   1908-9
Anderson   2A   1908-9
Stefansson (with Natkusiak)   3   1910-2
Stefansson (with Anderson)   4   1913-8

The search for Sir John Franklin had virtually completed the map of the Canadian Arctic. Still the north challenged adventurers, and exploration there went on. In 1878-9, the Northeast Passage was first navigated by **Nils Nordenskjöld** (1832-1901) in the *Vega* and, in 1879, **George Washington de Long** (1844-1881) passed through Bering Strait in the *Jeannette*. Beset off Herald Island, the *Jeannette* drifted nearly to the New Siberian Islands before being crushed by the ice. Of three parties that left the ship, only one survived. De Long, and most of his men, died.

Three years after the *Jeannette* tragedy, **Fridtjof Nansen** (1861-1930) read that wreckage from the ship had come ashore in Greenland, and concluded that the ice drift might be used to reach the North Pole. Nansen, who had already made an Arctic voyage to find zoological specimens, sailed north in 1893 to test his theory.

Nansen's ship, *Fram*, was frozen in north of the New Siberian Islands, and began to drift with the ice. In time, however, it became clear that the ice drift would not carry it far enough north, and in 1895 Nansen and **Frederic Johansen** (1867-1923)

left the ship to make an attempt on the pole by sledge. Unable to reach their goal, the two men retreated to Franz Josef Land, where they wintered unprepared. In 1896, they met a British expedition, and returned home in its ship, *Windward*. The *Fram,* commanded by **Otto Sverdrup** (1855-1930), emerged from the ice in August 1896, and sailed back to Norway.

Nansen's observations told the world much about the Arctic. It was he, too, who revealed the true nature of the Greenland icecap when he made the first crossing of Greenland in 1888. His researches there were continued by **Robert Peary** (1856-1920), who made his first expeditions in Greenland before trying for the North Pole. Peary was the first explorer to adopt Eskimo traveling techniques. In 1900, with **Matthew Henson** (dates unknown), his Negro servant, and companion on all his journeys after 1887, Peary reached the northern tip of Greenland, and in 1905-6 only the ice condition prevented his attaining his goal. In 1908, however, he again traveled north, and on 6 April 1909 he reached the North Pole.

In 1903-6, **Roald Amundsen** (1872-1928) first navigated the Northwest

Passage, sailing from Lancaster Sound to Bering Strait. The year he completed his voyage, **Vilhjalmur Stefansson** (1879-1962) set out into northwestern Canada. Between 1906 and 1912, Stefansson lived with and studied the Canadian Eskimos, and with an Eskimo named **Natkusiak** (dates unknown) he visited tribes on Victoria Island who had never seen a white man. On one of his journeys, Stefansson was accompanied by the zoologist **Rudolph Anderson** (1876-1961) who also carried out independent research. In 1913, Stefansson was appointed leader of the Canadian Arctic Expedition, the principal object of which was to chart the Beaufort Sea. Much valuable scientific work was accomplished, and Stefansson showed the potential importance of the Arctic regions to the world.

The Arctic was explored, but several "firsts" would still be accomplished. In 1958-9, the United States submarine *Nautilus* crossed the Arctic Ocean *under* the polar icecap while, 10 years later, **Wally Herbert** (born 1934) led the British Trans-Arctic Expedition in the first surface crossing of the Arctic Ocean, completing one of the last great journeys on earth.

The Great Southland

The world believed for centuries that there was a continent in the Southern Hemisphere—it was known as Terra Australis Incognita, the unknown southern land. The fabulous Terra Australis proved only a figment of men's imaginations but, deep in the unknown south, an undiscovered land mass did exist. Hidden behind the Antarctic ice pack, frozen and snowbound in summer and winter, the continent of Antarctica lay waiting to be explored.

Wilkes' men land on Antarctica, while one of his ships lies offshore amid the ice. Neither ships nor men were adequately prepared for their Antarctic voyage—the ships were not reinforced against the ice, the government-purchased clothing was too thin, and the stores were insufficient. This painting is based on a sketch made by Wilkes himself.▼

The first knowledge of the Antarctic was gained during the search for Terra Australis. Early in 1773, during his second Pacific voyage, **Captain Cook** made the first crossing of the Antarctic Circle and later, in the South Pacific Ocean, he pushed south to latitude 71° 10'. The ice forced him back on both occasions, but on the second he sighted ice mountains, and concluded that to the south must lie land. He also discovered South Georgia, and the South Sandwich Islands.

The first land within the Antarctic Circle was discovered by a Russian expedition led by **Fabian von Bellingshausen** (1778-1852), who in 1820-1 circumnavigated the world almost entirely south of the 60th parallel. Bellingshausen named his discoveries Peter I Island and Alexander I Land, but the latter is now known to be an island, separated from the mainland by an icebound strait.

On his voyage, Cook had noted how many seals there were in the South Atlantic and, by the time of Bellingshausen's expedition, sealers were regularly hunting in those icy seas. In 1823, **James Weddell** (1787-1834), in search of new sealing grounds, crossed the Antarctic Circle and, with good weather and no ice, succeeded in sailing south to 74° 15'—214 miles nearer the South Pole than Cook. Weddell made scientific observations, naming the sea he had sailed over after King George IV of England. Today, it is called the Weddell Sea.

In 1839, the Frenchman **Jules Dumont d'Urville** (1790-1842) tried to surpass Weddell's southing but that year the pack ice extended farther north, and D'Urville had to turn back. Sighting the northern part of Graham Land, he named it Louis Philippe Land, and the islands of D'Urville and Joinville he called Joinville Land. Both these "discoveries" had, however, been sighted before. The following year, sailing south from Hobart, D'Urville discovered Adélie Land.

An American expedition commanded by **Charles Wilkes** (1798-1877) was in the Antarctic at the same time as D'Urville. It was perhaps the worst prepared of all Antarctic expeditions for the conditions there, and Wilkes accomplished far less than D'Urville. Two of his ships explored the Bel-

lingshausen Sea and, afterward, Wilkes coasted Antarctica south of Australia, claiming many new discoveries. Most of these have since been disproved, but, in his memory, the region west of Adélie Land is today called Wilkes Land.

James Clark Ross—already famous for his work in the Arctic—sailed in 1839 for the Antarctic with the ships *Erebus* and *Terror*. His second-in-command was **F. R. M. Crozier,** who, with both the ships, was to disappear on Franklin's tragic 1845 expedition. Ross penetrated the ice pack to reach open sea off the shores of Antarctica. He discovered Victoria Land and the Ross Ice Shelf, a vast sheet of permanent sea ice extending from the Antarctic mainland, and named an active volcano Mount Erebus and a nearby mountain Mount Terror, after his ships. Ross even landed on the Possession Islands, and Franklin Island.

In 1841, Ross set sail from New Zealand, and despite difficult conditions, he reached nearly 78° 10' south. In December 1842, he sailed from the Falkland Islands to try to surpass

SOUTH ATLANTIC OCEAN

Mean limit of pack ice

SOUTH GEORGIA

SOUTH SANDWICH ISLANDS

ANTARCTIC CIRCLE

INDIAN OCEAN

FALKLAND IS.

SOUTH ORKNEYS

WEDDELL SEA

Amery Ice Shelf

West Ice Shelf

TIERRA DEL FUEGO

SOUTH SHETLAND IS.

DECEPTION I.

Graham Land Palmer Pena.

Filchner Ice Shelf

ANTARCTICA

80°

Shackleton Ice Shelf

PETER I I.

BELLINGSHAUSEN SEA

SOUTH POLE

Wilkes Land

PACIFIC OCEAN

Ross Ice Shelf

Sabrina Land

ROSS I. MT. EREBUS MT. TERROR McMURDO SOUND FRANKLIN I.

Victoria Land

Adélie Land

ROSS SEA

POSSESSION IS.

BALLENY IS.

AUCKLAND IS.

Hobart VAN DIEMEN'S LAND TASMANIA

NEW ZEALAND

AUSTRALIA

Cape Town

© Geographical Projects

Cook	1a	1772–3
(parts of his second voyage)	1b	1773–4
	1c	1774–5
Bellingshausen	2	1819–21
Weddell	3	1822–3
D'Urville	4	1837–40
Wilkes	5	1838–40
Ross, James C. (with Crozier)	6a	1839–41
Ross, James C. (with Crozier)	6b	1841–2
Ross, James C. (with Crozier)	6c	1842–3

0 200 400 600 800 1000 Miles

this record, but the ice pack halted him at 71° 30′ south. Ross had, however, already pushed farther south than any of his predecessors, besides making important discoveries and scientific observations.

After Ross's voyage, interest in the polar regions was concentrated on the Arctic, and no great contributions were made to knowledge of the Antarctic for nearly 60 years. Then, in 1900, the Royal Geographical Society commissioned an expedition under **Robert Scott** (1868-1912). Scott was accompanied by **Ernest Shackleton** (1874-1922), **Edward Wilson** (1872-1912), and **Frank Wild** (1873-1939). His expedition showed for the first time what the Antarctic plateau was like. In 1902, Scott established a new southerly record by sledging south to 82° 17′, and the following year he traveled 300 miles into Victoria Land.

Three years after Scott's return, Ernest Shackleton led an expedition to the Antarctic and, with a party including Wild, he pushed south to within 97 miles of the South Pole. Shackleton was forced to turn back by a shortage of provisions, and by bad weather, but **Douglas Mawson** (1882-1958) reached the South Magnetic Pole, and a party led by **Raymond Priestley** (born 1886) climbed onto the interior plateau at much the same point as Scott.

Shackleton had all but reached the South Pole, and in 1910 Robert Scott set out to conquer it. That same year, however, **Roald Amundsen** also set his sights on the pole. After wintering at the Bay of Whales, Amundsen set out for the South Pole, which he reached on 14 December 1911 after a comparatively easy march. Scott, however, suffered setback after setback on his journey southward and he, Edward Wilson, and three companions reached the pole only on 17 January 1912. The disappointment of finding Amundsen had got there first, combined with bad weather, made the return journey a nightmare and before reaching their base all five men died. So great was this tragedy that at the time it obscured the success of the scientific work carried out by Scott's ship *Terra Nova* and by Raymond Priestley's Northern Party on shore.

In 1914, Ernest Shackleton set out to cross Antarctica from the Weddell Sea to the Ross Sea, but he never managed to land on the Weddell Sea coast. As his ship *Endurance* sailed west, the ice grew thicker and in January 1915 the *Endurance* was beset. In November, crushed by the ice, it sank.

Shackleton and his men managed to reach Elephant Island then, leaving Frank Wild in charge, Shackleton and five others set out in the *James Caird*, an open boat 22 feet long, to cross the 1000 miles of open sea separating them from South Georgia and help. They reached South Georgia, but to get to the whaling station Shackleton had first to cross the island—the first time this had been done. He got there, though, and in time all his men were rescued too.

In 1921, Shackleton sailed once more for the Antarctic but he died in 1922 of a heart attack and was buried on South Georgia. The voyage, which resulted in only a few soundings, was continued in the *Quest* by Frank Wild.

In 1911, Douglas Mawson led an expedition to the Antarctic in the *Aurora*. He made his base at Commonwealth Bay and sledged east with **B. E. S. Ninnis** (1888?-1912) and **Xavier Mertz** (1883?-1913). King George V Land was added to the map, but both Ninnis and Mertz died. Meanwhile, sledging west from Shackleton Ice Shelf, Frank Wild reached Queen Mary Land. In 1929, Mawson led an expedition to Antarctica in the *Discovery*, carrying out oceanographic research and discovering Princess Elizabeth Land and Mac-Robertson Land. In 1930-1, he coasted Antarctica from Commonwealth Bay nearly to Enderby Land.

The first man to use airplanes for Antarctic exploration was **Sir Hubert Wilkins** (1888-1958) who, in 1928-9 and 1929-30, made flights over Graham Land and west of Peter I Island. Other pioneer flights were made by **Richard Byrd** (1888-1957) who, in 1928-9, in the first American expedition to Antarctica since that of Wilkes, made the first flight over the South Pole and established the Little America base at the Bay of Whales. In 1933, Byrd made a number of flights from a support ship off Antarctica, and the following year he set up a base 123 miles south of Little America to take weather measurements. For nearly five months during the Antarctic winter, Byrd manned it alone.

In 1957-8, Shackleton's dream of a crossing of Antarctica was accomplished when, from Shackleton base on the edge of the Filchner Ice Shelf, **Vivian Fuchs** (born 1908) traveled via the South Pole to McMurdo Sound. His expedition had been carefully prepared—Shackleton base was set up in 1955 and only in 1956 did the body of the expedition sail from England. In 1957, while Fuchs traveled south from Shackleton, **Sir Edmund Hillary** (born 1919) laid out food depots south from McMurdo Sound to the pole.

Fuch's journey took place during the International Geophysical Year, a year of international—and peaceful— scientific experiments. Numerous scientific stations were established in Antarctica and, in 1959, a treaty was ratified stating that no country can exclude another from performing peaceful scientific experiments there. Today, it is by these researches that the blanks on the map are being filled.

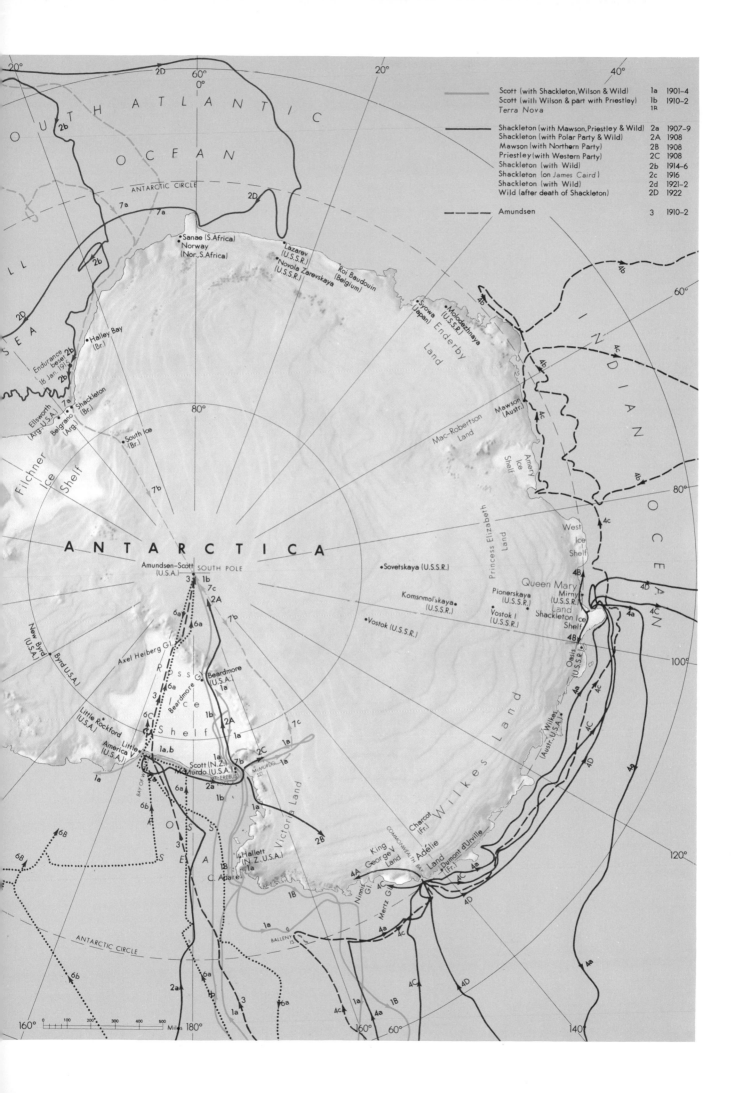

12 The Seas and the Oceans

Nearly three-quarters of the surface of the earth is covered by the oceans. Beneath the waves there lies a world as varied and thriving as that of the continents and islands but, until relatively recently, it was a world unknown and unexplored. Mariners sailed over the ocean, divers penetrated the shallow coastal waters, but, of the vast mass of ocean waters, nothing was known. Immense developments in scientific research techniques were necessary before man could explore the depths of the sea.

We know today that the seabed is as uneven as the land. Under the sea, there are plains (basins), mountains (seamounts), mountain chains (mid-ocean ridges)—the peaks of which often appear as islands above the surface—and deep valleys (trenches) with occasional even deeper declivities called deeps. The average depth of the water on the continental shelves—the part of the seabed adjoining most continents, and made up of rocks similar to those on land—is around 600 feet, but in the deep ocean it is in the region of 15,000 to 18,000 feet. In comparison, the average height of the land is a mere 2760 feet.

Much of the ocean floor is covered by a thick blanket of sediments, deposited there over millions of years. On the continental shelves, these are mainly terrigenous sediments (sediments from the land), but in the deep ocean most are pelagic sediments (sediments which fall to the seabed from the surface waters). Pelagic sediments are further subdivided into oozes, formed from the remains of animals and plants, and clays, made up of inorganic material. From a study of the different layers of sediment on the seabed, scientists can learn much about the history of the earth. Researches have also shown that the undersea world is not always peaceful. Undersea volcanoes erupt violently, and landslides roar down undersea ridges, or down the continental slopes into the deep ocean, smothering marine life.

The waters covering the undersea world are salt, but the degree of salinity varies from place to place. At the surface, their temperature varies too, but with depth it becomes more uniform until, in the

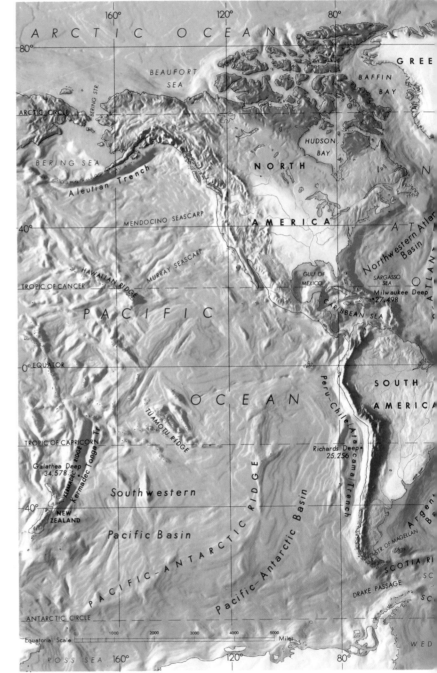

deepest ocean, it is almost constant at a few degrees above freezing point. Within these waters flow great currents, distinguished one from the other by the temperature and salinity of their waters, and by their speed, size, and strength.

Under the sea, the pressure of the water is immense. For every foot of depth, pressure increases at a rate of 0.442 pounds per square inch, so that, at a depth of 30,000 feet, the pressure is between 700 and 800 times as great as at sea level. Sunlight penetrates only a few hundred feet, and below that the ocean is dark.

What of life in the undersea world? Plants need sunlight to survive, and

sea plants are not found below the light barrier, but research has proved that there is animal life even in the very deepest spots in the ocean, although the greater the depth, the fewer animals there are. The sea creatures can survive at water pressures that would soon crush a human being, for the fluids in their bodies are at the same pressure as the surrounding sea. The animal life of the sea is generally divided into three groups—nekton (swimming organisms), benthos (organisms living on the seabed), and zooplankton (drifting organisms). Another branch of plankton, phytoplankton, is made up of minute drifting plants.

Today, as the world becomes increasingly overcrowded, and the natural resources of the land are exhausted, men are looking with ever increasing interest at the sea as a source of life. Their visionary plans carry into the future the work of their predecessors—the men by whom the oceans have been explored.

175

The Challenger Expedition

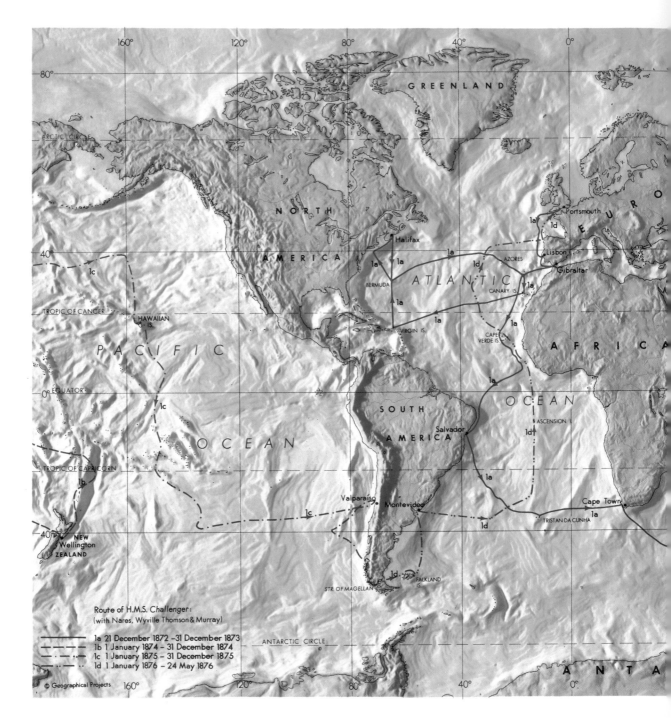

Route of H.M.S. Challenger:
(with Nares, Wyville Thomson & Murray)

```
————————  1a 21 December 1872 –31 December 1873
– – – – –  1b 1 January 1874 – 31 December 1874
–·–·–·–·–  1c 1 January 1875 – 31 December 1875
··········  1d 1 January 1876 – 24 May 1876
```

© Geographical Projects

In May 1876, a British warship, H.M.S. *Challenger*, sailed up the English Channel toward Portsmouth. It was returning home after a 3½-year-long circumnavigation of the earth, during which it had sailed nearly 69,000 miles over the world's oceans. The motive of its voyage—to explore the depths of the sea.

The *Challenger* expedition was organized with the help of the British Admiralty and the Royal Society, but its inception was largely due to **Charles Wyville Thomson** (1830-1882), a naturalist who had dredged the sea-bed in the Atlantic at some depth, and who wanted to dredge all the world's oceans, to investigate deep-sea life.

On the *Challenger*, Wyville Thomson led a scientific team which included four naturalists, **John Murray** (1841-1914), Rudolph von Willemoes Suhm, Henry Moseley, and J. J. Wild, and a chemist, J. Y. Buchanan. The *Challenger's* commander was **George Nares** (1831-1915).

H.M.S. *Challenger* sailed from Portsmouth in December 1872 on the first, Atlantic, leg of its voyage. Four traverses were made of the Atlantic, then the ship sailed from Cape Town for Melbourne, pushing far enough south to encounter the barrier of pack ice off the shores of Antarctica. From Melbourne, its route lay via New Zealand, the East

Indies and the Philippines to Hong Kong, then south to New Guinea and north again to Yokohama. In the Pacific, Hawaii and other islands were visited. Coasting southernmost South America toward the end of 1875, the *Challenger* passed through the Strait of Magellan, then, early in 1876, from the Falkland Islands, it sailed for home.

The voyage of the *Challenger* opened a new world for study, for with its voyage the science of oceanography was born. Although some scientists had previously studied the ocean, until the 1800's their equipment was primitive, and much work had to be based on conjecture. The

researches of the *Challenger* scientists showed for the first time what the oceans were really like. At 362 stations (stops), soundings were made to determine the depth of the water, and the ocean bed was trawled to bring up specimens of life in the depths. Ocean currents, the sediments on the seabed, and the temperature and composition of seawater were investigated too.

The soundings made from the *Challenger* showed that the physical features of the ocean floor are as varied as those of the land, although the contours in the ocean basins are less pronounced, owing to the deposition of sediments on the seabed. It was

Murray who first classified these sediments as terrigenous or pelagic. The deepest sounding made was 28,850 feet near the Mariana Islands. (The deepest recorded sounding today is 37,780 feet, in the Mindanao Trench near the Philippines.) Water temperature was measured by means of a thermometer recording only maximum and minimum temperatures, and readings showed that it remained constant at great depths.

Animals were brought to the surface in the trawl net from down to 16,500 feet—depths far below those where life had previously been supposed to exist. Through his experiments, Buchanan proved how the

creatures of the deep ocean could survive immense water pressures, and thus demonstrated that life was possible at any ocean depth. Plants, however, were shown to be nonexistent below a few hundred feet. Studies were also made of plankton, the "wanderers" of the sea.

After the *Challenger's* return to Britain, reports of the expedition's findings were compiled, reports that ran to 50 volumes, so revolutionary was the work. These 29,500-page reports have been called the "oceanographer's bible" for on them all future study of the ocean would be based.

The World beneath the Waves

The *Challenger* expedition drew back a long-closed curtain by obtaining definite and accurate information about the depths of the sea. Its revolutionary discoveries inspired new oceanographic researches by such men as John Murray, a naturalist on the *Challenger;* Louis Agassiz, professor of natural history at Harvard; Agassiz' son Alexander; and Prince Albert of Monaco, a generous patron of oceanography, as well as a practical oceanographer. Their investigations, and those of the oceanographers who followed them, covered many different subjects—life in the depths; seawater, its composition and movement; the seabed, and its importance to a study of the earth.

Early in the 1900's, the Norwegian oceanographer and fishery scientist Johan Hjort made a number of oceanographic expeditions on board the *Michael Sars*, and in the same years studies of edible fishes were carried out by Johannes Schmidt. It was Schmidt who, in 1922, on an expedition in the *Dana*, revealed the migration pattern of the eel, which swims to the Sargasso Sea to spawn.

For Britain, a study of whales was vital to the future of the British whaling industry, and in 1925 an expedition was sent to the South Atlantic in the *Discovery*. The scientific team under **Stanley Kemp** (1882-1945) and **Alister Hardy** (born 1896) carried out various researches, the most important of which were an investigation of the species of whale, and studies of whale migration and of plankton, which most whales eat.

A German expedition on board the *Meteor* was in the Atlantic at the same time as the *Discovery*. Its main object was to investigate the possibility of extracting gold and silver from the sea to pay Germany's war debt, but in this it was unsuccessful. However, under **Alfred Merz** (?-1925), until his death in August 1925, and afterward under **Captain Spiess** (dates unknown), the team made numerous observations, measuring the depth, temperature, and the various properties of seawater, and studying the features of the ocean floor, and the blanket of sediments that cover it. Through their work, they contributed more to basic understanding of the ocean than any expedition before.

A vital question remained unanswered by all these oceanographic researches. Was there, or was there not, life in the deepest parts of the sea? In 1950, a Danish expedition led by **Anton Bruun** (1901-1961) set out in the *Galathea* to find the answer. In the Mindanao Trench in the Pacific, the *Galathea* trawled the bottom at more than 33,000 feet, and from that depth the trawl brought back living creatures—strange and hitherto unknown species, which had adapted themselves to the darkness and pressure of the depths.

Long before the birth of oceanography, sailors had been familiar with ocean currents, and in particular with the Gulf Stream, whose current flowing east across the Atlantic could delay ships sailing west. In 1930, the Woods Hole Oceanographic Institution was founded at Cape Cod, Massachusetts, and as one of its first projects it planned an investigation of the Gulf Stream. During the following years, the voyages of the Woods Hole ship *Atlantis* revealed much about the composition and volume of that "river in the sea".

The Gulf Stream Drift Mission planned for 1969 would, however, carry out experiments impossible on the *Atlantis*, for its researches were to be conducted from *under* the sea. The expedition's ship was the *Ben Franklin*, a mesoscaph (boat for medium depths) designed by **Jacques Piccard** (born 1922) to explore the ocean at depths up to 2000 feet.

In Piccard's month-long voyage, his mesoscaph traveled with the Gulf Stream from West Palm Beach, Florida, to a point 360 miles southeast of Nova Scotia. Its six-man crew

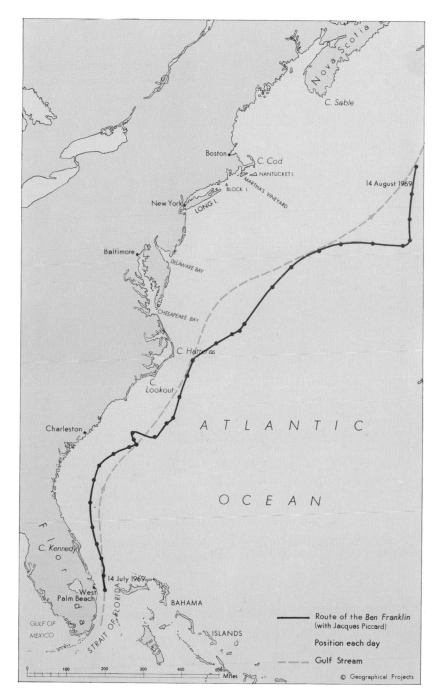

measured and recorded every physical characteristic of the Gulf Stream, and observed its animal life. They also acted as guinea pigs for the National Aeronautics and Space Administration (N.A.S.A.) to demonstrate how men would react to prolonged confinement in a small space.

Revolutionary new techniques have today transformed the science of oceanography, enabling more accurate and detailed studies to be made. Depth is no longer measured with a weighted chain, but with an echo sounder, which bounces a pulse of sound off the seabed. From the time the pulse takes to descend and return, depth can be calculated. Pulses of sound sent down not vertically, but at an angle, bounce back echoes from which a picture of the ocean floor can be drawn. Dredging is no longer the only means of obtaining bottom samples, for holes can be drilled into the seabed, and cores of sediment drawn up intact.

A geological core sampler was first used in 1947-8 by the University of Göteborg's expedition on the *Albatross*, and cores of sediment extracted which were up to 65 feet long. Deposits settle so slowly on the seabed that it would have taken several million years for the sediment blanket to attain that depth. From the composition of such cores, and the depth of the layers of sediment in them, scientists can learn much about the history of the earth.

Another method used to study the seabed is seismic-refraction, in which depth charges are used to create energy. Some of the energy generated by the explosions travels down to the seabed, and to the various layers of sediment and rock beneath. From each layer, an echo bounces upward, and these help geologists to judge the depth of the layers, their angle, and even to deduce their composition. This method was successfully used on board the *Vema*, a research ship specializing in geophysical observations. It was the *Vema*, with the aid of the Precision Depth Recorder (which traces a constant outline of the seabed), that charted the mid-ocean ridge, a great chain of undersea mountains encircling the earth.

Cores had been obtained from the seabed, but scientists wanted to probe deeper. Plans were laid to drill a hole into the ocean floor thousands of feet below the surface of the water, a hole so deep that it would cut right through the earth's crust. The preliminary drillings of Project Mohole, as the venture was known, were made in 1959, and led to the building of the **Glomar Challenger**, a ship designed especially for underwater drilling. Since the *Glomar Challenger* set out on its first voyage in 1968, it has obtained hundreds of cores from the seabed. From a study of these cores, scientists are learning new and fascinating facts about the earth.

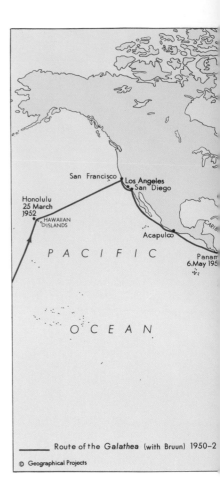

Route of the Galathea (with Bruun) 1950-2

© Geographical Projects

The purpose of the Galathea *expedition was to trawl at the deepest points in the ocean, to discover whether life existed there, and, if so, to what extent. Its findings*

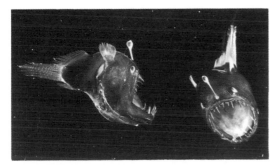

Four species of fish discovered at depths below 4200 feet—deep-sea prawn (above); deep-sea hatchet fish (above right); gulper eel (right); deep-sea anglers (below).

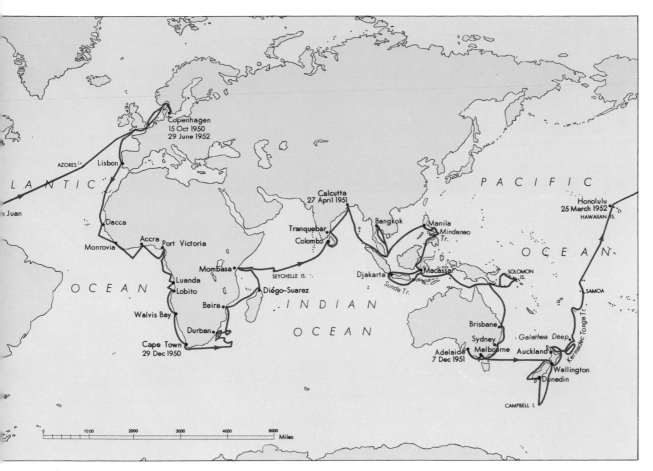

proved conclusively that there are ▲ living things even at the bottom of the ocean, and showed that they are especially adapted to life in their dark and pressurized home.

The Glomar Challenger was built specifically as a deep-sea drilling ship to obtain sediment cores from the seabed at great depths. The ship ▼ is able to drill in many thou-

sands of feet of water without anchoring because of its automatic positioning system. This holds the Glomar Challenger in place directly over the hole being drilled.

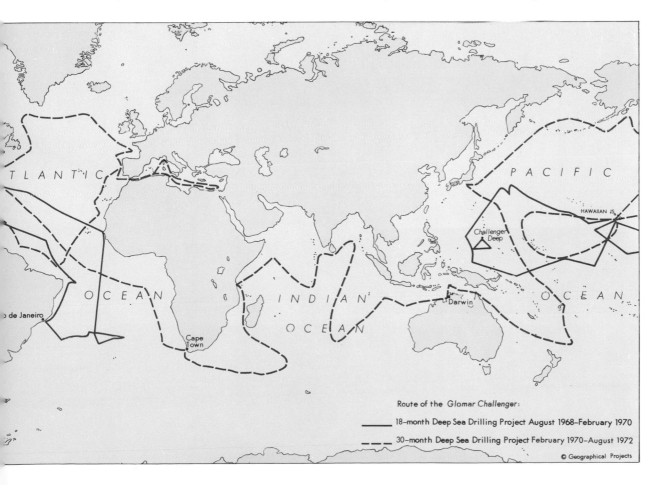

Route of the Glomar Challenger:

———— 18-month Deep Sea Drilling Project August 1968–February 1970

– – – – 30-month Deep Sea Drilling Project February 1970–August 1972

© Geographical Projects

181

Man in the Sea

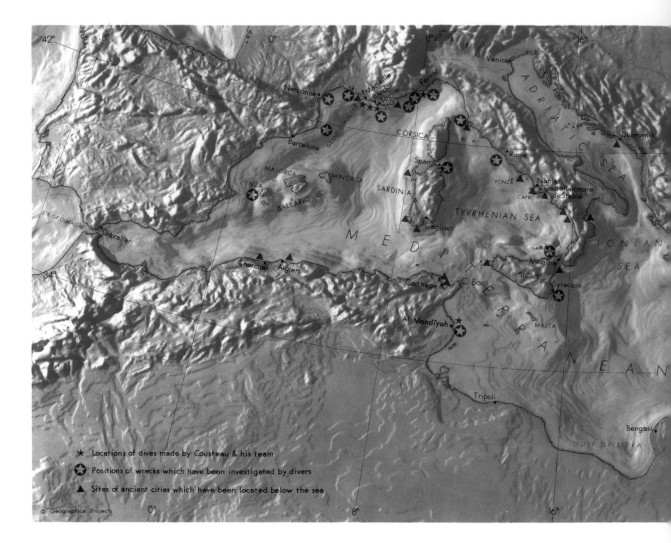

★ Locations of dives made by Cousteau & his team

⊛ Positions of wrecks which have been investigated by divers

▲ Sites of ancient cities which have been located below the sea

© Geographical Projects

Man's natural habitat is the earth. Without air, he cannot breathe, and the depths of the sea were therefore long forbidden him. Yet he was fascinated by the world under the water, the world of "inner space".

In classical times, the Greeks dived for sponges, for mother-of-pearl, and coral, and divers were employed in surprise attacks in war. Some Greek divers used short breathing tubes to enable them to swim undetected underwater, and the Greeks also invented a primitive form of diving bell. This was an air-filled bell, open at the bottom, which was lowered into the water, and into which the diver could poke his head to take a fresh breath. In an attempt to provide divers with a constant air supply, the Renaissance artist Leonardo da Vinci designed a diving helmet linked by an air tube with the surface. But his apparatus would not have worked below five feet, as water pressure would then have prevented the lungs expanding to take in air.

With the diving bell, however, there is no problem of water pressure, for as the water rises within the bell, the air is compressed to the same pressure as the water outside. By the 1500's, large diving bells were being used for underwater descents, but it was not until the end of the 1600's that a method was invented of pumping air into a bell at the same pressure as the water outside. This pushed down the water level in the bell, meaning that divers could reach greater depths. Individual bells, linked by airlines to the main bell, were used for underwater work.

One of the earliest practicable diving suits was made in 1715 by John Lethbridge, and by 1749 Lethbridge had descended in it to 72 feet. The forerunner of the modern diving suit was designed by Augustus Siebe. In 1819, Siebe produced his "open dress", a helmet fed with pressurized air from the surface, and attached to a jacket, which was open at the bottom to allow used air to escape. In 1837, Siebe developed this into a full diving suit. A much simpler form of diving apparatus was invented by Benoît Rouquayrol and Auguste Denayrouze between 1860 and 1865. It was a hard rubber mouthpiece, linked to a canister of pressurized air carried on the diver's back. The

canister was supplied from the surface by an airline.

Nearly 80 years passed before the airline could be dispensed with. Then, in 1942-3, **Jacques-Yves Cousteau** (born 1910) developed the aqualung. Like the Rouquayrol-Denayrouze device, it consisted of a mouthpiece linked to an air canister, but the air canister contained compressed air, and a demand regulator ensured a constant air supply at the same pressure as the surrounding water. The aqualung gave divers new freedom—which they used to investigate and salvage wrecks, and explore ancient cities lying under the sea.

The aqualung freed divers from the airline, it did not free them from danger. In 1870, the cause of decompression sickness—"the bends"—which takes the form of pains in the joints, paralysis, and even death, in divers who ascend too fast from great depths, had been explained, and thereafter the bends were usually avoided by making a gradual ascent. But with the invention of the aqualung, new symptoms were felt by divers who descended deep. Nitrogen narcosis—"the rapture of the depths"

182

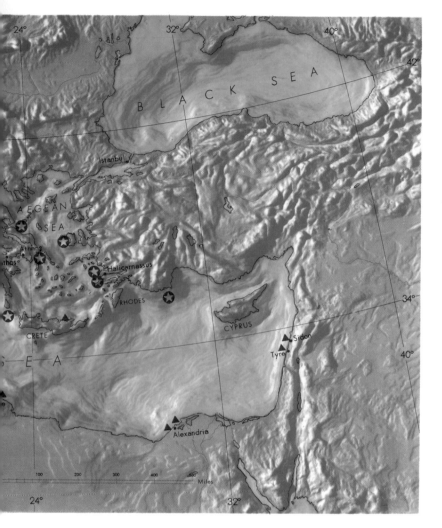

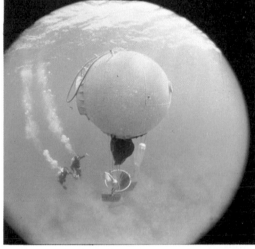

—is experienced as a feeling of drunkenness, which can make divers forget they are underwater, take out their mouthpieces, and drown.

No diver can penetrate the ocean's deepest reaches, and even before the invention of the aqualung, attempts had been made to devise a machine that could do so. The first successful depth machine was the brainchild of William Beebe, a naturalist whose interest in the ocean made him want to descend beyond the limits imposed by a diving suit. Beebe's bathysphere, which he built with Otis Barton, reached 800 feet on its first dive in 1930, and in 1934 a record of 3028 feet was set up. In 1948, in a new machine, the benthoscope, Barton reached 4462 feet.

The bathysphere and the benthoscope were lowered into the sea on a cable, and could only be moved by that cable. The first free-floating "deep-sea ship" was Auguste Piccard's bathyscaph. The cabin of the bathyscaph was attached to a float filled with lighter-than-water gasoline, and the machine carried lead shot as ballast. To descend, gasoline was emptied from the float, and to ascend,

lead shot jettisoned. In 1948 Piccard's first bathyscaph *F.N.R.S.2* reached more than 4500 feet unmanned, and in 1954 the *F.N.R.S.3* attained 13,287 feet. In 1960, his *Trieste*, piloted by his son Jacques and Donald Walsh, reached 35,800 feet.

Following the success of the bathyscaph, other deep-sea ships have been designed, many with specific functions in mind. Some are rescue vehicles, intended to help submarines in trouble, some are workboats, and some reconnaissance vessels, and even underwater "buses" have been planned. For the pioneers of underwater exploration, and in particular Jacques-Yves Cousteau, are no longer thinking simply of reaching great depths. Cousteau's latest projects all involve man living under the sea.

Cousteau's *Conshelf* stations of the 1960's were man's first underwater habitats. There, divers lived and worked for weeks at a time. Similar were the U.S. Navy's *Sealab* habitats, where men also lived deep under the sea. For the future, Cousteau envisages great cities built under the water, and populated by a new race of aquatic men.

▲ *The aqualung (top) gives the diver freedom to explore and work under the water. The bathysphere (center) is used for research at depths that no diver could reach. Beaver IV (bottom) is a submersible built to operate at depths of up to 2000 feet carrying out maintenance work on underwater wellheads for the oil and gas industries.*

13 The New Frontier

In October 1957, the Soviet Union launched the earth's first artificial satellite, Sputnik I. In April, four years later, the first man flew in space. But although the exploration of the universe is a comparatively recent enterprise, man's interest in the heavens can be traced back thousands of years.

The first astronomical observations were made in Mesopotamia and in Egypt in the early days of civilization, and it may have been from the Egyptians that the Greeks first learned astronomy. The Greeks discovered that the earth rotates on its axis, and that the moon revolves around the earth and, in the 200's B.C., Aristarchus of Samos propounded the theory that the earth and the other planets revolve around the sun. A century later, however, Hipparchus placed the earth at the center of the universe. His concept was elaborated by Ptolemy, and belief in the Ptolemaic system, implying as it did man's importance as center of the universe, persisted until the Renaissance. Even in the A.D. 1500's, when Copernicus revived Aristarchus' theory, his "new" notion was at first disbelieved.

Late in the 1500's, using a quadrant, Tycho Brahe made the first ac-

In 1590, Thomas Hood (dates unknown), mathematical lecturer to the City of London, published The use of the celestial globe in plano, set forth in two hemispheres. *To accompany and explain his work, he designed ▼ two charts of the heavens, which*

were engraved by Augustine Ryther. Hood's charts show the constellations and stars of the Northern and Southern celestial hemispheres, but their strange, pictorial form is far removed from the scientific detail of a celestial chart of the present day.

curate measurements of the positions of the stars and planets, and his contemporary Galileo adapted the telescope to observe the universe. Johannes Kepler, a mathematics professor, and Brahe's assistant, calculated the orbit of Mars from Brahe's figures, and went on to discover three laws governing planetary motion. More fundamental laws of motion, showing why the bodies in the universe move

in the way they do, were laid down by Isaac Newton. Newtonian laws of motion, as they are called, form the basis of modern rocketry.

Rockets were invented by the Chinese, who were using them as fireworks by the A.D. 100's, and who by the 1200's had developed them as weapons. Their use in warfare spread to Europe, then, toward the end of the 1800's, the Russian Konstantin

Tsiolkovsky applied the science of rocketry to space travel. His work was theoretical, as was that of the German Hermann Oberth who, in *The Rocket into Interplanetary Space*, published in 1923, discussed the technical problems of space flight. It was left to the American Robert Goddard, the "father of modern rocketry", to build the first liquid-fuel rocket, the forerunner of today's space booster.

185

To the Moon–and beyond

When World War II broke out in 1939, Germany had been carrying out rocket research for a number of years. In 1937, the Peenemünde experimental rocketry station had been established and there, during the war, Wernher von Braun and a team of scientists developed the V-2. The V-2 was a liquid-fuel rocket that was used against London and other targets. It was the first modern rocket, and its development considerably advanced rocketry technique.

The story of man's journey to the moon is a relatively short one, for less than 10 years passed between the first manned space flight and the first lunar landing. Each space flight was a monument to technical achievement and to human courage; some were also milestones on the way to the moon. The diagram below shows some ▼ *memorable space "firsts".*

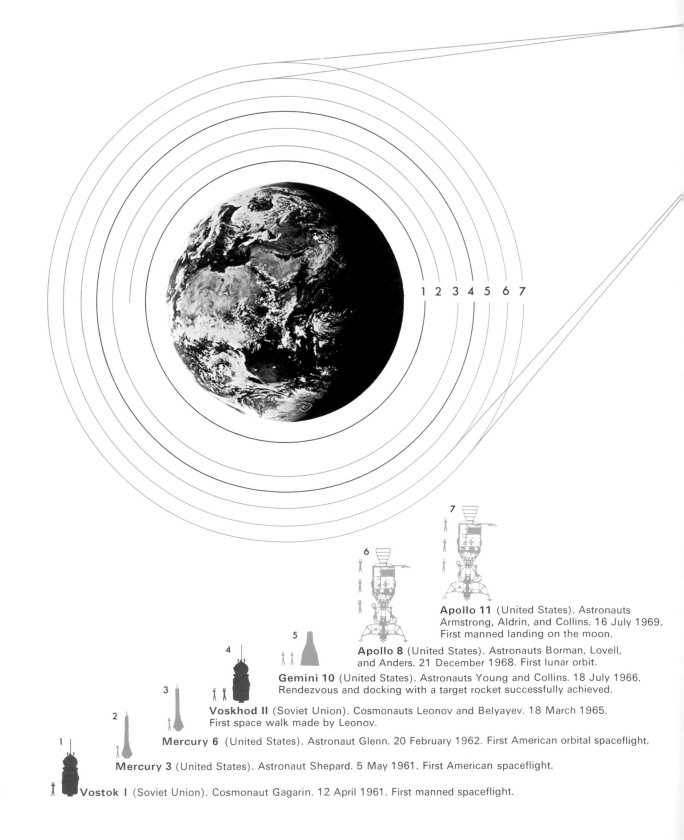

Apollo 11 (United States). Astronauts Armstrong, Aldrin, and Collins. 16 July 1969. First manned landing on the moon.

Apollo 8 (United States). Astronauts Borman, Lovell, and Anders. 21 December 1968. First lunar orbit.

Gemini 10 (United States). Astronauts Young and Collins. 18 July 1966. Rendezvous and docking with a target rocket successfully achieved.

Voskhod II (Soviet Union). Cosmonauts Leonov and Belyayev. 18 March 1965. First space walk made by Leonov.

Mercury 6 (United States). Astronaut Glenn. 20 February 1962. First American orbital spaceflight.

Mercury 3 (United States). Astronaut Shepard. 5 May 1961. First American spaceflight.

Vostok I (Soviet Union). Cosmonaut Gagarin. 12 April 1961. First manned spaceflight.

▲ *Edwin Aldrin walks on the moon.*

After Germany's defeat, many Peenemünde scientists surrendered to the Allies, and it was in the service of the Allies that they continued their research. In the United States, Wernher von Braun and his team worked on missiles for the army. From these they developed a booster capable of putting a satellite into space. Both the United States and the Soviet Union planned to launch satellites during the International Geophysical Year in 1957-8. The Soviet Union was first with Sputnik I in October 1957.

In January 1958, the United States successfully launched its first satellite, Explorer 1, and that same year N.A.S.A.—the National Aeronautics and Space Agency (now Administration)—was created. Two years later, Wernher von Braun became director of N.A.S.A.'s George C. Marshall Space Flight Center.

On 12 April 1961, the Soviet Union launched **Yuri Gagarin** (1934-1968) into space in Vostok I. Less than a month after this first manned space flight ever, the Americans' first manned space flight was made. Unlike Gagarin, however, **Alan B. Shepard, Jr.** (born 1923) made only a suborbital flight. Not until 1962 did **John H. Glenn, Jr.** (born 1921) become the first American to orbit the earth.

Shepard's and Glenn's flights were part of the American Mercury project, which, in six flights between May 1961 and May 1963, proved that man could survive the unfamiliar conditions of space. In 1962, meanwhile, the Soviet Union made the first group flight of the space age with Vostoks III and IV. The following year, in Vostok VI, Valentina Tereshkova became the first woman in space. In October 1964, the Soviet Voskhod program began. Voskhod II, launched in March 1965, carried two cosmo-

nauts, **Alexei Leonov** (born 1934) and **Pavel Belyayev** (born 1925). During their flight, Leonov left the capsule and "walked" in space.

The United States had announced a moon-flight program, which they called Project Apollo, as early as 1960, and the 1965-6 Gemini series of space flights showed that astronauts could survive flights long enough to take them to the moon. Gemini also perfected the rendezvous and docking maneuvers that would play a vital part in lunar missions. Gemini 10, manned by **John W. Young** (born 1930) and **Michael Collins** (born 1930), was the first to achieve perfect docking, for although Gemini 8 linked up with its target, the docked capsule and target went into a perilous spin, and the flight had to be abandoned.

On 27 January 1967, disaster struck the American space program. During a rehearsal for the first flight in the Apollo series, a fire started in the space capsule, and astronauts Gus Grissom, Edward White, and Roger Chaffee were killed. Not until October 1968 did N.A.S.A. consider themselves ready for the first manned Apollo flight—Apollo 7. In 1967 too, tragedy marked the Soviet space program when Vladimir Komarov was killed during reentry in his capsule, Soyuz I. In October 1968, the Soyuz program was resumed, and in January 1969, Soyuz IV and V made the first docking of two manned spacecraft.

At Christmas 1968, in Apollo 8, **Frank Borman** (born 1928), **James A. Lovell, Jr.** (born 1928), and **William A. Anders** (born 1933) became the first men to orbit the moon. During the Apollo 9 flight, the separation and redocking of the lunar module, which would make the moon landing, and the command module, were tested in earth orbit, and on the Apollo 10

flight a similar test was made in lunar orbit. Then, on 16 July 1969, Apollo 11 was launched. **Neil A. Armstrong** (born 1930) and **Edwin E. Aldrin, Jr.** (born 1930) made man's first landing on the moon, while Michael Collins remained in lunar orbit in the command module.

After the moon landing, N.A.S.A.'s budget was cut, and the Apollo program reduced from 10 flights to seven. All were successful, apart from Apollo 13. During that mission, an explosion damaged the service module, the moon landing had to be abandoned, and the astronauts were lucky to return to earth alive. On the Apollo 15 mission, in July 1971, a lunar rover was used for the first time. This self-propelled vehicle, especially designed for use on the moon, enables astronauts to explore up to several miles from their spacecraft.

In April 1971, the Soviet Union boosted the 24-ton Salyut orbiting laboratory into earth orbit. Salyut was initially unmanned, and four days after its launch, Soyuz X, crewed by three cosmonauts, rendezvoused with it. On this occasion, however, no crew transfer took place. In June, Salyut was manned for 24 days by cosmonauts from Soyuz XI, but all three men died when their capsule depressurized during reentry.

With the U.S. cutbacks in space spending, and the Soviet secrecy about their plans, future programs are uncertain. And most existing projects are for earth orbital flights, rather than flights to the moon or planets. In its 1973 program, the U.S. is to pioneer Skylab, an earth-orbiting laboratory. Besides carrying out important experiments, Skylab might be the precursor of space stations which could provide a jumping-off point for manned exploration of deep space and

187

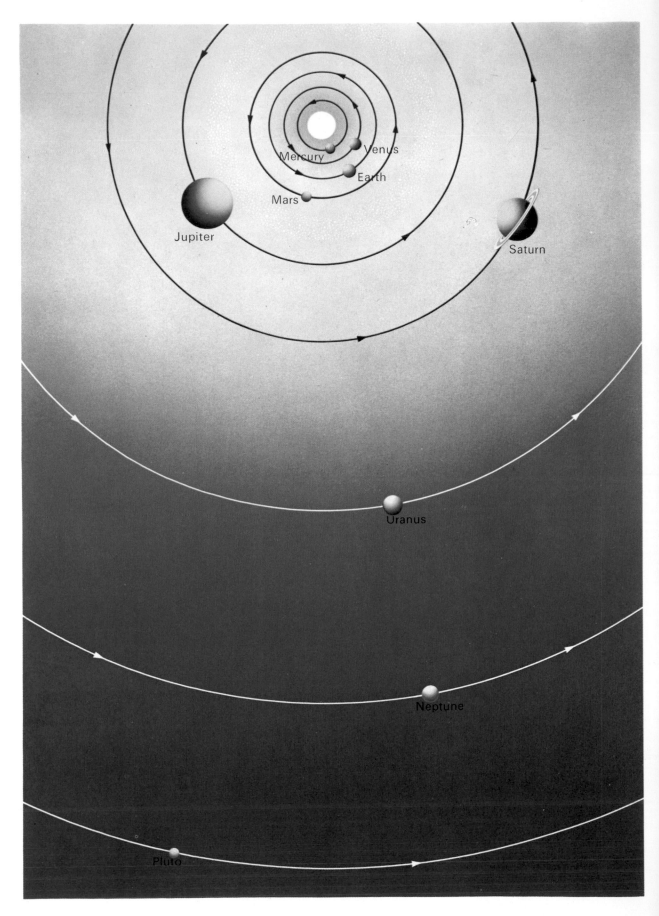

the solar system. The space shuttle, a reusable rocket booster which N.A.S.A. hopes would place space flight on a similar footing to civil aviation, could be operational in the 1980's. But perhaps the most important project planned is one that would involve cooperation between the United States and the Soviet Union—an Apollo-Soyuz docking in 1975. Whatever its result, it seems certain that now there is the basic technology for manned space flight, men will continue to push back the new frontier.

▲ *Man's journey to the moon is short in comparison with the vastness of the solar system, but no manned flights to the planets are yet planned. Unmanned probes have, however, been sent to Mars, Venus, and Jupiter, and a flight to Mercury is planned.*

Reference

Throughout this reference section, italic type is used for map entries, Roman type for text entries, and bold type where map and text entries occur on the same page.

191

Illustration Credits

CANDY

CALECVTH

GOA

DAMASCO

IERVSA

ASIA
noviter delineata
Auctore
Guil: Janssonio

EVRO
PÆ
PARS

Syri

Arabes

Armenius. Perse

Balaguatæ

Insulani Sumatriæ

GRÆCIA

MARIS

MEDITERRANEI PARS

Candia

Cyprus

Pontus Euxinus siue Mare Magior

NATOLIA

Mare de Sala vel Bachu seu Chualensko more

TARTARIA

NOVA ZEMBLA

TAR

Tumen

Kaski Thrtani

Ioughoria

PERSIA

PARSIA

MARE RVBRVM

EGYP PARS

AFRI

ABIS SINÆ PARS

CÆ PARS

ARABIA DESERTA

AYAMAN olim

ARABIA FELIX

Aden

Caldei el Calde

MARE

ARABICVM et INDICVM

Maldiva

OCEANVS

Æquator

ORI

EN

Zanziber

Pemba

Monfia

I. de Natal